COMMUNITY COLLEGE OF
ALLEGHENY COUNTY

Library Management Cases

by
MILDRED HAWKSWORTH LOWELL

The Scarecrow Press, Inc.
Metuchen, N.J.   1975

Lowell, Mildred Hawksworth.
　Library management cases.

　　Includes indexes.
　　1. Library administration--Case studies. I. Title.
Z678.L647　　658'.91'021　　75-23077
ISBN 0-8108-0845-5

Copyright © 1975 by Wayne R. Lowell

Manufactured in the United States of America

TABLE OF CONTENTS

	Page
List of Cases	v
Preface	vii
I Organizing Cases (Cases 1-21)	1
II Planning and Decision-Making Cases (Cases 22-51)	56
III Controlling Cases (Cases 52-71)	143
IV In-Basket Cases (Cases 72-76)	193
Title Index to Cases	251
Subject Index to Case Content	254

LIST OF CASES

Case Number	Case Title	Page
1	Need for Organizational Change	2
2	Flexible Scheduling	6
3	A Despotic Supervisor	9
4	The Memo Writer	13
5	Selection Committee	16
6	Baby-Sitting Service	18
7	Identify Yourself	19
8	Inflexible Rules	22
9	Interference with Student Discipline	23
10	Work Assignments	23
11	Central Information Desk	25
12	Data Packets	28
13	A Schedule Change	30
14	Resignation	32
15	Fractionated Time	33
16	Hemlock High Resource Center	34
17	Too Many Supervisors	38
18	Participative Management (Role Playing)	40
19	Busy, Busy, Busy	47
20	Volunteers (Role Playing)	52
21	An Organization Chart	54
22	Problems Inherited by a Young Administrator	59
23	Wanted: A Mover's Manual	66
24	Reorganization of Children's Services	67
25	"Innovative" Cataloging	73
26	A Technical Services Department	75
27	Momentum (Role Playing)	78
28	Popular Materials in a Research Library	81
29	Education Division vs. Library	82
30	Special Funding	83
31	A Branch in a Low-Income Neighborhood	84
32	Mission of Research Libraries (Role Playing)	89
33	Short- and Long-Range Planning	94
34	Gift Appraisals	101
35	A "Bargain"	104

36	Church and State (Role Playing)	109
37	A Fire	110
38	A New Community College	113
39	"Bandaid" Work	115
40	Faculty Reading Lists (Skit)	118
41	Staff Concern	121
42	"The Shelf"	123
43	School Reorganization	126
44	Study Center Requested	127
45	Individual Recognition (Role Playing)	128
46	Research Library Public Service	130
47	Arbitrary Architect	132
48	Clearance Policy (Role Playing)	133
49	Planned Expansion	135
50	Who Controls Library Space?	137
51	No Textbooks!	139
52	A Penitentiary Library	144
53	Confrontation (Role Playing)	148
54	The Scribbler	150
55	A Senile Public Library Board	151
56	Fund Accounting	152
57	A Gift with Stipulations	155
58	A Faculty Library Committee Member	157
59	A Pilferage Racket	158
60	Harassment at Stonechat Branch	161
61	City Hall	166
62	Overdues	172
63	Censorship	174
64	Control of Special Appropriation	175
65	The Sealed Envelope	176
66	How Much Autonomy Should a Branch Librarian Have?	178
67	Misuse of Seabrook College Library	180
68	Too Much Advice	182
69	The Tupelo Family	184
70	Service to High School Students	187
71	Questionable Practices	189
72	International League Library	196
73	Technical Information Center	207
74	Shawn Public Library	218
75	Tyson Hospital Medical Library	228
76	May County Library System	238

PREFACE

Of the cases in this volume, some are new; the remainder were published originally either in my The Process of Managing, in Role Playing and Other Management Cases, or in The Case Method in Teaching Library Management. Many of the previously published cases have been revised, updated, refocused, or completely rewritten--hopefully to make them better teaching instruments in library school management courses; and for use in various types of management training seminars, workshops, institutes, and continuing education programs for librarians.

When I wrote the cases for the four-volume Management of Libraries and Information Centers, very few, if any, "administration" courses in library schools utilized the case method as one of the teaching methods. Hence, I modeled the cases I wrote on those found to be successful in the teaching of management in schools of business and in public administration. The former varied in length from brief incidents to long, even sequential, cases. Public administration cases were invariably long and complicated and often constituted the main fabric of a whole course. To ascertain whether or not my cases met librarians' needs and requirements, feedback from library educators and leaders of continuing education programs was necessary.

To make this revision as useful as possible for librarians, I made a sample "market survey" in 1974. The librarians were asked: 1) what uses they had made of the four volumes; 2) what they found most and least valuable for their purposes; and 3) what they would like in a revised edition. The replies were most helpful and the suggestions have been incorporated in the revision.

The feedback from this survey, from conversations and correspondence with many librarians, and from other sources of information, indicated that librarians preferred shorter cases which focused on one concept or principle rather than complicated many-faceted cases which would require extensive analysis. For this reason, none of the long cases in the earlier four volumes were chosen for inclusion here except that several library educators requested that the in-basket cases be retained in this volume. The in-basket cases have been updated and revised.

All types of libraries are represented in these cases: academic, public (municipal, county, state, federal), school, and special. The fact that a problem or situation is presented in one type of library does not mean that it is unique to that type of library; the same problem might well occur in any other type of library.

The general structure of this volume and the sequence of parts follow the phases of management: organizing, planning, and controlling. Cases about the fourth essential phase of managing--leading and motivating--are to be published in a companion volume, Library Personnel Cases.* This division was dictated by the feedback from librarians. Although human factors cannot be separated from organizing, planning, and controlling, the cases in this volume focus more on other management problems than on personnel problems.

In the first edition, I did not place questions at the end of cases because I felt this would channel reader thinking to those questions and perhaps inhibit consideration of other issues. Librarian feedback indicated that, in this revision, questions would be a welcome addition. They have therefore been included for each case.

Cases written especially for role playing have been so marked. Other cases could also be role-played effectively before a group or class. When students and others go through the decision-making process of analyzing cases, they are, in effect, role playing, since they must perceive themselves in the role of the chief character in order to conceptualize alternatives and to decide on a solution. They bring to the case discussion their perceptions of the environmental setting, the problems involved, and their role as the chief character.

All of these cases are based on facts which were acquired through personal interviews, records of court cases, confidential library reports and files, correspondence, grievance hearings, and numerous printed sources. To protect the confidential nature of the data acquired, disguises of various kinds were used in writing the actual incidents and experiences into cases--such as size and type of library, age and sex of characters, and geographical location. The focus has been on the problem. For names of places, libraries, and surnames of characters, the names of colors, fabrics,

---

*Publisher's note: The author died while this volume was in preparation, and it is unlikely that Library Personnel Cases will now be completed.

trees, nuts, flowering plants, birds, rocks, and minerals were used. Given names of characters were selected at random from a list of names for boys and girls. If data about the same type of problem were acquired from several sources, the facts, incidents and characters were woven into a composite to exemplify that type of problem.

The reader may well ask why this volume is limited to cases and does not include lecture outlines, suggested readings, and bibliographies as did The Process of Managing. The reason is that times have changed and there seems no further need for such a provision.

The format and content of the first edition were dictated by the late Dr. Ralph Shaw, who at that time was Vice President of The Scarecrow Press. He was a pioneer in advocating and applying basic management principles to the administration of libraries. He believed that library school courses in "administration" needed a complete overhaul. At the time, these courses could be characterized in one of two ways: 1) a "library economy" course which was a catch-all for materials and subjects not covered elsewhere in the curriculum, such as charging procedures and methods, order routines, statistical record keeping, and preparation and care of materials; or 2) functions of library operations with which the library administrator dealt on a day-to-day basis such as physical plant, legal involvements, control of operational functions, and budget. In addition, in nearly every library school, courses on "administration" of types of libraries proliferated, as though the process of managing varied according to type of enterprise. Actually, these courses were not "administration" but descriptions of activities and problems in public, academic, school, or special libraries. Management as a field of serious study in librarianship remained underdeveloped. The literature of library administration remained basically uninfluenced by transfer of insights and knowledge of management as developed in such areas as public administration and business.

Dr. Shaw wanted to see management courses taught in library schools which would present the latest concepts and research findings of management wherever developed. So, he asked the writer to prepare two syllabi which could be put in the hands of library educators to assist them in teaching either a basic management or a personnel course. He hoped these would replace both the "library economy"-type course and the "administration" of types of libraries courses. The Process of Management was essentially the basic library management course I taught in the Graduate Library School at Indiana University and included lecture outlines, background information, suggested readings, bibliographies, and cases to accompany each unit. Personnel Management had the same format and recorded my course in personnel. In addition to these two syllabi, Dr. Shaw wanted a "how-to-do-it" volume about teaching by the case method which he thought might give library educators confidence in utilizing this method if they had not used it previously. This was published as The Case Method in Teaching Library Management.

In 1974, there seems no need to update the background information, the lecture outlines, or the bibliographies for three reasons:

First, since the first edition was published, management has become a discipline in its own right, applicable to any area of society and to all organizations. Whereas in the past, management concepts were rigorously applied in private firms, today they are applied wherever effective managers are needed, such as in space agencies, urban transport, wildlife refuges, hospitals, churches, schools, the armed forces, civic and service organizations, government, business, and libraries. In fact, in the very near future we may see interdisciplinary management departments in universities which will blend together whatever has been learned for educating managers in every type of enterprise.

Secondly, management textbooks now are interdisciplinary and so broad in scope as to be equally suitable for non-profit social organizations and institutions as for profit-oriented agencies. These textbooks are kept up to date by frequent revisions which incorporate the latest research findings and are accompanied by books of readings which amplify concepts in the texts, and by teachers' manuals which offer substantial help to those who have limited background in the subject. To integrate what is learned from these textbooks, librarians need library cases to exemplify principles and concepts--and this is the function of this volume.

And third, several library schools have either faculty members from schools of business teaching their management courses or librarians who have studied all phases of management and personnel. Other library schools are likely to employ such persons in the near future because today's master's graduates are thrust into administrative positions early in their careers and they need to be prepared in this area.

       Mildred Hawksworth Lowell, Ph.D.
      Professor Emeritus of Library Science
         Graduate Library School
           Indiana University

CHAPTER I

ORGANIZING CASES

The objective of organizing is to establish an activity-authority environment in which individuals can perform most effectively. Whether the number of employees is large or small, their effective cooperation requires organization. Organizing is the grouping of activities necessary to accomplish goals and plans, the assignment of these activities to appropriate departments, and the provision for authority delegation and coordination. Two elements are invariably present in organizing: dividing the work into jobs and, at the same time, making sure that these separate clusters of work are linked together into a total team effort. The success of any enterprise depends to a significant degree on how skillfully their managers assign tasks so that they result in integrated, purposeful action.

To help visualize organization structure and relationships among units in a formal organization, organization charts are normally employed. These show the major functions and their respective relationships, the channels of formal authority, and the relative authority of each person. Such charts may be vertical, horizontal, or circular.

In most libraries, staff manuals are an essential part of the organization structure and are normally prepared for use at every level of supervision.

Here are some basic principles of organizing:

Objective: An organization must have objectives.

Specialization: The work of each person should be confined to a single function.

Unity of direction: One head and one plan should be provided for each group of activities.

Unity of command: Each person should receive orders from one person and be accountable only to him.

Authority and responsibility: A person held responsible for certain results should be given authority to achieve them.

Delegation: Each decision should be delegated to the lowest possible level.

Span of managerial authority: Consists of the number of persons whom one superior can supervise and who have access to the superior.

Scalar principle or chain of command: A hierarchy of jobs and a line of authority proceeds from the chief executive to his immediate subordinates and so on down to the lowest employee in the organization.

Balance: Various parts of the organization should be in balance so that none of the functions are given undue emphasis at the expense of others.

Exception principle: Recurring decisions should be handled routinely by lower level managers, whereas problems involving unusual or exceptional problems should be referred to higher levels.

Case 1

NEED FOR ORGANIZATIONAL CHANGE

Recently a dental research foundation received a large grant from the National Institutes of Health to continue and enlarge its research program. In addition, revenue from royalties and the sale of publications had created a more stable financial base for the foundation than it had had in its first twenty years of existence. For years the staff of the foundation had been dissatisfied with the organization and operation of its library, which had grown to 25,000 bound volumes of books and journals and many thousands of pamphlets, reprints, manuscripts, and reports. The library also contained many uncataloged kodachrome and glass slides, X-ray negatives, and a few motion pictures. An expanded research program demanded the skill and knowledge of a professional librarian to assist the staff.

The foundation library had originated as a private collection in the office of the first director and founder of the research program. As the collection grew, it was moved first to an outer office under the supervision of the director's secretary, and then to a separate "library room" tended by a full-time clerk.
For the past eight years the library had been operated by Mrs. Williams, an attractive, cultured widow in her late fifties. Her three children were grown and lived quite a distance away, so almost her whole life centered around the library. Flowering plants, ferns, and trailing vines on every window sill, desk and piece of equipment were evidence of her interest in growing beautiful things. She also was an art enthusiast and had decorated the walls with pictures and artifacts. Just keeping the plants watered took an hour or more each day. She was very possessive about "her" library and the various housekeeping and decorative details. She spent hours "mending" books, "reinforcing" paperbacks or fragile books (to the detriment of the books), and labeling books in beautiful, precise lettering. Reference service to the staff was minimal and inadequate. It usually consisted only of Mrs. Williams' memory of something she had handled.
Because of a large budget and a stepped-up research program, the foundation staff urgently needed a better organized library with a complete and accurate catalog. There was need for an aggressive and thorough selection and acquisition program, which would include searching out everything published in any language about dental research and obtaining either the publications or reprints or photocopies of them. The staff would need abstracts of the most pertinent dental publications, supplied at regular intervals, and also high-level literature searches and research assistance.
The director explained to Mrs. Williams the new roles the library and librarian must fill and the necessity for employing a professionally educated librarian. Diplomatically, he told Mrs. Williams that she would have to adjust to many changes in "her" library and to the work assignments which the new librarian would give her. He assured her that she would be retained on the library staff or in some other place in the foundation with no decrease in salary until her retirement in six years. Mrs. Williams was upset by the news.
In a few months the director hired Miss Bruce, who had not only a master's degree in library science but also eight years' experience in a medical school library. She had completed a sixth year in library school, where she had specialized in science literature and the administration of special libraries. When she came for a personal interview, Miss

Bruce was dismayed at the situation she found. Nevertheless, she liked administrative challenges, she wanted to live in this part of the country, where both mountains and ocean were close by, she was interested in dental research, and she believed that she would be mentally stimulated by working with the foundation staff. The director told her that she would have a free hand in reorganizing and revitalizing the library. She realized that the job would be a difficult one.

When Miss Bruce began her duties, she faced these problems:

Classification System: Many years ago the first director had devised a system based on fifteen letters of the alphabet, each of which stood for a general subject, such as anatomy, surgery, or law. Such a classification was satisfactory for a small office collection, but was hopelessly inadequate for a collection of more than 25,000 volumes. An alphabetical arrangement by author would have been much more useful. There was no consistency in the use of classification letters. Frequently, Mrs. Williams had classified second copies of books with a letter different from that used for the first copy.

Miss Bruce found that at least two-thirds of the collection covered subjects which were not strictly dental literature; related subjects represented included anaesthesia, legal decisions, and child psychology, among others. She decided that the Dewey Decimal Classification would be the easiest system for the staff to use, but that she would classify the purely dental material according to the system devised by Dr. Arthur D. Black, late Dean of Northwestern University Dental School in Chicago. To avoid the constant repetition of 617.6, the Dewey number for dentistry, and to shorten the numbers, Dr. Black had substituted the letter D for 617.6 and had worked out the following classification:

D DENTISTRY
D1 Dental anatomy, histology, and physiology
D2 Operative dentistry
D3 Prosthetic dentistry
D4 Orthodontia
D5 Oral hygiene
D6 Oral pathology
D7 Oral surgery
D8 Dental jurisprudence, ethics, and economics

Each of these numbers was then subdivided in the same manner as the Dewey system.

Serials Record: An inspection of the serials record

and a spot check of holdings against the record revealed that it was inadequate and incomplete. There was no procedure for claiming missing issues or routing new issues to the staff. Miss Bruce ordered new rotary wheel equipment and devised a color coding system for a new check-in system.

Museum Collection: Miss Bruce found in the library some large, high, locked bookcases, with glass doors, which contained plaster models of teeth and jaws, skulls and bones of animals and humans used in comparative anatomical dental research, and various other specimens and artifacts related to teeth and dentistry.

Card Catalog: The form of entry used on the catalog cards was based on a style used for footnotes in medical journals at the time the first cataloging was started many years ago. Because the style was so inadequate and failed to provide the information needed for present-day use, the foundation staff rarely used the catalog. Since neither Mrs. Williams nor any of the clerks preceding her had ever heard of a subject heading list, most of the subjects chosen for subject headings were identical with the broad classification categories. For example, "anatomy" was the heading used for two drawers of catalog cards. Whenever the author's name was not clearly evident on the title page of a book, Mrs. Williams had used the word "anonymous" as the author. Two catalog drawers contained cards attributed to this ubiquitous author. Miss Bruce decided that she would have to start a new catalog and eventually discard all the cards in the present catalog.

Librarian's Office: The room which Mrs. Williams had used for an office contained one desk, one table, three filing cabinets, a sink, and wall shelving. When Miss Bruce became librarian, she found both the desk and the table piled about two feet high with an accumulation of cards, pamphlets, periodicals, papers, and books. The size of the pile and the yellowed pages indicated that they had been there for quite some time. Filing cabinets and window sills were crowded with plants and the walls were decorated with hanging brackets containing more plants. The shelves were crammed with all kinds of publications not yet "cataloged." Because the only telephone in the library was in this room, Miss Bruce decided that for the time being this would have to be her office.

Moving out of "her" office to a smaller one on the other side of the stacks, away from the entrance to the library, was a blow to Mrs. Williams' pride. Although Miss Bruce had all the plants and pictures moved to Mrs. Williams' new office so that she would not miss them, she felt

6 / Library Management

demoted and somewhat degraded. Knowing that finding a new role for Mrs. Williams would take tact and patience, Miss Bruce tried to involve her as much as possible in analyzing conditions in the library and in discussing alternative solutions for improving organization and service. But Mrs. Williams did not understand the terminology or concepts, and she could see no reason for any of the changes Miss Bruce suggested. After spending endless hours trying to give Mrs. Williams the background information essential for making various decisions, Miss Bruce finally gave Mrs. Williams a pile of library science publications and asked her to read them. Mrs. Williams pouted and complained, and either did not read them or had difficulty comprehending what she read.

Believing that Mrs. Williams would "lose face" by being transferred from the library to another job in the foundation, Miss Bruce hoped to find a niche in the library where Mrs. Williams could not only contribute to an on-going, vital library, but also find work which would interest her. Miss Bruce had employed two full-time clerks whom she was training to handle all serials, binding preparation, circulation, descriptive cataloging, and some literature searching. She had had Mrs. Williams try each of these duties but found her either incapable of or undependable in doing any of them.

* * *

Can you suggest priorities for bringing about a complete organizational change for the library? Has Miss Bruce been too solicitous about Mrs. Williams' feelings, to the detriment of effective organization?

Case 2

FLEXIBLE SCHEDULING

Midwest Electronics employed approximately five hundred employees who worked Monday through Friday from 8:00 a.m. to 5:00 p.m. with an hour for lunch--a total workweek of forty hours. The plant cafeteria couldn't accommodate all the employees at one time, so lunch hours for the different departments or assembly lines were staggered between 11:30 and 2:00. The plant was located on the outskirts of a medium-sized city and employees arrived either by bus or by private car.

Learning from friends and from newspaper articles about "flextime" being adopted in other plants in the area, several employees started promoting the idea among their fellow workers. This plant was unionized, so any changes in work schedules had to be approved by the union and included in the union contract. At the next union meeting, the promoters of flexible scheduling suggested that a committee be elected to meet with management to discuss the possibilities.

The spokesman for the group explained to the membership what was meant by flexible scheduling or flextime: "An ideal flexible schedule would permit employees to choose their own working hours, but such an ideal is impossible to achieve in practice because of the need to maintain supervision and communication among employees. However, it is possible in some work situations to broaden the range of choices considerably beyond that found in the standard five-day week and still maintain management's control over the quality and quantity of production. An employee working a flexible week might not wish to have each day begin and end at the same time, or he might prefer to shorten his daily time at work by extending the number of working days to six or seven; or he may have some other preference. The most common flexible week is the four-day week, in which work previously done during five working days of equal length is accomplished in four working days. For example, five eight-hour days and four ten-hour days both make a forty-hour work week. The four-day week saves transportation costs to and from work for one day a week, provides the employee with a three-day weekend for leisure or work at home, and gives the employee one weekday for personal business such as medical or dental appointments."

A committee was elected to meet with management, and a meeting was held after work three days later. Management pointed out that 90 per cent of the employees at Midwest worked on assembly lines which required that everyone begin and end their jobs at the same time. It would be impossible to operate the plant with employees coming and leaving at different times because the work flow would be interrupted, thus slowing down the next line, and supervision would be most difficult. After more meetings with their union, the committee asked management about the possibilities of a ten-hours-per-day, four-day week. Management asked that all employees vote on this.

The results of the vote were: 77 per cent voted for the 7:00-5:30, four-day week, ten hours per day with half an hour for lunch, and 23 per cent voted to retain the present

8 / Library Management

five-day schedule with one hour for lunch. On the basis of this vote, management agreed, for a trial period of two months, to operate the plant 7:00 a.m.-5:30 p.m. Tuesday through Friday with half an hour for lunch. If the shorter rest period at noon and the longer day increased worker fatigue, with consequent lowering of quality and quantity of work, the management reserved the right to go back to the standard five-day week. The motto of the plant was "zero defects" and the workers were very proud of their record on quality control. The pace of the assembly line had been determined by many tests and union negotiations in the past and was written into the union contract. If worker fatigue caused by longer hours made it impossible for workers to keep up with the assembly line or if the quality of the product dropped, then the plant would go back to the standard week.

A research library served the engineers, research staff, and officials of the plant. Prior to the adoption of the four-day week, the library had been open 45 hours per week, the same hours as the plant (i.e. 8:00-5:00, five days a week). The staff consisted of Mrs. Ben, head librarian, four librarians, one part-time translator, and two clerk-typists. Each of the five librarians worked at the circulation desk one day a week plus one noon hour. One librarian was responsible for acquisitions; one for cataloging; one for serials, continuations, indexing services, technical reports, and patent literature; one for reference, literature searches, interlibrary loans; and Mrs. Ben was responsible for supervision, public relations, attending staff meetings with the engineers and research staff, and service to their clientele. One clerk-typist worked for the acquisitions librarian and the cataloger; the other did secretarial work for Mrs. Ben, answered the telephone, typed bibliographies, and any other work assigned to her. The translator was always busy translating articles from foreign languages for the research staff and had no responsibility for any library work.

Now, with the plant's new four-day week schedule, the library was open 42 hours per week and the circulation desk had to be covered for this number of hours. The old vertical pattern of scheduling for the circulation desk would no longer fit the changed number of days.

* * *

Devise what you consider would be an ideal schedule for service at the circulation desk. Remember that each staff member has half an hour for lunch.

Case 3

A DESPOTIC SUPERVISOR

In his search for a new circulation librarian, Dr. Kenneth Martin, director of libraries at North State College, had obtained placement papers from library schools for several candidates and had interviewed applicants at the annual meeting of the American Library Association. His first choice was Jack Sherwin, a man in his thirties who for five years had been assistant to the circulation librarian in a state university. Both library school professors and past employers considered that Sherwin had exceptional capabilities: initiative, dependability, responsibility, and administrative ability. The circulation department at North State had been operating most inefficiently for several years; a person with Sherwin's knowledge, experience, and capabilities was needed to reorganize it. Sherwin was therefore invited to the campus for an interview, he was offered the position, and he accepted.

During the first few weeks on the job, Sherwin discovered that as circulation librarian he was primarily responsible for the operation of the public desk, but that he had little or no control or responsibility over the personnel who worked in the closed stacks. Control of the latter was retained by Homer Grant, head of public services and Sherwin's superior. Grant had been "inherited" by Dr. Martin from the former librarian, had neither a college nor library degree, and had had no experience in any other library. At one time he had gone to a two-day personnel management conference. He obviously did not consider his lack of intellectual accomplishment a handicap. He had opinions on every subject and enjoyed sharing them with anyone who would listen. Consequently, most of the staff avoided him.

To develop and improve communication between the circulation department and the faculty, Dr. Martin suggested to Sherwin that he have lunch in the faculty dining room and in other ways get to know as many faculty members as possible. Sherwin soon learned, to his consternation, that librarians did not have academic status but shared the same position as maintenance and clerical workers on campus. In the administrative structure of the university, they reported to the head of non-academic personnel. As a result of this status, the library staff had to park two or three city blocks from the library, although an ample parking lot for the faculty was located immediately behind the library.

10 / Library Management

Dr. Martin asked Jack Sherwin to recommend improvements and changes in the circulation department and in other areas of public service, and encouraged him to report progress frequently. The first project that Sherwin thought essential was simplifying the charging system. After studying various systems in use at other libraries, he decided that the marginal punch cards would best serve the needs of this library. Martin enthusiastically agreed with the recommendation and instructed Sherwin to act on it. Grant, however, had difficulty in understanding how the system worked. Sherwin explained the system in painstaking detail, but Grant still did not understand the system or even the need for improvements. Sherwin was somewhat frustrated, since Dr. Martin had specifically instructed him to effect improvements.

Designing the new charging system and composing policies and procedures for the department required time away from the public desk. Grant told Sherwin that he was neglecting the most important aspect of his job. "That's where the public is, and that's where you should be to give them the best possible service," he said. Sherwin replied that any improvement in record keeping directly affected service to the public and that he could not accomplish much on the project when at the desk. As a result of this conversation, Sherwin worked at the desk for his regularly scheduled hours and designed the charging system during off-duty hours. Within three months all records were transferred, and the charging system was functioning smoothly.

One morning shortly afterward, Sherwin came in five minutes late. Mr. Grant called him into his office and said, "You must always be on time as a good example to your staff." Sherwin thought that this attitude and the manner in which it was expressed were suitable for a foreman in a factory but not appropriate at the professional level. Another morning, after a relief break, he was again called into Grant's office and was told that staff association rules specified that no staff member should leave the building except during lunch without the permission of his immediate supervisor, and that employees in the public service department were further restricted by Grant to taking their breaks only in the staff room. To Jack Sherwin these regulations appeared unreasonable, but he agreed to abide by them in the future.

The library had no orientation program for part-time employees. Students assigned to the circulation desk were told only a few basic principles about the files and the procedures for handling requests. Because of a shortage of professional staff in the circulation department, student assistants were often on duty alone, particularly in the evenings and on Saturday afternoons. Also, often at these times no reference librarian was on duty. Having received some complaints about service when only student assistants were on duty, Mr. Sherwin decided to work out an orientation program for the entire circulation process, including interpretation of the public catalog. The program would take about three hours of a student's time.

As a part of this program he designed a series of questions which student assistants were to answer by consulting the public catalog. Most of the questions were very elementary and were designed: 1) to teach how to distinguish between an author, title, or subject heading; 2) to give the student some comprehension of a dictionary catalog arrangement; and 3) to point out the necessity for following up "see" and "see also" cross references. Several students had taken the test without any problems. One day a young man who was to work in the department was given the test while Sherwin was on his lunch break. When Sherwin returned, a note on his desk asked him to report to Mr. Grant's office immediately. Grant, in a rage, questioned the justification for giving such a test to student assistants. "I don't think we can really expect students to take tests of this sort. After all, they are employed to do routine assignments and are not expected to be professionals. Why, even I can't answer this problem. Who told you to do this? No one ever told me anything about it." Sherwin explained why he thought the test was necessary and added that it was commonly done in libraries; in fact, he had given similar tests in his former job.

"Inasmuch as I am circulation librarian, I consider the department my responsibility to administer. I did not think it necessary to inform you about the orientation program. Dr. Martin expects me to improve the circulation department in any way I think best," said Sherwin.

For more than ten years virtually nothing had been done about the many books which were recorded as missing. At least 7,000 cards in the circulation files indicated books had been missing for various periods of time. Frequent calls came to the desk for many of these titles. Mr. Sherwin was embarrassed in answering patrons' questions because of the numerous inaccuracies in this file. To improve the service, he decided to reorganize this phase of the work by developing a procedure which would eliminate the file. He had observed that his student assistants did not have enough to do at the desk during slack times; they could work on this missing book project then. It would not be necessary to employ any additional clerks. He devised this procedure:

12 / Library Management

1. Student assistants remove charge cards for missing books from circulation file and check with shelves. After checking shelves, give all cards to Sherwin with notes about what has been learned in the course of the search.
2. For those titles found on shelves: Sherwin will make any necessary changes in records and notify proper departments (if that is necessary).
3. Cards for books not found on shelves: Sherwin will assign a student assistant to check shelflist to see whether there are other copies and if so, how many. Return cards to Sherwin.
    a. If title is not in demand and the library has more copies, Sherwin will send circulation file cards to cataloging department, requesting that they mark these copies "withdrawn."
    b. If book is not in demand and library has no other copy, Sherwin will decide whether to buy or withdraw.
    c. If book is in demand, Sherwin will ask order department to reorder.

Before starting the project, Sherwin discussed the utilization of student help and the proposed procedure with Martin, who said, "Excellent! I am pleased that you are doing this job which has been needed for a very long time. I suggest, though, that you route to my desk the cards for books that are not in demand and that are single copies. I may know of some reason why the book should be reordered or of some future use for the book, although there is no demand at present." Sherwin made this change in 3b. of his procedure.

The project was started in the spring and proceeded slowly. By August, when Sherwin was to take his vacation, the project had not been completed. He instructed the student assistants to continue checking the missing cards against the shelves (item 1 in procedure) and to place all cards so searched on his desk for action upon his return. He told Mr. Grant about his instructions to the students.

When he returned a month later, he learned that the cards had not been put on his desk but instead had been placed on Martin's desk. Martin, of course, thought that the intervening steps in the procedure had been completed and proceeded to make decisions about withdrawal or reordering. When the order department staff started working on the orders, they found that the library had other copies of many titles. As that department was short-staffed and

overworked, the head of the department complained bitterly to Dr. Martin about the inaccuracy of the checking done by the circulation department.
Mr. Sherwin was sharply criticized for carelessness by Grant. Although the student assistants had made the error, this fact did not lessen the emotional tension. Sherwin considered such criticism unwarranted and unjustified. He was dependent upon untrained part-time student help, and these student assistants had not followed instructions.

* * *

In most libraries, is supervision of stacks normally one of the responsibilities of the circulation librarian? In what ways did Dr. Martin ignore the chain of command in this situation?

Case 4

THE MEMO WRITER

For eleven months John Carleton, the librarian of a U.S. government research library, had been watching the civil service lists for a GS-9 cataloger. When he learned that Miss Gladys Sprague qualified for the position, he hired her on the strength of her standard government application, because he desperately needed another cataloger to work on the accumulated backlog. Although she had no library degree, she had a bachelor's degree in chemistry, a capability the position required, had had excellent inservice cataloging training, and about nine years of experience as a cataloger in other government libraries. Since she had just arrived on the mainland from her last position with an overseas armed forces activity, where she had worked for four years, Mr. Carleton could not quickly check her references. He reasoned that anyone who had worked that long as a cataloger in other government libraries should be satisfactory for his library. Subsequently, he did check her references and found that she had had difficulty with previous supervisors and had resented being told what to do and how to do it.
Almost from the day she started to work in the library she complained about real or imaginary problems. The library was in an old World War II barracks which had

been renovated for library use. The original windows had been left unchanged, however, and they opened and closed with great difficulty. Normally, the library staff never opened the windows but depended on the heating-ventilating system in winter and on individual window air-conditioners in summer. Claiming that she needed plenty of fresh air, Miss Sprague went over her supervisor's head to write to Mr. Carleton complaining about the "intolerable and overwhelming heat." She wanted the windows open winter and summer. From previous experience over the years the staff had found that if the windows were wide open in the winter, they inevitably came down with colds and flu because of drafts and uneven heating; in summer, they were much too warm and the air-conditioners would not function properly.

 Mr. Carleton informed Miss Sprague that he was referring her memorandum to her supervisor, Mrs. Irene Rey, and that she should take up future complaints with her. Mrs. Rey relocated Miss Sprague's desk next to some windows, so that Miss Sprague could either use the mechanical ventilation or open the windows next to her desk. Miss Sprague next complained that since there was too much draft near the windows, she wanted to get away from them but she still wanted the windows open. Mrs. Rey again rearranged all the work stations in the cataloging department to get Miss Sprague out of the "drafts." Each of these moves annoyed the rest of the staff.

 Mrs. Rey, who had been head cataloger for five years, had a reputation of being a firm but fair administrator. She had very little turnover in her staff, had a better than normal ability to handle people, and was tolerant, patient, and understanding.

 A few months later Miss Sprague located herself and her equipment and furniture in a small, little-used room of the library away from everyone else, claiming she could work better by herself. This was done without Mrs. Rey's permission or knowledge, but all personnel in the department mutually agreed it was a beneficial move, since it eliminated a source of constant friction. After four weeks, however, she rejoined the rest of the catalogers, indicating that she thought they "needed her."

 In general, Miss Sprague resisted advice and guidance in her work. She persisted in using her own subject headings. Consequently, Mrs. Rey had to revise her work constantly. Ignoring Mr. Carleton's directive to go through channels with her complaints, Miss Sprague sent a second memorandum to him as follows:

Organizing Cases / 15

To: Mr. John Carleton From: Gladys Sprague
In re: Mrs. Irene Rey Date: -----

Because I could not endure the overheated, dry room in which the catalogers work, I had to open windows and turn on fans. Mrs. Rey resented my doing this and decided to get even with me in every way she could think of.

I am sure you understand Mrs. Rey's intense passion for our subject headings authority file, but I doubt if you have had the opportunity to observe how completely obsessed she is with it--to the point of not allowing any other member of the staff to add headings without her approval. Her desire for consistency and perfection doesn't give her license to impair cataloging procedures just because she doesn't have time to approve every term we need to use at the moment.

Her every action is directed toward her self-aggrandizement, which makes her a poor supervisor. I could get along with her beautifully if I cared to cater to her, but this I cannot do. She is arrogant and has an overbearing manner.

Mr. Carleton ignored this memo. When he had to fill out the forms recommending annual increments for his staff, he tentatively turned down an increment for Miss Sprague. Ninety days before the final report was due, he and Mrs. Rey individually and collectively talked with Miss Sprague, pointing out her failures and suggesting ways in which she could improve her work and her spirit of cooperation. Mr. Carleton told her that if she improved during the ninety days, he would approve her raise. A written statement of the conferences was given to her so that there would be no question as to what the complaints were. Her performance did not improve. Mrs. Rey informed her that she had not approved her within-grade raise. Mr. Carleton got another memorandum:

To: Mr. John Carleton From: Gladys Sprague
In re: My step increase Date: -----

I really don't know whether you are being influenced by what Mrs. Rey is saying about me and my work. However, if my step increase is withheld, I will be compelled to talk to the personnel division about it, or go even beyond them if necessary.

16 / Library Management

Mr. Carleton again ignored the memorandum. A few days later another memorandum was placed on his desk early one morning before he had arrived at his office:

To: Mr. John Carleton   From: Gladys Sprague
In re: Mrs. Rey   Date: -----

I would have no concern about the way Mrs. Rey spends her time on the job if it were not for the fact that I am a victim of her viciousness. At least while she is wasting her own and other people's time she is not nagging me about spaces, indentations, periods, and commas. Here is a reasonably accurate and verifiable account of the way she spent her day yesterday....

From this list of activities, you can see that she wasted most of her day in gossiping with other members of the staff or doing personal reading. I can understand her need for personal attention, but that is no excuse for using library time for trivial and personal things. She tried to engage me in conversation three different times by asking personal questions, but I had work to do and didn't answer her. It almost seems that she would prefer my paying a lot of personal attention to her rather than keeping at work.

This is only to let you know the kind of person who is recommending that my step increase be withheld, and who is bitterly opposing the upgrading of my job.

*   *   *

In what ways did Miss Sprague ignore the chain of command? Were Mr. Carleton and Mrs. Rey justified in withholding Miss Sprague's step increase?

Case 5

SELECTION COMMITTEE

Joan Peters began working as one of five elementary school librarians in the River County school system last year. Her immediate supervisor was Alice Longford, the director of the River County Instructional Materials Center.

Organizing Cases / 17

Each librarian was responsible for four school libraries and worked in each school one day a week; on the fifth day she worked in the Center. On the days when no librarian was present, the library was staffed with sixth-grade students who were trained by the librarian. Because all processing was done in the Center and materials were sent to the schools ready for the shelves, students could handle the clerical routines and the shelving. Although this arrangement was less than perfect, it did insure that each elementary school received some professional service.

The book selection committee for the twenty elementary schools consisted of the five librarians and two teachers. The committee met in two sections: one section, consisting of two librarians and one teacher, selected books for the primary grades; the other, consisting of three librarians and one teacher, selected books for the intermediate grades. The book budget was apportioned arbitrarily between the two committees; any unspent balance at the end of the year was used for instructional materials or equipment.

The two sections of the committee met regularly, studied various reviewing journals, and selected books which they believed desirable. They then exchanged lists so that all five librarians would know what was being considered. When the lists had the final approval of both sections of the committee, review copies were ordered from a local bookstore. The manager allowed the Center to keep the review copies as long as the committee wished and accepted without charge all books which it decided not to buy. All books finally chosen were purchased through this bookstore.

Each committee member was responsible for reading and reviewing approximately one-seventh of those selected for review; in other words, each member was to read an equal number. As far as possible, each one chose first the titles she was interested in and then whatever other titles were left. Miss Longford insisted that each book must be read and reviewed before it was purchased. Because the books belonged to the bookstore and were not the property of the school system, she said that they could not leave the Center. Reading several hundred titles a year at the Center was an impossible assignment because each librarian was there only one day a week and had many other responsibilities while there. Consequently, the reviewing was not well done.

By the end of the year Miss Peters was frustrated and unhappy about her work on the selection committee. In the school system where she had worked before coming to River County, all books could be taken home for reading and each librarian was responsible for only one subject area. In addition to sending in requests for new books for that area, each person studied the collection to fill in gaps and to discard outdated titles. These librarians also met and heard each other's reviews, so that they got to know the collection better.

Early in the fall of her second year at River County, Miss Peters decided to talk with her colleagues and sound out their opinions about the work of the selection committee. She learned that all of them were also dissatisfied. After some discussion they decided to work out new procedures and regulations. Miss Peters was asked to be the chairman and to present their plan to Miss Longford.

* * *

If you were Miss Peters, what procedures and regulations would you recommend? Remember that supervision of four school libraries is a very heavy work load.

Case 6

BABY-SITTING SERVICE

The Willow County Library was in the business center of a large city. The staff of the heavily used children's department included three professional librarians, two full-time clerks, and part-time high school pages. During the week many men and women working in the downtown area borrowed and returned books for their children. Story hours for preschool children were held two mornings a week, and at the same time programs were provided for the mothers. Elementary school children came to the department on regularly scheduled visits and programs. Saturdays were especially busy.

Several times in the past a woman had brought her five children, who ranged in age from two to ten years, and had asked if she could leave them while she did an errand. Whenever a parent made a request of this kind, the staff asked for a telephone number and address where the parent could be reached. The librarian told the parents that children usually got restless if left longer than half an hour and that it was impossible for a busy staff to keep a close watch on them. The mother of the five children had always returned promptly.

One Saturday she came in at 2:00 p.m., left the children, and handed a staff member an address and a telephone number. About an hour later a staff member had to reprimand two of the younger children, who were noisily playing tag around the tables. A little later another librarian noticed that the two-year-old had fallen asleep on the story-hour rug and that two other children at a table had their heads down on their arms. She called the number which the mother had left but got no answer. She repeatedly called all afternoon, but the children were still in the library at the 6:00 p.m. closing time. One librarian took the children to the entrance and waited there with them for twenty minutes. When their mother still had not come, the librarian called the police. Just as the police were helping the children into a prowl car, the mother appeared. She was furious that the police had been called and was abusive in speaking to the librarian.

* * *

Should this department have stricter rules and regulations concerning unattended children? If so, what do you suggest? Did the librarian at 6:20 have any other choice but to call the police?

Case 7

IDENTIFY YOURSELF

A lifelong resident of Cold Harbor, Robert Phyfe had been the director of the Cold Harbor Community College library for two years. His previous library experience had been acquired as a student assistant in cataloging while he was attending graduate library school.

Because the library was open to adult residents of the town and high school students, Mr. Phyfe was concerned that books might circulate to those who needed them less than the college students did. He instructed his clerks at the circulation desk that anyone wishing to check out material should "identify himself." A policy of the library made the loan privilege the same for faculty members and students because the college and its library were so new and the collection was still quite small. Until the collection could be strengthened and enlarged, the director of the library thought that faculty members could supplement their personal libraries by using the interlibrary loan service which he had taken great trouble to provide. (A large state university less than 100 miles away provided loan service.) Because of his limited budget, Mr. Phyfe did all that he could to reduce losses.

One day Mr. Phyfe received an irate telephone call from Miss Electra Johnson, a distinguished faculty member. She was furious that a student at the circulation desk had refused to let her borrow a book because she could not provide identification. She asked Mr. Phyfe for an explanation. She pointed out that she was a faculty member, the senior ranking professor of her department, and a native of Cold Harbor, where her family had lived for generations. Not to be recognized was unthinkable.

Mr. Phyfe immediately mailed to Miss Johnson a copy of the lending code of the library, which stated among other things, that "all persons are required to identify themselves." As he was very busy, he did not take time to write her a note. In the mail next morning Mr. Phyfe received this letter from Miss Johnson:

> Dear Mr. Phyfe:
> Thank you for sending me the lending code. However, the statement that it makes about identifying oneself is precisely the point I tried to make to you on the telephone the other day. I thought at the time, because you were in such a hurry to get to a meeting, that I did not make myself clear.
> I did identify myself by checking the appropriate box on the charge card. As you know, the card provides space for a borrower to write his or her name, address, and telephone number and to show his or her connection with the college, if any. This I did most willingly, and, I may add, in very clear handwriting.
> I should think that since faculty members are never provided with or asked to carry any identification that proves their connection with Cold Harbor Community College, the circulation desk of your library should have easily accessible a list of the faculty. When I asked the young woman at the desk to check my name in the faculty directory, she replied that she didn't have one.
> Is it not possible that this young person could have had access to such a list in your office? I

suggest to you that perhaps one of your duties is to provide some measure of service, the least of which would be to allow us to charge out a book occasionally. At the very least, I should think that you would find it advisable to train your staff to have good manners and to show common courtesy.

Mr. Phyfe's reply read:

Dear Miss Johnson:
We will in the future require all faculty members of the Cold Harbor Community College to identify themselves by showing a driver's license.
Thank you for your interest in the library. I am always interested in hearing from anyone who does not receive good service from the Cold Harbor College library.

Miss Johnson's answer read:

Dear Mr. Phyfe:
Surely you cannot be serious, but I suppose you must be. Since I do not have a driver's license, I shall do my best to find someone who will lend me one whenever I wish to check out a book from the library. Actually, my friends tell me that there is little hope that I shall ever be a borrower again. Driver's licenses, I am informed, do not reveal the occupation or business address of the holder.
Should I try to pass as a student? Perhaps this would be the easiest, although scarcely honest, way out of my predicament. I had thought until I joined the Cold Harbor Community College faculty that a library tried to encourage its use by faculty and students.
Sincerely yours,

Electra Johnson

cc: President Bates, Cold Harbor Community College
Dean Alden, Cold Harbor Community College

*   *   *

1) Consider the public relations aspect of this case, 2) Mr. Phyfe's handling of the situation, and 3) his instructions to desk attendant.

Case 8

INFLEXIBLE RULES

    Like most universities, Colburn University has a large reserve book room. Each instructor who wishes to put a book on reserve for his students must fill out a form for each book. Reserve book librarians have come and gone at Colburn, but this procedure has remained the same for many years.
    When she was promoted to the job of supervisor of the reserve book department last spring, Jane Holden had had three years' experience in the circulation department as a clerk; two of these had been spent as the supervisor of a large number of student workers. She was a competent employee, and both she and the library administration were satisfied with her promotion.
    During the first week of the fall term, a professor of philosophy who had been on the faculty for twenty years arrived at Mrs. Holden's desk with at least twenty-five books in his arms. He requested that they be put on reserve for one of his classes. Mrs. Holden asked him if he had filled out the reserve form for each book. The professor replied that he had not had time to do so and he did not have time then. "In that case," said Mrs. Holden, "I cannot put the books on reserve for you until you do have time to comply with our rules," and she went back to her desk.

*   *   *

    Was Mrs. Holden being very officious in her treatment at this professor? Couldn't she have had a student assistant fill out the forms and thus create a better public relations image? How inflexible are rules and procedures?

Case 9

INTERFERENCE WITH STUDENT DISCIPLINE

Students are reported to the dean of students office by the assistant librarian at State University Library whenever they fail to return library materials or do not pay fines. These reports are made at the end of each semester and summer session. Such a report does not prevent a student from registering the following semester, but after this one semester of grace, the student cannot register until he settles his account with the library.

Occasionally, when a student has been informed that he cannot register until he clears his record at the library, he goes to the library director's office and tells his tale of woe. The director, a lenient and gentle person, is quite often influenced by the student's story and overrides the staff recommendations for discipline. Such action by the director damages staff morale, especially that of the clerks at the circulation desk who bear the brunt of these problem students.

* * *

Enforcing the library rules and regulations in regard to circulation has been delegated to staff members at the circulation desk. After a decision has been delegated, has a higher line administrator any right to make counter decisions?

Case 10

WORK ASSIGNMENTS

The College of the Bible is a coeducational Christian college offering undergraduate preparation in the liberal arts, biblical and theological studies, and church vocations to one hundred and sixty students. A core major in the Bible and theology is included in each of these programs, which are taught by four full-time and three part-time instructors.

Because its student body was so small and its library so inadequate, the college failed to receive accreditation from the Accrediting Association of Bible Colleges. Plans to improve the library, which had had a succession of non-professional librarians at its head for the last fifteen years, included hiring as head librarian a newly ordained minister with wide non-professional experience in both public and seminary libraries. Mr. Johnson was given the rank of assistant professor and was to teach a course in the spring semester in addition to directing the library. Before the fall semester began, he took the basic courses in cataloging and classification, selection, and reference at a nearby graduate library school.

One of Mr. Johnson's first projects was a book inventory, which involved comparing the shelflist with the books on the shelves. He found many books not listed on the shelflist and many titles in the shelflist not represented on the shelves. After comparing the shelflist with the card catalog, he found that the card catalog did not agree with either the books on the shelf or the shelflist. Cataloging was so inadequate that one could not be certain that a card represented the book it appeared to be describing. Moreover, only one-third of the collection has been cataloged.

Mr. Johnson decided that Library of Congress cards should be ordered for all books; the use of these cards would eliminate the need for individual cataloging and card duplication. Before any cataloging was started, the Dean and Mr. Johnson weeded the collection and eliminated superseded editions, out-of-date religious tracts, and other unsuitable books which the library had received as gifts. Such materials composed about one-fourth of the collection. The library was kept open 8:00-5:00 Monday through Friday and 9:00-12:00 on Saturdays--a total of 48 hours per week.

Six students were assigned to Mr. Johnson to help in processing books, ordering Library of Congress cards for both new books and those already in the collection, and reclassifying books; this work involved removing Cutter numbers from book pockets, catalog cards, and shelflist cards. Students worked ten hours a week in the library as part of a scholarship program. The limited budget of the college did not provide for a student worker at the circulation desk. As a result, the desk was unmanned and a bell was placed on it for students to summon help. All student workers spent at least one hour a day on technical services projects. The schedules were arranged so that the students could spread their working hours over the week and would not have to work more than two hours in any one day. The schedules were also arranged, not according to blocks of time, but according to free periods which the students felt

Organizing Cases / 25

would not interfere with their studies. As a result, student assistants never worked two consecutive hours.
Mr. Johnson saw between four and six of his student workers each day. Since each student worked only for a short time, he found that he had to have several persons working on the same job. He also had to explain the same job to each student as he reported for work. Often the explanations took up at least a fourth of the student's working time. And by the time the student returned to work the next day, he had forgotten a great deal of the procedure because he had not worked long enough on the previous day to be thoroughly familiar with it. Mr. Johnson then had to spend more time explaining the procedure again. Another problem with student assistants involved the coordination of the various stages in technical processing and card ordering. Workers often had to be trained to do operations which were behind schedule before they could proceed with the part of the technical processing that they had originally been trained to do.
As a result of this constant supervising of student workers, answering reference questions, taking care of calls for reserve and stack books at the circulation desk, and answering the telephone, Mr. Johnson found it difficult to carry on his own work. When he got behind in his part of the processing, a bottleneck was created. He found that at least ten per cent of the work done by the students was inaccurate. Consequently he spent much of his own working time checking students' work. After the beginning of the second semester, when Mr. Johnson began teaching the course which he was preparing for the first time, the work in the library fell hopelessly behind.

* * *

How effective is Mr. Johnson as a supervisor and in organizing his own time? How would you divide the work among the six student assistants? Should a staff manual be prepared? Each of the six students worked ten hours a week--and the library was open 48 hours a week. Devise a weekly schedule for the six students.

Case 11

CENTRAL INFORMATION DESK

The central information desk of the Metropolitan

Public Library was part of the reference department and handled all incoming telephone questions as well as questions from patrons at the desk. Quick reference questions were answered from the basic collection of several hundred volumes shelved at the desk. Problems requiring longer searches or more specialized material were referred to other members of the reference department located in another room where there was a large collection.

The information desk was open until ten o'clock every night, including Sunday. Its services were heavily and constantly used, even in the late evening hours, and especially during school holidays. The telephones were always busy, and frequently lines of patrons were waiting.

Mrs. Norma Johnson was in charge of the desk and of scheduling her staff of clerks and professional librarians. At all times at least one professional librarian was scheduled for duty and was assisted by experienced clerks, most of whom had worked at the desk for several years. Mrs. Johnson made out the schedule a month in advance. Night, holiday, and Sunday schedules were fairly divided among the staff, so that each one had about an equal number of the less desirable hours of work. A week before making out each month's schedule, Mrs. Johnson always asked each staff member for a list of any special dates and times (birthday celebrations, concerts or plays, dental appointments, etc.) when he or she preferred not to work. After working out the monthly schedule, Mrs. Johnson consulted individually with each staff member before posting the schedule to be sure there were no mistakes. She was not always able to give each member the exact preferences for hours and days, but she tried to. The schedule for the next month was posted ten days before the beginning of the month.

On the day before and the days after Thanksgiving, Sarah Martin, a professional librarian who had worked at the information desk for about seventeen months since she had graduated from library school, was scheduled to work as follows:

> Wednesday: 1-5 p.m., 6-8 p.m.
> Thursday: None (library closed)
> Friday: 8:30 a.m.-12 noon, 6-9 p.m.
> Saturday: 8:30 a.m.-12 noon
> Sunday: 12 noon-4 p.m.

At ten o'clock on Wednesday morning Miss Martin hurried into Mrs. Johnson's office. Her rapid footsteps, the excitement in her eyes, and the color in her cheeks were all signs to Mrs. Johnson that this was no ordinary call. With a note of urgency in her voice, Miss Martin said, "I am scheduled for twenty hours of work today through Sunday, but I have twenty-eight hours of overtime which I accumulated for working last month when Mr. Smith was out with his appendectomy. I would like to go home today and return to work Monday morning."

"Since you're scheduled to go to work in three hours, this is certainly a last minute request! Why didn't you tell me about this a month ago so that I could have arranged these days off for you?"

"I didn't know about this then--you see, my mother just called an hour ago to tell me that my brother Dave, who is in the Navy, has leave from his ship and will be home for Thanksgiving and the weekend. That's why I want to go home. I haven't seen Dave since his leave after boot camp a year ago. You know I live four hundred miles from here and it will take me all day today to get home. I probably can't get a plane reservation, so I'll have to go by train or bus. And it will take most of Sunday to get back again."

"I can sympathize with your wanting to go home, Sarah, but how can we cover the schedule? You know how many high school and college students use the facilities of the information desk both by phone and in person over a holiday. I was counting on you to cover the hours you are scheduled."

"But I have the time coming to me."

"We appreciated your pinch-hitting for Mr. Smith last month; but I just don't know how I can cover your schedule."

Sarah Martin burst into tears and ran out of Mrs. Johnson's office.

*　　*　　*

How can a supervisor evaluate emergency priorities? Was Sarah Martin's emergency of less importance than Mr. Smith's appendectomy? What provisions should be made for a back-up staff to step in when emergencies occur. Was Miss Martin correct in her assumption that because she had worked extra hours for Mr. Smith, she was entitled to an equal amount of time off at her discretion?

Case 12

DATA PACKETS

Since 1920 the library in a state-supported university has provided "data packets" to persons in the state. One can obtain information on such diverse subjects as flower arranging, biographies, communism, or United States diplomatic relations with Argentina by writing directly to the library. The patron then receives by mail an envelope of clippings and pamphlets from the files maintained by employees of the data packets department. Sometimes a book or two is included, but even with this addition, the material has a somewhat limited usefulness because the file collection is weeded infrequently and not very carefully.

The head of the data packets department, Mrs. Finley, is also the head of the reference department. At one time she had been the director of the library. But several years before, when a new library building was being planned, Mrs. Finley, at her own request, relinquished her position as director. Mr. White, a librarian with experience in planning and building, was employed to replace her, and she then was appointed head of both the reference and the data packets departments. This arrangement was very much to her liking because she had no interest in planning a new building. She felt no animosity toward the new director, who had been hired only after she had turned down the job.

During the planning process Mr. White decided to make several changes in the internal administration of Mrs. Finley's departments. He believed that the usefulness of the data packets could be greatly increased if the collection were drastically weeded and brought up to date. Since the extension division of the state library had been offering almost identical service for many years, he suggested that the services should be coordinated and that the requests for the packets should go wherever possible through local libraries. Mr. White believed that much of the information in the data packets could be found in pamphlet files in libraries all over the state. He also knew that the amount of staff time spent on the preparation of the packets should be greatly reduced. Mrs. Finley now employed what she called "subject specialists" to do the clipping. Many of these women, none of whom had professional training, were being paid almost as much as the professional librarians on the staff, although their jobs could easily be done by clerks, or even by part-time student help. Mr. White also wanted a review of all subscriptions for periodicals which were clipped because he thought many were so popular that they could be found in almost any library or by any patron at his local newsstand.

Because the reference collection was divided by subject, the files for the data packets were kept in two separate locations. Periodicals were divided between the two rooms and bound volumes were shelved in the bookstacks adjacent to the rooms. All periodicals were received and checked by the periodicals librarian in the technical processes room and then were taken to the two reference rooms each day. Duplicate copies of periodicals that were to be clipped were also sent each day to the appropriate room where they were examined, clipped, and stored away in the bulging files. (Mrs. Finley kept a duplicate checking record, although it was easy to reach the periodicals librarian by telephone.)

For the convenience of students she also kept materials in the reference rooms which were not strictly for reference purposes. Mr. White could see no real need for this arrangement because the bookstacks were adjacent to the reference rooms. Furthermore, he thought putting non-reference materials into an area designated for reference purposes was a questionable library practice.

Mr. White discussed his ideas for changes in several private conferences with Mrs. Finley. Her invariable answer was, "Why, I guess I'm of the old school, Mr. White. You're of the new, and never the twain shall meet." Mr. White knew that somehow the twain were going to have to meet, but he was uncertain how, when, or where this would occur.

Since plans for the new building were well underway, decisions had to be made about the size and location of rooms and the services to be rendered in these areas. Limiting the size of the rooms would effectively stop the growth of the data packets, but would hardly be in the best interests of the reference services now or in the future. Mr. White wanted to move the entire data packets operation to the state library extension division, but he knew that it would be difficult to convince Mrs. Finley and some of the other older department heads of the need for this change.

* * *

Should the objectives and goals of a state-supported university include data packet service to the state? If

30 / Library Management

diplomacy fails, should Mr. White impose his decision about room sizes, staff utilization, and functions of departments on his staff even though he may hurt the feelings of some staff members?

Case 13

A SCHEDULE CHANGE

When John Carlson became head of the circulation department of the Fremont County Library three years ago, he changed the charging system, but he made few changes in the daily schedules. Clerks assigned to the circulation department had traditionally worked from 9:00 a.m. to 6:00 p.m. three days a week and from 1:00 p.m. to 9:00 p.m. two days a week. Mr. Carlson saw no reason to change these hours because it seemed obvious to him that the desk should be manned only when the library was open to the public. On the other hand, the clerks in technical services and in several other departments worked from 8:00 a.m. to 5:00 p.m. This also was a satisfactory schedule because these employees rarely had direct contact with the public.

Several times during the past year some members of the circulation staff had asked Mr. Carlson if their hours might be changed to eight to five on the three days they worked the early shift. Each time Mr. Carlson had refused. He explained to the clerks that it was necessary for them to work when the library was open to the public and that there was no need for them to be at the desk earlier than 9 a.m.

Three months ago, Alice Haynes, a long-time library employee and a frequent spokesman for the other clerks in circulation, made an appointment to see Mr. Carlson. She again requested a change of hours for all the circulation clerks; Mrs. Haynes told the department head that all the clerks preferred to start work an hour earlier, so that they could have more free time in the evenings when they were not on the one-to-nine shift. She said that she would like to arrange an earlier dinner hour for her family. When Mr. Carlson refused the request without hesitation, Mrs. Haynes left his office quite angry.

Although Mr. Carlson did not tell Mrs. Haynes, he thought that much time would be wasted by the clerks if they worked unsupervised from eight to nine in the morning. He was certain from his experience on a former job that the early hour away from the circulation desk would be spent largely in getting ready for work, talking, and drinking coffee. He believed that most of the clerks worked well only under close supervision and that working in public kept some of them from wasting more time than they might otherwise. He also thought Mrs. Haynes was a trouble-maker. He knew that she had been critical of the new charging system. She had openly questioned many of his decisions, and although she ultimately conformed to the changes, she did so with obvious reluctance.

Two weeks after the conference with Mrs. Haynes the Welfare Committee of the staff association, which was made up of representatives of both the administrative staff and the clerical workers in the library, met with Mr. Carlson. The committee told Mr. Carlson that the clerks in the circulation department had asked the committee to study the possibility of his changing their working hours on the early shift from nine to six to eight to five. Mr. Carlson was asked to state in writing his objections to the change of hours and to submit them to the committee.

Mr. Carlson identified three problems: the lack of need for service to patrons between eight and nine because the library was closed to the public at this time; the lack of sufficient work away from the desk between four-thirty and six, a busy time in the library.

The Welfare Committee passed the objections on to the clerks for study and possible rebuttal. In a month's time the clerks sent back to the Welfare Committee a list of routine duties that might be done more efficiently in an uninterrupted hour before the clerks at the circulation desk became busy with patrons. They also had kept circulation records for a month covering the period between 4:30 and 6 p.m. These records indicated that the major after-school rush hour was over before that time.

When Mr. Carlson received this information he polled the circulation staff by secret ballot. The vote was overwhelmingly in favor of the change in hours. The change was approved by the administration on a trial basis.

* * *

Can you suggest more flexible scheduling than that reported by the circulation clerks--e.g., a split shift once a week for each clerk or only evening duty one day a week or some other combination of hours? Or, could each cataloger be scheduled at the circulation desk for half a day each week?

Case 14

RESIGNATION

On the strength of her cataloging experience in a small college, Nancy was hired as head cataloger in the Garfield system. Although she had no administrative experience, she did have good references from her former supervisor and an excellent record as an undergraduate and as a graduate student in library school.

She proved to be somewhat disappointing as a cataloger of public library materials. She was a perfectionist about some aspects of the cataloging procedures, but she had difficulty managing her time and that of her staff, professional and clerical. A backlog of uncataloged materials began to accumulate.

After she had worked two months she requested sick leave so that she might return to her hometown to have some dental work done. The rules of the library stated that no employee was eligible for sick leave until he had completed a full year on the job. No exception was made for Nancy.

Three months later, she requested leave with pay for a trip home for Christmas. She explained that she was unable to get her dental repairs in Garfield because no dentist was competent enough to handle her difficult problems, and she wanted to get this work done over the Christmas holidays. She was given the leave, but without pay.

During the next few months her problems with staff scheduling and work assignments became more acute; the backlog grew. Both the director and his assistant were inclined toward a "let's-wait-and-see" attitude. Nancy had been working for less than a year; she had had no supervisory experience and catalogers were difficult to find. Both of them suggested ways of improving organization and tried to help Nancy as much as possible. She seemed resentful of their attempts to help her.

In June, almost a year after she had come to Garfield, Nancy told the director that she had decided to take a job in a small college near her hometown. Although the job would not be open until the first of September, she gave the library a month's notice, so that she might take a short trip abroad. The director was not sorry to have Nancy leave and was happy to help her with her arrangements to go abroad. He identified her so that she could obtain her passport and gave her suggestions for hotels and sightseeing.

On the day that Nancy was to leave the library, the director's secretary filled out an income tax withholding form indicating the total wages she had been paid that year and took it, and her final check, to Nancy. The director was dumbfounded when Nancy announced that she had decided not to take the college job, that she had cancelled her trip, and that she planned to stay on the job. He told Nancy that her employment with Garfield was officially terminated on the first of July. Nancy said that she would check with a friend of hers on the board of trustees.

At the next board meeting the director was ordered to keep Nancy on the payroll until she got another job or until the first of September, whichever came first.

* * *

Does a public library board have the authority to make decisions about library personnel?

Case 15

FRACTIONATED TIME

In addition to customary reference service, the reference department of State University Library provides orientation tours of the library. Because of a student body of more than 25,000 and a faculty and research staff of about 5,000, this tour service has become a heavy drain on the time of the reference librarians. The reference department consists of nine professional librarians, a clerk, a typist, and part-time students.

The reference staff train guides from other library departments to give tours for new students at the beginning of each semester and each summer session. For some classes the reference staff give intensive tours and for some even prepare bibliographies of material pertinent to the subject of the course. Compiling these bibliographies and preparing for each tour takes from one to fourteen man-hours of staff time per class.

The reference department staff are also responsible for answering telephone and mail questions, indexing several serials, selecting new reference books, and covering the reference desk during the ninety-three hours the library is open. The work involved in these activities is so great that the reference staff should be spending all of their time on them. If you were chief of this reference department, would you: 1) Try to allocate only a certain number of hours a week to tours? 2) Persuade the director of libraries that some other department of the library should have responsibility for tours? 3) Explore the possibility of making a motion picture to be shown to new students and abolishing the orientation tours?

* * *

What should be the goals and objectives of a university library reference department? How are one's priorities established?

Case 16

HEMLOCK HIGH RESOURCE CENTER

The community of Hemlock is located just off a major interstate highway and is about an hour's drive from a large city. Farming in the area has declined in importance, a few small industries employ about one hundred persons, and the city provides employment for many more. Two elements make up the population: an older, conservative group which has lived in the area or community for many years and includes many retired farmers; and a growing number of younger families (young executives on the way up) with children of pre-school and elementary school age. The population has grown slowly through the years but many persons believe that residential housing projects could "mushroom" at any time and consequently increase the population substantially. With little industry and few wealthy families, the tax burden rests squarely on the home owners. The people of the community are proud of their school system but are not willing to increase taxes in order to further improve the schools.

The school system is considered progressive in leadership and programs. For more than ten years, homogeneous or ability grouping, foreign language through all grades, and trades and industries in the high school have all been a part of the system's program. In the past five years a number of innovations have been introduced into the schools:

team teaching, special education, modular scheduling, advanced and enriched summer studies, programmed instruction, and learning phases. The system is divided into four schools: a primary school (kindergarten through third), an intermediate school (4th through 6th), a junior high (7th and 8th), and high school (9th through 12th). The high school has a four-track program: general, college preparatory, commercial, and vocational. Forty-nine per cent of the graduates go to college. Besides the usual high school courses, the school provides courses in trades and industries, advanced math, four years of Spanish, psychology, sociology, and college English. Enrollment is about 1,700 and the faculty numbers 65.

The high school is located in a rural setting and the site has ample room for expansion and development. The building was built five years ago on an austerity budget which required many compromises and omissions. One of the neglected areas was the Resource Center. Because no librarian was consulted in the planning, the Center is too small, poorly arranged, and quite inadequate to serve the needs of the curriculum, the students, and the faculty. The Center has approximately 8,500 books (of which about 1,700 are fiction in very bad condition), 45 periodical subscriptions, 60 phonorecords, 40 phonotapes, a large number of filmstrips, mounted pictures, pamphlets, clippings, and slides. Seating space is provided for 60 students. Equipment includes a microfilm reader, "wet" and "dry" carrels, filmstrip viewers, record turntables, tape decks, and several types of projectors (motion picture, opaque, and overhead). All motion pictures used in the school are rented.

The hall outside the entrance doors is wide enough, according to fire regulations, for display cases and a library bulletin board, but there are none. Priorities on the limited budget have not permitted the purchase of these items and evidently no one has thought of having them built in the shop classes. The Resource Center is reached through a cheerful double-doored entrance of light oak. The windows on the north and west outside walls are high enough to allow for shelving (forty-two inches high) below them, which somehow creates a top-heavy effect. Wherever there are no shelves, light blue ceramic tile covers the walls for sixty inches above the floor. Some visitors to the library have compared these tiled walls to a hospital corridor or the London underground. The floors are covered by an expensive but practical tan carpeting. The librarian believes that, instead of investing in carpet, it would have been better to have put the money into the collection because the latter is so sub-standard.

36 / Library Management

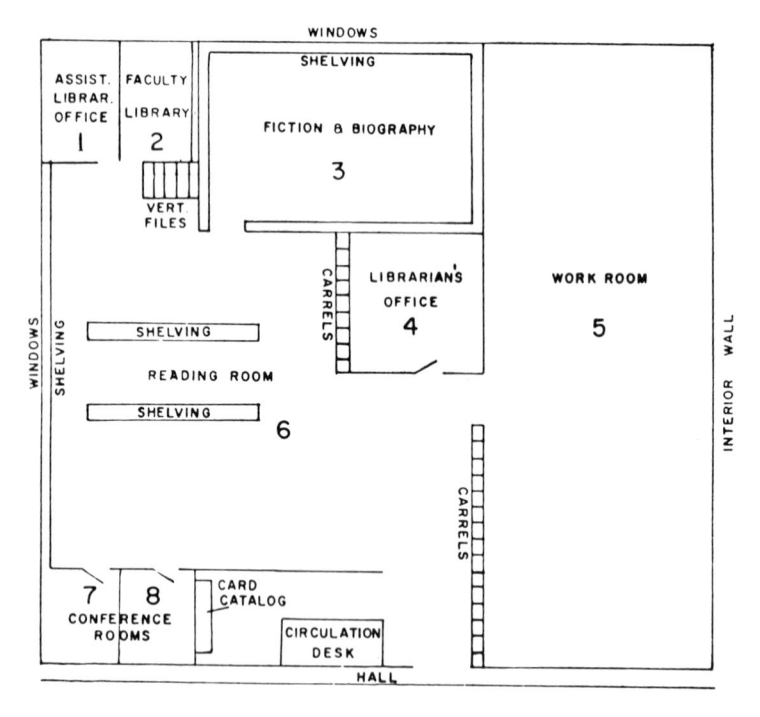

HEMLOCK HIGH RESOURCE CENTER
Fig. 1

    The glass-enclosed librarian's office (4) is directly ahead of the entrance. Theoretically, some work could be done in the office while supervising the reading room and student assistants at the circulation desk, but the librarian keeps the curtains drawn over the upper half of the west wall to shut out the glare from the overhead lighting in the reading room. The study carrels, along the west wall of the librarian's office, block the lower view into the reading room. The students and faculty feel that the librarian is isolating himself from them by operating from a removed and quiet office.
    The assistant librarian's office is back in the northwest corner (1). Evidently, the reason for this location was so that each professional could supervise a different portion of the library. Unfortunately, they cannot properly supervise

the main reading room from their offices, let alone carry on a program of service.
Until now, the second librarian has seemed content to do minor clerical work connected with the technical processes. Her typist, however, is housed in the workroom (5). The hidden corner office, along with the lack of a definite time when she is scheduled to be on the floor assisting patrons, encourages the disassociation of the second librarian from all professional library activities. The students who staff the circulation desk are the only persons visible for library service in the main reading room. The students are responsible for the current periodicals which are housed behind the circulation desk.
The fiction and biography room is primarily used by teachers who bring in entire classes to do library-connected work. The student who simply wants to come in and browse finds little space or encouragement. The shelves are crowded and provide no room for desperately needed additions to bring the collection up-to-date.
The faculty library (2) contains a reasonable stock of up-to-date professional education materials and has a pleasant view of the grounds. To prevent losses the door is kept locked; a teacher must find one of the librarians to unlock the door to gain access to the collection. Needless to say, it is not used very much.
Two small conference rooms (7,8) west of the circulation desk open off the reading room. Because the doors are solid, there is no means of supervising activities within these rooms, so the doors are kept locked. Only students with written passes from faculty members may use them; a staff member must take time to check the passes and to unlock the rooms.
The workroom (5) is very crowded and is used for processing new materials, for housing back issues of periodicals, for typing, and for storing all the different types of projectors used in the school.
The present building design prevents the Center from being open evenings and Saturdays. The lack of an outside entrance directly into the library is partially overcome by the fact that the main library entrance opens from the main entrance foyer. However, there is no way to block off the hallways to prevent access to other parts of the building. Extended hours seem almost a necessity since the facilities, services, and resources of the public library are very poor.
The space situation is desperate. This so-called "resource center" was not large enough to be a book-oriented library under the old 1960 Standards for School

38 / Library Management

Library Programs of the American Association of School Libraries. It is even less adequate in meeting the Current Standards for School Media Programs. The area was not planned with any understanding of the services and needs of a true resource center. The main reading room and the fiction and biography room are so crowded with tables and chairs in order to meet the regional accrediting association's seating requirements that it is difficult to move easily through the rooms. Unfortunately, the financial situation is such that extensive remodeling is out of the question, and the classroom situation is such that no nearby room is available.

* * *

You have just accepted the position as head librarian of this Resource Center. What reorganization, rearrangements, and changes would you make to improve utilization of space and staff and to provide better service? Draw a floor plan showing changes. Assume that you have a modest budget for some remodeling.

Case 17

TOO MANY SUPERVISORS

Carl Locke started working in the Sterling College Library ten years ago. He was an honors graduate of Sterling, where he had majored in mathematics. Despite his outstanding record in school, he had been unable to get a job in business or industry because of a severe speech impediment. He had been a stammerer since childhood. Over the years he had undergone various kinds of treatment and training by many speech therapists. Recently he had been under the treatment of a psychiatrist. Although there had been some improvement, his stutter still became aggravated by emotional stress. Whenever he was upset, his speech became almost incoherent and was often accompanied by facial contortions and breathing irregularities. He frequently dropped things.
    He still lived with his family, was quite withdrawn socially, and had few friends. He spent most of his free time taking courses at a neighboring university.
    Since he had been at the Sterling Library his time

had been apportioned among three supervisors, two of whom expected all of their employees to perform consistently at top speed and efficiency. Mr. Locke's work schedule was:

8:00 a.m. -	Files catalog cards.	Supervisor A
9:15 a.m. -	Sorts morning mail and distributes it to various offices and departments in the library	Supervisor B
10:30 a.m. -	Checks in, sorts, and arranges periodicals and serials	Supervisor B
12:00-1 p.m. -	Lunch	
1:00-1:30 -	Files catalog cards	Supervisor A
1:30 p.m. -	Sorts afternoon mail and distributes it.	Supervisor B
2:30 p.m. -	Assists in gift section	Supervisor C
4:30-5 p.m. -	Picks up mail from offices and departments	Supervisor B

Supervisor A supervised him closely and gave him detailed instructions for each part of his job. Supervisor B had the reputation of being one of the most demanding and ill-tempered supervisors in the library. Many of his employees had quit because he was brusque and dictatorial. No matter how quickly and accurately Mr. Locke did his work, Supervisor B believed that it could be done more efficiently. It was in this department that Mr. Locke experienced the most difficulty with his speech.

Over the years the supervisor of the gifts section, Mrs. Rivers (Supervisor C), had become confident of Mr. Locke's ability and had entrusted more and more responsibility to him. She had put him in charge of the correspondence files and the card files, and he frequently answered many letters himself. He also was extremely accurate in checking the collection for duplicates. Because he obviously felt relaxed in Mrs. River's section, he occasionally was able to talk without stuttering and even to indulge in a pun or two.

One afternoon when he arrived in the gift section, obviously under great stress, he told Mrs. Rivers that he was quitting his job in the library. Although he liked his work with her, he could not get along with the other two supervisors. Because he was so upset it was difficult for Mrs. Rivers to understand what had happened. She suggested that he leave early and told him that she would telephone Supervisor A to arrange for someone else to pick up the afternoon mail.

Mrs. Rivers hated the thought of losing Mr. Locke's assistance and wondered what she could do to help him.

* * *

This situation violates a basic principle of organization, usually called "unity of command," which states that each person should receive orders from only one person and should be accountable only to him. Can you suggest a solution to this case?

Case 18

PARTICIPATIVE MANAGEMENT
(Role playing)

Members of the Forest Board of Education were active, alert, and community-conscious; they believed the schools should serve the needs of the city as thoroughly and completely as possible. Through the years they had funded the addition of various vocational curricula to increase the employability of high school graduates in the city's offices and industries.

A recent employment survey conducted by the Chamber of Commerce revealed the availability of jobs in a number of areas which require post-high-school training. The length of training required for the different areas ranged from two months to two years, depending upon the nature of the job and the type of skills to be acquired. The areas identified in the surveys as needing a continuous supply of new trainees were: electronics and data processing technicians, architectural draftsmen, teacher and hospital aides, pattern drafting and draping (apparel industry), medical records, dental assistant, fire protection technology, culinary arts, police science, and food service management.

In addition to the evident need for post-high-school training programs, the Board was receiving increasing pressures to provide academic college courses: 1) for those high school graduates who were inadmissable to the established colleges and universities of the state because they did not meet entrance requirements; 2) for those from low income families who could not afford to attend the established academic institutions; and 3) for those who were employed full time and wanted to work toward degrees by studying at night. Besides training and academic courses, there was also a need in the community for basic adult education courses in reading, writing, and speaking for non-English speaking and illiterate residents.

The Board conceived the idea of developing a community college system to serve these needs and to supplement the city's two academic programs offered in an extension center of the state university and in a church-related liberal arts college.

At the suggestion of the Board, a local newspaper publicized the community college idea and provided a blank for readers to fill out and send in if they were interested in any of the programs described. Local radio and television stations also carried spot announcements asking for expressions of interest. The tabulated results indicated a potential student body large enough to establish community colleges at three different population concentrations in this city of about 700,000. The Board decided to start one as soon as possible; then, depending upon enrollment, interest of the residents, and success of the curricula, start a second one in about four years and a third several years after that.

Since the student body would probably consist of students from low-income families who were dependent upon public buses for transportation, the Board decided to establish the first college in the downtown area, as near as possible to a point where all city bus routes converged. They found and purchased a large empty building in this location and employed an architectural firm to renovate it. Next, they searched for and employed a president who was knowledgeable about the learning requirements of the type of students and curricula envisioned for this new college. They found such a man in Dr. Ira Crane.

Dr. Crane believed that a majority of the students would lack communication skills in reading, writing, and speaking and hence would respond better to a multi-media approach to learning rather than to one that was verbally oriented. Hence, he searched for a librarian who had experience in selecting, organizing, and utilizing all communication media. He believed a high school librarian would probably have better background in all media than an academic librarian, so searched for a school librarian who had both the necessary academic preparation and work experience and also had an interest in cooperating in the development of an innovative learning program.

He employed Mrs. Sarah Willow, a childless widow of about forty who was head librarian in a unified school district media center where she supervised two librarians, an audio-visual technician, and a number of clerks and pages. Her school library program had included a number of audio-visual courses and she had tried to keep up-to-date in this area through summer workshops.

No job description of her position had been written, as Dr. Crane expected her to evolve an innovative instructional learning resources center and he felt incapable of defining the parameters of such a position. He described to her the Board's proposed plans for developing two more community colleges, and his goals for this college. He delegated to her full authority: 1) to work with the architect in planning, adapting, and renovating the floor assigned to the library; 2) to plan for and choose the furniture; 3) to search for and employ the library staff; 4) to develop policies for collection building; 5) to supervise all operations; and 6) to work with the faculty in coordinating library services and collections with the curriculum and the instructional program.

Mrs. Willow was employed in July and instruction was to start fourteen months later. Her first concern was to employ a professional staff capable of creating an instructional learning resources center. She decided that initially she needed three persons who would represent competencies to supplement hers: an academic librarian, a special librarian, and a media specialist. Although the collection in the high school media center, which she had developed, was in many respects essentially a liberal arts collection, she thought a person with academic library experience would bring to this staff a perspective, a point of view, and a knowledge of printed materials suitable for a college collection, especially reference books, serials, and government publications. A special librarian with experience in abstracting, in providing information services to his clientele, and in justifying continuously the existence of a special library should bring to the staff the expertise to "market" and "sell" the multi-media approach to faculty, students, and Board of Education. To select, service, and repair all the audio-visual equipment, the background and experience of a media specialist were necessary.

After much searching and many interviews, Mrs. Willow employed the following who reported for work on October 1: Mr. Earl Falcon (academic librarian), Miss Shirley Veery (special librarian), and Mr. Howard Fulmar (media specialist).

Role for Mrs. Sarah Willow, chief librarian:

You see your role in this community college library as a planner, a policy maker, and a coordinator. Your abilities are more suited to innovation and conceptualization than to implementation. You are impatient with detail and unconcerned about operations. You are vigorous, aggressive, emotional, and strong willed. You are media-oriented and dedicated to the total learning resources concept. You are determined to have all media thoroughly integrated into one total operation. You expect the catalog to be an index to all media so that users have only one place to look for all material in whatever form on the same subject.

You are a staunch advocate of participative management and look on this new position as an opportunity to experiment fully with this managerial philosophy. When you assumed your most recent position as librarian of a high school media center, it was an on-going, well organized, smoothly running operation in which each staff member had clearly defined responsibilities delegated to her. You introduced more participation in decision making but could not make changes in the basic organizational structure. In this new community college library, you would like full staff participation in all decisions. To this end, you have written no job descriptions nor thought through staff organization or division of responsibilities. You have a vague notion that your three professional staff members can work democratically with you to make decisions on all problems as they arise. You expect your professional staff to respect each other's competencies which complement each other, to share abilities, to cross-fertilize ideas, and to coordinate and co-operate activities.

When you interviewed Mr. Falcon, Miss Veery, and Mr. Fulmar, you spoke of each being your assistant. You were thinking in terms of participative management, with all four professionals sharing in administrative decisions. Several recent comments and occurrences have led you to believe that each of them thought you meant he or she was to be the assistant director.

You did not think a cataloger or an acquisitions librarian were necessary because you envisioned purchasing pre-cataloged and pre-processed books from a jobber and depending upon the media specialist to catalog all non-print media. However, this has proved unrealistic as some cataloging and processing has already had to be done on the premises. You have employed a full-time typist to do all the typing for the four staff members as well as to type requisitions.

44 / Library Management

You have found Mr. Falcon, Miss Veery, and Mr. Fulmar very capable, efficient, and dedicated to creating the best possible instructional learning resources center. Each of them has had to change his traditional frame of reference and professional orientation because this situation is so different from their previous library experiences. The effect of this reorientation has at times resulted in their all going in different directions with little coordination or communication in sharing resources and expertise. They have requested a conference with you tomorrow morning-- it is now March and you have all been working together for five months.

Role for Mr. Earl Falcon:

You are thirty years old, are print-oriented, and have had eight years' experience in academic libraries: two years in the acquisitions department of a large university library; three years in the cataloging department of a well-organized, traditional, liberal arts college library; and the past three years as head of the reference department in the same liberal arts college library. Your ultimate goal, when you graduated from library school, was academic library administration. You believed that you needed experience in all areas of academic librarianship before you became an administrator--hence your choice of positions included both technical and public services.

When you were interviewed for the present position, Mrs. Willow implied that you would be assistant director, which would qualify you to be considered for head librarian in one of the other community colleges in Forest when they came into being. She said that the Board believed experience in helping to develop and administer this learning resource center would be the right background for developing a similar one in one of the other community colleges.

You are concerned about your status in this library administrative structure. You have learned that both Miss Veery and Mr. Fulmar think they are the assistant director. Their belief is based on impressions and implications received during their interviews with Mrs. Willow.

In addition to clarification of your personal status, you would like clear definition of work areas so that each professional has authority and responsibility in a specific area. You and Miss Veery have discussed this and have agreed that both of you should work on building the collection (materials in all media), that you should take charge of acquisitions and cataloging of all materials regardless of

Organizing Cases / 45

their format, and she should take charge of all circulation, reference, information retrieval, and dissemination of information (utilizing all media).
You have discovered that Mr. Fulmar is an expert in evaluating, selecting, operating, and repairing audiovisual equipment but his idea of descriptive cataloging of non-print materials leaves much to be desired. Whether the final form of the catalog will be film cartridge, computer print-out, card file, or something else has not yet been determined. But, regardless of form, the descriptive cataloging input will be the same and must be uniform and thorough. You would like the responsibility for cataloging all materials which the jobber does not or cannot do. The jobber can provide current, popular print materials but those represent only a small fraction of the items which must be acquired for this collection. These include all types of audio and visual materials, programmed learning kits, sets of workbooks and basic education readers, government publications, maps, retrospective printed books, microfiche, microfilm, and technical reports. You believe only a librarian experienced in cataloging can produce a satisfactory integrated catalog of all these diverse forms and types of materials. Furthermore, you are convinced that ordering these requires the skill of a librarian with experience in acquisitions and a knowledge of sources of supply. Expecting a typist to do this is unreasonable, unfair, and ineffective.
You are a bit skeptical about how all media can be integrated into the curricula to serve non-verbally oriented students but you are willing to try.

Role for Miss Veery:

You are thirty-two years old, ambitious, hard working and have creative ideas for service to the faculty and students. Your experience includes four years in U. S. Army libraries overseas, three years in a naval electronics facility, and three years in a federal aviation agency. Although you thoroughly enjoyed the work in federal libraries, you welcomed this opportunity to work in an academic setting and to improve the employability of young men and women from low-income families. In other words, the social service aspects of this position appealed strongly to you, as did the opportunity to get administrative experience in preparation for eventually becoming head librarian of another similar community college. You thought you were to be assistant librarian here and were disconcerted to learn that Mr. Falcom and Mr. Fulmar also think that each of them is assistant director. You want this matter cleared up for the sake of everyone concerned.

You like to work with people, all of your experience has been in public services and you would like to be responsible for this area in this library. As an academic librarian, Mr. Falcon's orientation and interest is more towards collection building and the provision of learning resources than it is to the dissemination of information.

You believe that the responsibilities of the person in charge of public services should include: 1) scheduling carrels and rooms for cooperative study, listening, or viewing audio-visual materials; 2) circulating all learning resources whether on paper, film, tape, or disc; 3) the housing and shelving of all materials; 4) the supervising of all microfiche, microcard, and microfilm readers and printers; and 5) planning and directing all reference service, including retrieval and dissemination of information. You are especially interested in the concept of information transfer whether the information is on IBM cards, magnetic tape, or print. You hope this library can participate in whatever networks of knowledge are available in this area.

Because of your experience in special libraries, you have a grasp of service which brings a unique approach to academic problems. You brought vigor and insight to this position which are valuable assets in the integrative approach to learning.

Role for Mr. Howard Fulmar:

You are twenty-eight years old and have academic background as a media specialist. You have had very thorough training in the operation, care, upkeep, and repair of all types of AV equipment as well as in the production of slides, transparencies, and graphic teaching materials. You have worked as assistant media specialist in this city's public schools. You have never worked in a library. You are ambitious and accepted this position because of the opportunity to develop a domain of your own.

In this library you believe there should be a sharp separation between print and non-print, including separate housing and control. You would like to see the floor assigned to the library divided physically into a media area and a book-periodical area. Since microfiche and microfilm are film, you think that these and the readers and printers should be in your area, as well as all AV materials.

You think librarians are much too fussy about cataloging, scheduling and circulating procedures; you want to take charge of these for everything except printed materials. And, of course, you expect to supervise all use and care of the machines as well as train and supervise the projectionists and technicians.

You are much less concerned with the organization and control of materials than librarians are. You don't think it is important to know where each item is at all times. You think the idea of listing all learning resources together in one catalog is the height of silliness. You want to generate and produce a separate title list for motion pictures, for slides, for tape recordings, and so on.

Your conception of your position is to produce all kinds of teaching aids to support the curricula: transparencies for opaque projectors, slides, graphics, tape recordings of lectures, and many others; also, to offer whatever services your staff will be capable of performing, such as setting up films and projectors, splicing and repairing film, photographing, instructing faculty members and students in the use of audio visual equipment, and promoting innovative instructional uses for all AV resources.

Case 19

BUSY, BUSY, BUSY

During his four years of undergraduate work, Silas Locust worked half-time in a medium-sized city public library. Starting out as a circulation reviser and shelver, he later was promoted to other positions as vacancies occurred and his competence increased: borrower registration clerk, circulation desk attendant, searcher in acquisitions, catalog filing clerk, and, finally, the last summer as substitute for branch librarians on vacation. Following graduation from library school, he worked as assistant librarian in a college library for two years before accepting the position as librarian of Eastern Lincoln State Normal School in 1935 at the age of 25. The College had been established by the state legislature to serve an area where no college existed. One building was erected, and a faculty (including Silas Locust) was employed as of July 1, 1935, to plan for the first classes which started the following September.

No librarian had been consulted in planning the large

room across one end of the building which was labeled "Library." Immovable wooden shelves around all walls, an enormous semi-circular charging desk, a carpenter's version of newspaper and periodical racks, and massive tables and chairs for readers were not ideal but this was the physical setting in which Mr. Locust started to develop a library collection and plan for library service. For several years he had only part-time student help. When the demonstration school was erected, he carefully planned the school library quarters and employed a certified school librarian to take charge. Eventually, as the student body and faculty increased, he gradually added clerks, subprofessionals, and professionals to the staff. But always the library was more or less a "one-man show," as Mr. Locust had originated every procedure, every service, every physical arrangement, and he closely controlled everything.

The original two-year teacher-training curriculum was gradually expanded to include two years of terminal and college preparatory junior college courses, then to a three-year teacher-training program, and then a four-year teacher-training institution. With the change in curricula came changes in name from Normal School to Teachers College to State College. In 1970 the institution was known as Eastern Lincoln State College, had a student body of about 12,000 enrolled in baccalaureate, master and specialist programs, and occupied many buildings on an attractive campus.

In the 1950's Mr. Locust took a leave of absence to study for an Ed. D. degree specializing in audio-visual materials and services. His title was changed to Director of Libraries to indicate his changed status and the fact that he supervised a main library, library science classes, residence center libraries, two demonstration school libraries, and a multi-media learning resources center. In 1970, the main library collection of about 300,000 volumes and the learning resources center occupied a recently completed building which was a monument to Dr. Locust's admirable planning: attractive, hospitable, well-furnished, functionally efficient, logically arranged, and economical to supervise. The learning resources center had more than fifty carrels wired for dial access, closed circuit television, a studio laboratory where recording could be done, many tape recorders, filmstrip readers, record players, and motion picture projectors.

According to the retirement regulations of the College, all administrators must retire from administrative duties at 65. Hence, Dr. Locust will give up his responsibilities as Director of Libraries and will teach library science courses.

Organizing Cases / 49

*   *   *

You, the reader, have been appointed as Director of Libraries to succeed Dr. Locust. Will you assume all of the responsibilities and duties which Dr. Locust performed? Or do you suggest some changes? Will you take on other responsibilities? Here is what you have learned about his activities, either from him or from your observations when you visited the library for interview, or from his staff:

Fine Money: All fine money is kept in a locked vault in Dr. Locust's office and he personally supervised all details including counting what went to the circulation desk, what was collected and put in the vault, what was sent to the Treasurer's office, and the locking and unlocking of the vault.

Staff Meetings: No staff meetings have ever been held--either total staff or department heads.

Organization Chart: No organization chart has ever been drawn up but the following head positions exist: acquisitions, cataloging, circulation, reference, media center, and two demonstration school libraries. However, any staff member with a problem doesn't necessarily work through his department head but has gone directly to Dr. Locust because any decision would be made by him and not by the department head.

Shelf List: From her glassed-in office, the head of the Cataloging Department can see only part of her department because of the position of the shelf list which blocks the view. She has requested permission from Dr. Locust to move it to another location, but he has refused because the present location is where he planned it to be when the floor plans were drawn. "He is very possessive about his library," she said.

Periodicals Department: Believing that anyone could check in periodicals, Dr. Locust employed about a year ago a housewife who had a B.S. degree in home economics to take charge of the periodicals section, which is part of the reference department. The reference librarian objected strenuously to the appointment and tried to make him realize how complicated that work had become and that it was even difficult for a professional. Dr. Locust said, "Oh, I think she can carry on all right after I show her what she should do." The home economist hadn't the vaguest understanding of library materials and refused to take advice from the reference librarian. She never did understand the intricacies of the job and finally he discharged her. Then, he spent the summer in that section, "cleaning up the mess" and weeding the collection. One department head who had some serious problems she needed to talk over with him said of those months: "I would ask if I could talk with him and he would just stand with a pile of periodicals in his arms and ask about the problem--never even suggest we go to his office and sit down to discuss it. He acted as though he were in another world and didn't want to be bothered with any other problems. So, I didn't even tell him what was on my mind and he went on with his sorting."

Card Catalog: Dr. Locust has always been most particular about the card catalog and specified how the cards should be reproduced and typed and the physical appearance of each one. His interference made more work for the Cataloging Department because the cards could be reproduced faster and cheaper by other methods. An example of his concern about the appearance of the catalog was cited by the head cataloger: "One day recently he came down to the Catalog Department and was absolutely irate. When checking the filing, he found two cards tied together with a granny knot instead of a square knot. He threw the cards on my desk and suggested that I reprimand the girls who had done this and see that it never happened again." Except for the two years he was on leave to work on his Ed. D. degree, he has always revised all filing in the card catalog. He won't trust this responsibility to anyone else even though he doesn't have the time to do this. Cards were filed daily by clerks from the Catalog Department but Dr. Locust was not consistent in the time when he would revise the filing so the cards just accumulated in the drawers above the rods. Patrons would pick up the loose cards and put them back any place or the cards would drop out on the floor. Consequently, some cards were probably lost and the filers got no feedback on their filing. If the Catalog Department got behind on filing, he would have a "filing bee" and have the entire staff of acquisitions and cataloging filing in the catalog at the same time.

Marking Books: Dr. Locust personally trains the students who put the call numbers on the spines of books. He wants the letter done with an electric stylus which gets very hot and produces blisters on the marker's fingers. He stipulates that the call number must be at a precise distance from the lower edge of the spine. Several months ago, after one marker left and he had not had the time to train another, the books awaiting marking were lined up on the floor across the whole end of the Cataloging Department. He does not approve of typed white labels affixed to the spine.

Ordering Supplies: Orders for supplies were placed only once a year because it was supervised personally by Dr. Locust. He would ask each department head to submit a list for his department. Then, if he thought the request too extravagant or too large, he cut it. As a result many supplies would be exhausted long before the end of the year. For example, recently, the Cataloging Department ran out of bookplates and paste for the pasting machine, which held up new books until these supplies were replenished. Another problem with once-a-year ordering was that when the supplies arrived, the bulk was so great that it was difficult to find storage space for them.

Paper Saver: As a result of his experiences during the Depression when nothing was thrown away which could possibly be used, Dr. Locust was a paper saver. The staff had memos from him about saving typing-size paper which had one good side for use as scratch paper. The memos were specific about types of paper to save. Wrapping paper from interlibrary loan packages was to be neatly folded and reused if the paper was not too rumpled or worn.

Dress Code: The college was located in a very conservative community and students were expected to be dressed in conventional styles of clothing. A dress code for the library was formulated several years ago. One item of the code stipulated that no woman wearing pants or trousers could use the library. The intent was to avoid sloppy, ragged, blue jeans and was adopted before dressy pantsuits and slacks became the vogue. Every person entering or leaving the library had to pass by the entrance guard and he was responsible for enforcing the dress code. The reference librarian told this story: "One day a young woman came in wearing trousers and the entrance guard quoted the dress code. He suggested that she put on a skirt and then he could admit her. She explained that she commuted to campus from her home forty-five miles away, she couldn't take the time to go back home, she had no place to go for other apparel except her home, and she desperately needed to use library materials for an oral report in class the next day. The entrance guard expressed his sympathy with her plight but told her he was expected to enforce the regulation. So, she proceeded to remove the trousers, rolled them up, stuffed them in her brief case, and proceeded to go about her work. The dress code had nothing to say about admitting a girl who wore only underwear partially covered by shirt tails, so the guard let her pass."

Case 20

VOLUNTEERS
(Role playing)

In the central library of a large city-county library system, an information desk was located on the main floor near the entrance. When assigned to this desk for the first time, each staff member was put through a thorough orientation by the floor supervisor, because this person represented the library to the public and, consequently, was expected to be well groomed, polite, courteous, cheerful, patient, and well informed. In addition, the person had to know the layout of the building, the location of departments and collections, library rules and regulations, extension services offered by the library, and who was employed in the system. Many telephone calls were also handled at this desk.
    One morning the personnel officer for the system, Mr. Wren, approached the desk and introduced a fashionably dressed young woman to the staff member on duty, Miss Enid Adler. Mr. Wren said, "This is Mrs. Jones who will be working at this desk for the next two hours. Each member of the Junior League has volunteered to spend four hours working in the library. These women will be assigned to this desk at various times during the next three weeks and thus release the regularly assigned staff members for other work. They will talk to patrons when they come to the desk and will answer the telephone. We are very grateful to these Junior League members for this volunteer service." As he spoke, Mr. Wren beamed approval at Mrs. Jones.
    For Enid, this was a most frustrating and annoying two hours. Inasmuch as she was responsible for the desk, she could not leave without permission of the floor supervisor. Being very conscientious, she did not feel she could leave the desk in the hands of a stranger even long enough to go to her supervisor and ask for advice. Mrs. Jones had received no instructions, no orientation, no idea of what she was supposed to do, yet here she was seated at the desk as though she were the staff member in charge. Enid stood around awkwardly. Mrs. Jones proved at once that she could not man the desk by herself--she would listen to a patron's request and then turn helplessly to Enid for the answer. To top it off, she started smoking a cigarette. Enid promptly told her to put it out and informed her that

Organizing Cases / 53

no library employee could smoke when on duty in a public area. Mrs. Jones refused and said she had been told by Mr. Wren that it would be all right to smoke. Enid was concerned about the impression her smoking would make on the patrons because most of them knew the staff rules about smoking on duty as well as did the staff. There was no ash tray at the desk so Mrs. Jones used the waste basket for her ashes.

As soon as Enid was relieved at the desk by the next librarian scheduled to work there, she reported the conversation with Mr. Wren and the presence of the Junior League volunteer to her floor supervisor, Mrs. Belle Vireo.

Role for Mrs. Belle Vireo:

You had not been informed about the request of the Junior League to do volunteer work in the library, nor had you been consulted about their being assigned to the information desk. Enid's report is the first you had heard of the project and you are wondering who in the administration made this decision. You are angry that Mr. Wren ignored the chain of command in placing someone to work on your floor without your approval or consent. You are a line officer responsible for all personnel and operations on this floor, whereas Mr. Wren is in an advisory staff position where he should provide service to the line officers but should never interfere in line operations.

You are going right up to Mr. Wren's office to confront him with his overstepping his authority. You consider the information desk a crucial post which cannot be turned over to anyone not especially trained for the work.

Role for Mr. Wren:

You have no idea of what really goes on at the information desk. Since only attractive, personable, outgoing staff members are scheduled there, you have assumed that the person plays hostess to greet patrons as they come in. It seemed the ideal place to put these attractive Junior League women because they were gracious and charming and would make beautiful hostesses. You believe the only qualification for the person at the desk is to have a pleasant voice and manner, a pleasing personality, and an ability to communicate--and surely these women had these qualifications.

You thought Mrs. Vireo would be delighted to have all this free help to relieve her staff for more important duties. You knew that she was always complaining about not having enough staff. In your enthusiasm for pleasing the Junior League members, you sort of forgot about the organizational chain of command.

Case 21

AN ORGANIZATION CHART

When you assumed the position as head of the Circulation Department of Sycamore University Library, the staff was composed of the following:

>one professional in charge of fines and overdues
>>(full-time)
>
>eight subprofessionals (full-time)
>>circulation desk day supervisor
>>circulation desk night supervisor
>>stack supervisor
>>carrel attendant--in charge of some 450 carrels
>>tracer (searched for missing books)
>>filer and sorter
>>two check out desk attendants
>
>forty part-time students

All eight of the full-time staff report directly to the head of the department. The library is open 92 hours a week but the two circulation desk supervisors work a total of 80 hours, so for at least twelve hours a week only student assistants are at the desk. Actually only student assistants are at the desk for more than twelve hours because they have to cover rest breaks and any other times the supervisors are not at the desk (staff meetings, illness, and absences). The former head of the department was scheduled for desk duties on weekends, one evening, and emergencies.

* * *

Reorganize the department to: 1) reduce the span of authority; 2) provide backup for each key position; 3) give more responsibility to the professional member of the staff; 4) clarify the chain of command so that each person reports to someone; and 5) relieve the head of the department of any scheduled desk duty. You can add two full-time subprofessionals. Draw an organization chart.

CHAPTER II

PLANNING AND DECISION-MAKING CASES

Planning is a basic management function along with organizing, leading, and controlling. Planning is an activity essential to good management. A plan is a commitment to a course of action believed necessary to achieve specific results. Guides and courses for future actions, prior to performance, are required in order to achieve goals. Plans may be short- or long-range. Planning and the responsibility for planning should be engaged in by all supervisors whether they are at the top, the middle, or the bottom of the organization structure. In other words, everyone employed in any kind of supervisory capacity should be concerned with planning, from the director of libraries down to the clerk in charge of after-school pages who do the shelving. Good planning considers the nature of the future in which decisions and actions are intended to operate.

Cases in this section exemplify such areas of planning as decision-making and courses of action; objectives, goals, and mission; standing plans and planning instruments; and single-use plans--programs and projects. Hopefully, these cases will provide some vicarious experience in understanding the facets of planning and decision-making, the roles of staff members in the planning process, the importance of planning, and the necessity of flexibility in adapting to change. Budgets are one type of plan for which no cases are provided because these are local and specific in nature.

1. Decision-making and courses of action

Some of the prerequisites in making planning decisions are: diagnosing a problem or situation, evaluating past experience in relation to today's problem, identifying and comparing possible courses of action, and allocating resources and time.

2. Objectives, goals, mission

Objectives are statements of purpose toward which organizing and controlling are aimed; they imply effort toward a preselected result. Objectives may change as conditions or circumstances change; they may be short-range objectives towards long-range goals. After top-level objectives have been set, then objectives for all units of a library need to be established which are consistent with all other objectives. The word "objective" covers long-range library aims, specific departmental goals, and individual assignments. Objectives are important in providing individual motivation to those who must fulfill the objectives, in giving direction to the library staff as a whole, in serving as a basis for delegating and decentralizing work to be done, in coordinating staff work, and in providing the basis for appraising results in terms of managerial goals.

A mission is an objective which implies moral compunction to achieve a result. Ideally, all well-thought-out-objectives should be accepted as missions.

3. Standing plans and planning instruments

Standing plans are designed to provide ready guides to action in dealing with recurring problems; they establish a structure of customary behavior for achieving results. One type of plan may be more useful in a given situation than another. The principal types of standing plans or planning instruments are: policies, operating procedures, rules and regulations, schedules and single-use plans (programs, projects, missions).

(1) Policies

Polices are broad guides to thinking, established to assist subordinates responsible for making plans. Policies delimit an area in which a decision is to be made and assure that the decision will be consistent with objectives; they must provide for some discretion and initiative, otherwise they would be rules. Examples of policies: Student assistants will be used only for tasks which contribute to their growth and learning. Insofar as possible, vacancies on the staff will be filled by promoting from within.

(2) Operation procedures

Procedures are guides to action rather than guides to

thinking; they establish a method for handling repetitive tasks or problems. Greater efficiency in routine jobs can be achieved through procedures which identify the one best way of getting the job done. Procedures tend to be more or less chronological in listing what is to be done. Examples of procedures: Searching for and ordering library materials. Inter-library loan procedures. Preparation of materials for the bindery.

(3) Rules and regulations

Definition: rules are the simplest type of plan and spell out a required course of action. A rule prescribes a specified action for a given situation. A rule reflects a managerial decision for or against action. Like procedures, rules guide action, but rules specify no time sequence (e.g., "no smoking" is a rule unrelated to any procedure). As distinguished from policies which guide thinking in decision-making by identifying the boundaries of discretion, rules are also guides, but they allow no discretion or initiative in their application. Some examples of rules and regulations:

> Librarians on duty must not eat, chew gum, or smoke.
> Only library materials may be copied on the library's xerox machines.
> Children may not use the elevators.
> No questions having to do with contests will be answered.
> Employees must remain on the premises during fifteen-minute rest periods.

(4) Schedules

Work schedules are vital to planning because they specify which employees are to work when and where, and what tasks are to be accomplished. A schedule may be annual, monthly, weekly, or daily.

(5) Single-use plans: programs, projects

A program is a comprehensive plan which: 1) may include objectives, policies, procedures, rules, standards, budgets, methods, and other elements necessary to carry out a major course of action; 2) usually encompasses a relatively large undertaking; 3) includes future use of resources in an integrated pattern; and 4) establishes a sequence of actions. Examples of programs: building program, library orientation for new students, in-service training for clerks, National Book Week promotion.

A project often is one step in a program and consists of a cluster of activities which is relatively separate and clear-cut. A project typically has a distinct mission which is designed to achieve a clear termination point.

Case 22

PROBLEMS INHERITED BY A YOUNG ADMINISTRATOR

Acorn State University is a rapidly growing institution with more than 16,000 students. The library building, although relatively new, is not very well planned either for service or operation but has adequate space for students and books for at least ten years. The library staff consists of 26 professionals, 55 clerks or typists and part-time student assistants. The collection contains about 750,000 bound volumes and about 15,000 microforms.

For several years the university administrators have received complaints from students and faculty members about library facilities, services, and collections. The student newspaper has frequently carried "Letters to the Editor" outlining specific complaints with details. The Vice President for Academic Affairs was aware of these complaints and talked with the library director several times about them. The library director always had plausible reasons or excuses to account for the deficiencies, and assured the Vice President that the staff were working to improve the situation.

Last year student government officers decided that if any changes were to be made in library operations, they would have to do something dramatic to get university administrators to take action. A student government committee was assigned to investigate long-standing student complaints about the library. The student senate, after hearing the committee's report, allocated enough student funds to hire three library consultants to come to the campus and study the situation. The consultants issued a twenty-page report which stated that they found morale low, students confused, many essential services lacking, and the main library basically unused. Their recommendations aimed at a score of problems, including what they described as a research-oriented library on a largely undergraduate campus. That factor, plus student confusion in locating books and a poor study environment in the main building, led students to use the public library and its branches. The consultants urged the library staff to take a new look at the basic role of the library, to speed the flow of books through technical services, to buy more books needed for courses, and to improve services.

Although the consultants pin-pointed problems often cited in the past by students and faculty members, their unbiased, outside influence acted as a catalyst for action by the university administration. The Vice President for Academic Affairs appointed a task force consisting of three students, three faculty members, and three library staff members to implement these recommendations. In the face of such widespread criticism and publicity, the library director resigned.

A search and screening committee was appointed to search for a new director who would be capable of handling this difficult position. This committee did a very thorough job of looking nationwide for the right person for the job. The chairman of the committee even followed up written recommendations by phoning applicants' references and asking very pointed and personal questions about each applicant's credentials. Following is the story of the final choice:

I became director of this library two months ago, after receiving a Ph.D. in library and information science. I am 34 years of age and, prior to the three years of doctoral study, had had nine years of professional experience in academic libraries, of which four were in an administrative capacity as head of a department. When I was interviewed on the campus, the university administrators were frank in telling me about the library problems but assured me that the new director would have their support and adequate financing. My interviews with library staff members revealed many additional internal problems of which neither the students nor faculty members or administrators were aware. Management was my minor during my doctoral study, which included courses in higher education and courses in the School of Business in personnel, organizational behavior, and management. I was eager to apply what I had learned and this position looked like one in which I could utilize most of what I knew!

During the two months I have been here, I have visited every department as many times as necessary to assess the work of each; have had personal interviews with all 81 employees; have talked with many faculty members and student leaders; have made feeble efforts at flow-charting some operations (with little success); have attempted to make organization charts to determine who reports to whom; have studied library floor plans; have had frequent meetings with the Task Force Committee; and have read the fragmentary, incomplete files of departmental and director's reports for several years. Here are some of the problems which I have inherited:

Cataloging department:

　　　The situation here is explosive and is undermining the work of everyone in the department. About six years ago Mr. Kernel became head of the cataloging department after having had about 12 years of successful experience as a cataloger in two other libraries. At that time he was about 40 years of age. He is very intelligent, knows all there is to know about cataloging and classification and keeps up with all changes in catalog codes, etc. He sets high performance standards for himself and for his staff and is very industrious and hard working. He is forthright and honest, which to some persons makes him appear blunt, undiplomatic, tactless, and domineering. He has little tolerance or patience with inefficiency, inaccuracy, or carelessness. He inherited a poorly trained, inefficient, unsupervised, all-female staff. His predecessor was a poor administrator who let each staff member go her own way with no formal division of duties, which resulted in each person doing pretty much what she liked to do, when she wanted to do it, and in whatever way she preferred. Needless to say, the work was done in a most disorganized, haphazard, inaccurate way with many inconsistencies and discrepancies in classification, filing, and card forms. Mr. Kernel was incredulous! He proceeded to organize the department and insisted that each member of the staff follow the same procedures, codes, and rules which he specified. Actually, he found it necessary to teach them as though they were beginning students in cataloging and classification, only it was a more difficult teaching task because his staff had to unlearn so many wrong ideas.
　　　One of his professional catalogers and two typists resigned rather than comply with these changes--for which he was grateful because he could then choose suitable replacements. However, the oldest clerk-typist on the staff, and his greatest problem, did not resign. Being older than Mr. Kernel and having worked in the department for about ten

years, Elsie felt that she knew more about this department and how it should be run than he did. She was the wife of a faculty member and she and her husband were close friends of the library director--facts which she felt gave her a privileged position in the department. She was openly belligerent and argumentative, was the least competent of all the typists, and showed a lack of responsibility in assuming her share of the work. Frequently she went to the library director with spiteful complaints concerning Mr. Kernel.

For about six months after he became head of the department, Mr. Kernel tried patiently and with all the tact of which he was capable to change Elsie's attitude and work habits. He finally went to the director and asked that she be transferred to some other department in the University or be dismissed. He received no support from the director, either because of the director's administrative inability or his unwillingness to create any conflict in his social relationships with Elsie and her husband. He refused to transfer Elsie or to dismiss her. So Mr. Kernel had no choice but to live with the conflict, and over a period of about five years, a sour situation developed. Two camps developed-- a minority for Mr. Kernel and a majority for Elsie. This conflict, and the emotion associated with it, affected everyone in the department.

Both Mr. Kernel and Elsie came to see me during the first week I was on the job, and each presented his story. I promised to study the situation impartially and objectively and to come up with some sort of solution. I have decided that relations are such in the department that both individuals should be transferred, for if one is left, tension, bitterness and hostility will remain. I learned that Elsie is eligible for early retirement, although she will receive less retirement income than she would receive if she continued to work until age 70. I have recommended immediate early retirement for her, and she has agreed. Mr. Kernel is a tenured associate professor and, as such, cannot be dismissed. I have offered him a newly created position of bibliographer in charge of building collections, at the same salary he is currently receiving. Alternatively, I will be happy to recommend him for a cataloging position in another library. He is very upset about being removed from the cataloging department and has not yet decided what to do. I have appointed one of the catalogers as acting head.

Personnel records:

I have no personnel records nor annual reports from

staff members. I will have to work out a personnel data form for each staff member to fill out.

Classification and pay plans:

Seven years ago the president appointed a director of classified personnel. Prior to that time the University had no classification or pay plan. Classified personnel are all employees except faculty members. Since professional librarians have faculty status they are not included in this classified status.

For every non-faculty job on campus, this man wrote a job description after conferring with each employee and his supervisor, classified the various levels of jobs, and developed salary schedules to accompany the job classification. This involved going to every department on campus and getting the cooperation of the department head--maintenance, athletics, offices, library, etc. When he approached the library director, the latter told him, "Put them all in the same category, I don't want to worry about it or have you interfering with my staff." Then, later, the library director changed classification levels and salaries according to whim.

I have looked briefly at the payroll vouchers which my secretary prepares and I can see that many salaries are not commensurate with duties performed. So I have a horrendous amount of work ahead of me to get job descriptions for my staff. At a departmental heads meeting this morning I gave them an "Analysis of Duties" form which has more than thirty items on it and asked them to heave each member of their staff fill one out. Then, I will go over them with each department head later. From the blank looks on their faces, I am sure they don't understand what I want them to do, and that I will have to spend much time with each of them explaining the items on the blank. After I have written a job description for each employee, I will confer with the campus personnel director to be sure they are compatible with the job descriptions for similar positions on the rest of the campus--and eventually there will be a classification and pay plan for the library staff!

Organizational structure:

My predecessor's laissez-faire attitude resulted in no organizational structure and each person more or less went his own way. Also, all 81 staff members came directly to him with problems instead of taking them to their supervisors or department heads. I need a basic organizational framework within which I can establish a chain of command and delegate authority. My attempts at charting supervisory relationships in order to determine who reports to whom have not been fruitful. I will have to do much reorganizing in order to come up with a coherent, workable organizational structure. At the moment I can't visualize all the changes this will require. I do know that there will have to be some staff changes or transfers, little working cliques broken up, and space reallocations.

I would like to include the staff in decision-making, to introduce some participative management, but they are not ready for such democracy. I see my role at present as a change agent and, as such, must exert strong leadership.

Acquisition department:

Miss Maders, head of the acquisitions department, had excellent experience in acquisitions in a public library and an academic library before coming here four years ago. She is about fifty years of age, single, quiet and reserved, very considerate of others, gentle, pleasant, scholarly, and knowledgeable about the book trade. But she is not an administrator. A couple of the clerks boss her around as well as the other clerks and typists. I will have to replace her. In that position, I need not only someone who knows the book trade but also a person who can plan, organize, implement, and administer an acquisitions program that is responsive to the instructional and research program of the University.

We have a rather large book budget for an institution of this size. We have approval plans with several jobbers. However, we are not really approving; we are operating what I would call acceptance plans because there is no selection involved. If a title is not a duplicate, we buy it. I do not like this. Our profile with one jobber excludes such obvious areas as agriculture, religion, children's literature, cookbooks, and several other categories. Of course, the jobber tries to send books that are appropriate for academic library collections for institutional approval--only we are accepting rather than approving. I have asked Miss Maders to develop a responsible acquisitions program with procedures by which we can introduce selectivity and faculty participation into an approval acceptance plan. She doesn't respond to these suggestions; she seems satisfied with the status quo. Perhaps one factor in her lack of response may be her staff of clerks, all of whom have worked in this department from six to eleven years. If she were to change procedures, records, or files they might be very upset and unwilling to make the necessary changes. It may be that she has made the suggestion to them and they have vetoed the idea.

Here is an example of resistance to change in this department: when a faculty member wishes a book ordered, he fills out a request card which is then searched and verified by a clerk in acquisitions. This card is given to a typist who types a multiple order form when the book arrives. The catalogers would like the benefit of the searching information which is on the request form but they don't get it in spite of frequent requests by the head of cataloging. I have talked to Miss Maders three times about this and have asked that this request form routinely goes to cataloging. Cataloging still is not getting it.

For the sake of the library, I must terminate Miss Maders in this position and appoint some one who can administer the department adequately. She is not tenured. In this institution, at the end of five years, one of three recommendations has to be made: tenure, non-reappointment, or extension of the probationary period. She has been here four years. According to the AAUP standards on tenure, I must give her one year's notice if I am not going to recommend her reappointment. So, if I recommend termination to the president, she must be notified no later than next July 1. I will have to tell her that she is just not the person for this job and that she should look for another position. This may seem a little brutal because she is a fine person personally. But I have to, for the sake of the department and the library.

Resistance to change:

All of the professional librarians and about half of the clerks on this staff are older than I am. In fact, some are 20 to 30 years older than I. One department head has been in the same position for 25 years. I have the feeling that they think of themselves as more knowledgeable, wiser, and more experienced than I am, and that my ideas are out of books and are not practical. This makes for some resistance and complicates finding solutions to problems. They don't want to be jarred out of their comfortable "ruts."

Another attitude which I am finding hard to cope with is their "This is our library" philosophy, which I think is what the students were complaining about when they mentioned poor service and difficulty in locating books. How does an administrator orient such a staff to an awareness of user needs and to a philosophy of public service?

* * *

Criticize this young administrator's approach to his job, to his solutions or his suggestions for solution.

How would you tackle the problems if you were the administrator? To what problem would you give first priority? Does this staff need some form of continuing education?

Case 23

WANTED: A MOVER'S MANUAL

At 4:00 p.m. one hot afternoon Polly Backus sat at her desk in the library resting her feet and enjoying the air-conditioning. She had been working in a storage loft, arranging the books that had recently been moved there. She was trying to decide what to do next.

Several months ago, Mrs. Backus, the assistant librarian, and Mr. Jay, the librarian, had decided to move several thousand volumes to make room for a new fine arts department. Mr. Jay had made a rough estimate of how much space he needed and had rented two empty rooms above a store two blocks from the library. This would not be too far for a page to go for an item that a patron might call for.

Mrs. Backus seized the opportunity not only to weed the library's collection but also to separate little-used materials from those which circulated often. Not only would the library gain a new department, but the general collection would be made more useful and the appearance of the overcrowded library would be improved.

Because there was no shelving in the rented rooms, Mrs. Backus decided first to move the books out of the basement storage area in the library, where the new room was to be, and then to move the old shelves into the rented quarters. She and the other staff members, after having scurried around gathering a variety of boxes and cartons, hastily, but carefully, packed the books. While they were still packing Mrs. Backus decided that some of the older materials in the children's collection could be moved too. She instructed the children's librarian to weed the collection in her room and to pack anything she might want to store.

When all the materials had been packed, Mrs. Backus

hired several students to help move the cartons into the library truck and deliver them to the store, where they would carry them up the stairs into the rooms. The students quit after half a day; they complained that the work was too hard.

    Mrs. Backus was at a loss to know where to get help that was not too expensive for her budget, but when she asked Mr. Jay for advice, he suggested that she use the teen-aged sons of several staff members. They were hired, and the moving was accomplished on weekends and after school over a period of several weeks. This somewhat delayed the plans for the new fine arts department, but it allowed Mrs. Backus more time to weed the collection.

    When the shelves in the basement of the library were empty, professional movers removed the old stacks, delivered them to the storage area, and set them in place. All that remained to be done was to place the books on the shelves.

    It was then that Mrs. Backus discovered that books in several Dewey classes had been placed together in one carton. She had planned to use pages to shelve the books, but now she realized that she would have to supervise the shelving herself. After working in the storage area for several days she decided that it would probably be necessary to unpack all the boxes, put the books on the shelves, and then rearrange them according to class. After she and several pages had unpacked three-fourths of the cartons, she discovered that she did not have enough space on the shelves for the remaining books.

*   *   *

    What decisions should have been made by Mrs. Backus prior to moving a single book? List in order of priority. Should detailed procedures be worked out before starting this project? If so, identify these step by step. Criticize the quality of planning for this project.

Case 24

REORGANIZATION OF CHILDREN'S SERVICES

    Eight months before Miss Marble, head of the children's department of the Marathon Public Library, was due

68 / Library Management

to retire, the director of libraries, Mr. Paddock, started to search for her successor. He wanted a creative, imaginative person to be coordinator of children's services, who would not only be head of the department in the main library but would supervise, staff, and direct the children's services in the branches.

After interviewing many applicants, he chose Mrs. East, an outgoing and attractive widow in her forties. She had a bachelor's degree in elementary education from a university whose curriculum provided a broad liberal arts background and a minimum of educational methods courses. During six years of teaching Mrs. East had found herself becoming so interested in working with library materials that she took a year's leave of absence to study for a master's degree in library science at an accredited library school. After she had received her degree, she worked as an elementary school librarian in a progressive school system for several years; for the last five years she had been assistant to the director of children's services in a large metropolitan public library. In addition to this professional preparation and experience, Mrs. East had personal experience in using children's materials with her own three children, who, at the time of her appointment in the Marathon Public Library, were in their late teens.

Mr. Paddock set up Mrs. East's appointment so that she would start to work a month before Miss Marble was scheduled to retire. This would provide an opportunity for Miss Marble to orient Mrs. East into the work of the children's department and would give Mrs. East a chance to get acquainted with the personnel in all branches. Mr. Paddock's mandate to Mrs. East was to reorganize the children's department so that it functioned more effectively, to create system-wide children's services, and to study and improve the collections.

After two months on the job, Mrs. East had acquired the necessary information for making some decisions. On the basis of the facts she had gathered, she thought that she could write new job descriptions and begin to develop services and acquire materials.

The Marathon Public Library system consisted of a downtown main library and twelve branches, which served a population of approximately 725,000. The budget for library materials was below the national average for cities of comparable size. There was no written book selection policy. In the main library all books for every department were charged and returned at a loan desk at the entrance.

All personnel were included in a city civil service

system. Librarians at the two largest branches had master's degrees in library science. All the other branches were administered by clerks, none of whom had even a bachelor's degree. No branch had a children's librarian, or had ever had assistance or supervision from the children's department in the main library. None of the branches offered story hours or any other book-oriented programs for children. Every branch participated in the summer reading club and, to encourage high attendance, used the promotion techniques developed by the main library's children's department.

The Present Staff: Children's Department, Main Library:

1. Jane Marble, head, children's department: Seven years in present position. After two years in college, Miss Marble took the city civil service examination and qualified as a clerk-typist. Her first position was in the social welfare department, and during the following years she transferred to successively better positions as they opened up in various departments of the city government. After nine years she transferred to the order department of the main library. Several years later she qualified for entrance into the "librarian" series of the civil service classification by attending a summer school offered annually by the state library. Her only other professional training was an occasional workshop, institute, or librarians' meeting. Seven years ago, when the position of head of the children's department became vacant, she applied for the position. Although she had had no experience in working with children in or out of the library, and her only contact with children's materials had been as a clerk-typist in the order and cataloging departments, she was transferred to this position from the circulation department. The job description for the head of the children's department did not specify either a master's degree in library science or experience with children and children's materials. It did specify that the position must be held by a person holding a Librarian V classification, which Miss Marble possessed because of her seniority on the library staff.

Since her appointment, Mr. Paddock had become director and had worked with the city civil service commission in rewriting all "librarian" classifications. All of them now required a master's degree in library science; in addition, all of them above Library I required professional experience.

Miss Marble's duties included intra-departmental

communication, payroll, monthly reports, schedules, and hiring of pages and clerks in her department. She did all of the book selection from current recommended lists which had been checked by her assistant. She spent 98 per cent of her time in her office and rarely worked with borrowers.

    2. <u>Miss Karen Blue, professional assistant</u>: Two years in present position. Miss Blue received a master's degree two years ago from a good accredited library school. All of her electives were in children's materials and services, which included practice in story-telling and book-oriented programs. Although she came to this job directly from library school, Mr. Paddock hired her because of her superior professional preparation. He gave Karen's placement papers to Miss Marble so that she could see what courses Karen had had and could read the reports from the supervisor of her practice work in the university demonstration school library. He hoped that Miss Marble would use Karen's capabilities to improve services to children. Miss Marble had ignored the papers and returned them to Mr. Paddock with the remark that she was too busy to spend time on them. She made no attempt to utilize Karen's professional potentialities or her experience in story-telling and children's theatre.

    Karen's duties included filing cards in the children's department public catalog, recommending replacements for lost books, and weeding the collection by checking titles against standard lists. She also checked in the card catalog all children's books recommended in each issue of <u>Horn Book</u>, <u>School Library Journal</u>, <u>Booklist</u>, <u>Bulletin of the Center for Children's Books</u>, and other periodicals. Karen noted which books the department already owned, and from these lists Miss Marble then decided which titles would be added to the collection. Miss Blue also served the public, and, in her spare time, went through the collection checking each title on the shelves with the <u>Children's Catalog</u>, <u>Index to Children's Poetry</u>, <u>Index to Fairy Tales</u>, and several other bibliographies and indexes. When she found a book on the shelves listed in one of these, she stamped the flyleaf of the book with a rubber stamp bearing the title of the bibliography or index.

    3. <u>Sub-professional</u>: This employee had an A.B. degree from a local college and had been in this position for four years. Her duties included preparing displays, helping with the summer reading club, serving the public, and typing order cards. She also helped Karen with the weeding and checked in new books when they came from the catalog department.

4. Clerk. Full-time: This employee was a high school graduate. She typed, alphabetized, and filed order cards for the books Miss Marble wished to buy for the department. She alphabetized catalog cards when they came from the catalog department, but she did not file them. (Miss Blue did this.) Her job also involved helping patrons, some shelving, and page work. She did not have enough work to keep her occupied for a full day and was frequently observed sitting idle.

5. Part-time page: This position was filled by a high school boy who came in after school. He picked up books from the tables and shelved them, did errands to other departments, and did heavy jobs like moving furniture.

Programs and Routines: Main Library:

When Karen discovered that the department offered no programs of any kind to children, parents, or teachers, she offered to give book talks and other kinds of programs, to start a puppet theater series, and to have story hours for preschool children. Miss Marble said, "We're too small a department to do any of those things and we don't have time." Later, Karen showed her a list of activities which she was doing but which the idle clerk could do under supervision. Karen explained that she would then be free for activities which directly served the children. Miss Marble reprimanded her for the suggestion.

A series of story hours was conducted every summer by a volunteer women's organization. Complete authority for planning and carrying out the series was delegated to the organization. The head of the children's department took no responsibility for selecting and training the storytellers. All that the library staff did in preparation for the story hours was to notify the library's public relations secretary of the time and date, to ask the janitor to move some furniture before and after the story hour, and to get out and put away the mats on which the children sat during the program. Miss Marble had no control over what was told, the length of the story or stories, the age level of the listeners, or the number permitted to attend.

Listeners ranged from babies to sixth graders and the parents who brought the children. Selecting appropriate stories was difficult, if not impossible. As no preregistration was required, the library staff never knew whether there would be enough space for those who came. The number of listeners varied, but normally all of the eighty-five seating mats were in use and many children and parents were standing. The quality of the stories told and the delivery varied greatly according to the ability of the story-teller. Miss Marble usually ignored the crowd and stayed in her office. Karen Blue and the sub-professional served as disciplinarians and also tried to help other patrons who came for service during the program. Karen would meet the patrons at the entrance to the department to find out what they wanted, and then would make her way as quietly as possible through the children on the floor to find the books requested. A library auditorium, on the floor above, could have been used for the story hours, but it never had been. The story-tellers made no attempt to relate what they told to the children's reading, and very few children ever borrowed any books. Most of them arrived just before the scheduled time and left as soon as the story was finished.

For many years the children's department had sponsored a summer reading club. Much staff time was required during the spring for working on prizes, posters, and publicity for the club. During the summer the staff were so busy with clerical work that they had little time to work with patrons or the collection.

Selection of Materials:

Miss Blue checked the current reviewing media against the card catalog in the children's department at the main library and gave the titles of the books to Miss Marble, who had sole responsibility for selection in the main library's children's department. She had no authority, however, over selection in the branches. Each branch librarian came to the branch office at the main library once a week to select what she wanted from the titles which had been selected for the children's department in the main library. Miss Marble divided the books in the branch office into two groups: "Recommended for Branches" and "Not Recommended for Branches." The branch librarians were not limited to the recommended group but were strongly advised to choose from this list. The branch librarians were allowed to choose their own books because they were aware of the needs and interests of their patrons. Each week the professional staff of the main library cringed as they saw the best books (those recommended in Horn Book, or the Newbery and Caldecott winners) and books of local interest passed up in favor of marginal titles which could justifiably be purchased only by a large children's department. They frequently ordered too many new books when their basic collections were inadequate.

Cataloging of Children's Books:

For "easy" books, only a title card and an author card were provided. For all the other books, LC cards were used when available and the Dewey numbers used by the Library of Congress were assigned to the children's books. Many of the classification numbers were either too long and too complex or were not suitable for a children's collection. Mrs. East discovered that no one in the catalog department was responsible for children's books, and consequently the cataloging was not at all suitable for a children's collection.

*   *   *

Mrs. East has a formidable reorganization task ahead of her. If you were Mrs. East, where would you start with reorganizing and what priorities would you establish?

Case 25

"INNOVATIVE" CATALOGING

Bata College, a church-related, unaccredited liberal arts college, has a student body of about 800. The college library started with a reading room, developed a book collection of sorts, and eventually employed a "librarian" to replace volunteers and students. The organization of the library leaves much to be desired. Some semblance of order has been achieved in organizing for service and use, but the cataloging is done in a haphazard fashion.

Recently, as a result of a news story in a popular national periodical, money from benefactors and philanthropic foundations has flowed into the college. Inadequate and shabby buildings have been renovated, a student union and cafeteria building have been built, a science building is under construction, a library building is in the planning stage, and eight faculty members with Ph.D. degrees have been employed. The governing board and the officials of the college are hoping to qualify for state and regional accreditation in a few years.

To meet the accreditation standards for libraries, the Bata College Library must be greatly improved in every way. Consequently, the library's inadequate budget has been increased. Two capable, well-qualified, experienced college librarians have been employed as head librarian and cataloger.

With the spirit of a missionary or a Peace Corps volunteer, the cataloger, Miss Ilian, accepted the position as a challenge to her abilities. Now that she has assessed the chaotic situation, she wonders where to start. She has found an elderly woman busily "cataloging" books without checking either the catalog or the shelflist because the shelflist and the card catalog are in such a mess.

Miss Ilian has found accession books which are numbered 14,000 to 32,000. The accession records prior to 14,000 are missing. Many books are on the shelves but are not listed in either the catalog or the shelflist; they have been given call numbers, book cards and pockets have been inserted in them, but no catalog cards have been made. Almost one-third of the books on the shelves have call numbers on the spine but no cards or pockets. There may or may not be cards for them in the catalog. No shelflist cards have been made for about one-third of the collection.

As a result of inexperienced volunteer help and no processing procedures, many books on the shelves have typed catalog cards inside the covers. The cards fall out when the books are handled; many cards have been picked up off the floors and brought to the circulation desk.

No revising or checking had been done after catalog cards and book pockets and cards have been typed. Consequently, the call numbers on the spines of many books do not agree with the numbers on the catalog and shelflist cards. Several editions of many books are listed on the the same set of cards. All books written on the same subject and by the same author are frequently listed on one set of cards with one call number.

Because there has been no systematic way to check whether or not the library owns a title, many duplicate copies have been purchased. If the library owns several copies of a book, each copy may bear a different call number.

The entry form on the catalog cards agrees with no standard cataloging method. All cards are individually typed and there is no consistency in their format.

No inventory of the collection has ever been made, and shelf-reading has never been systematic. The collection contains hundreds, perhaps thousands, of donated books which should never have been put on the shelves or cataloged.

* * *

What decisions does Miss Ilian need to make in order to proceed in an orderly and efficient manner?

Case 26

A TECHNICAL SERVICES DEPARTMENT

Mr. Emil Dexter has just retired as chief of technical services in the Woodrow University Library. He was appointed to the library staff in 1941 when he was working in the university's purchasing department. Because the librarian thought that his experience and knowledge of purchasing procedure would be useful in ordering library materials, he was put in charge of ordering within the library. He had worked as a student assistant in the library during his undergraduate days and had received an A.B. degree in liberal arts. During two summers following his library appointment he was given a leave of absence to take some library science courses at a local teachers college which trained school librarians. Mr. Dexter was a member of a family well known in the community; some of his forebears had been influential members of the university's board of trustees. His original appointment to a minor position in the purchasing department had been obtained primarily because of his family connections. The library appointment may have been made for the same reason.

At the time he was hired in the library, an efficient, experienced cataloger was in charge of cataloging and classification. About eight years ago when she retired, Mr. Dexter became head of both ordering and cataloging, chiefly because both departments were housed in one room. He knew little about either classification or cataloging; direction of the catalogers was concerned chiefly with the paper work required by the head office for budgets, records, reports, appointments, absences, and promotions. He also divided the workload among the catalogers.

The cataloging staff were efficient and capable but could have turned out much more work had they had better direction. Since the library had several departmental libraries as well as subject reading rooms in the main building, a number of subjects and languages had to be represented among the skills of the catalogers.

Mr. Dexter participated actively in the alumni association of the university and during the last five years was chairman of a fund-raising campaign for new university buildings. During much of his work day he was either using the telephone to straighten out details of the campaign or having conferences with people who came to see him. Because of the crowded conditions in the technical services room, most of the staff overheard conversations and were distracted from their work. He was often absent because of speeches or meetings. As a result of his alumni activities, the technical services department received little of his thought or time.

Mr. Dexter was not a good manager, and he was not interested in becoming one. He was a fine public speaker, but communication with his staff was minimal. He had neither personnel policies nor goals for the work of the department. This lack of planning and interest, complicated by very crowded conditions, resulted in low staff morale. The arrears in cataloging were tremendously large; both faculty members and students were "screaming" for materials.

A professional staff of four and eight clerks were crowded into the space assigned to technical services (see Fig. 2). Receiving, binding, acquisitions, cataloging, and the national and trade bibliographies used by the public and other library staff members were housed in one room. No room dividers or low partitions had been installed; no draperies or other sound-deadening devices had been provided; desks and files were jammed together as closely as possible; no private nook had been provided for the chief of the division, and everyone could hear every word spoken in the room.

A well-qualified, experienced director of libraries was appointed two years ago. She soon discovered the deplorable conditions in this department, but decided to wait until Mr. Dexter's retirement to make any changes in technical services. After she had studied the qualifications of all members of the library staff, she decided that no one could be promoted to the department head position. She therefore contacted the library schools. The job description specified a master's degree in library science from an accredited library school, some knowledge of management and personnel, and experience in technical services.

You have just accepted this position. The librarian has promised cooperation and financial support for purchasing equipment which will improve the working environment and lessen the noise. She has obtained permission from the

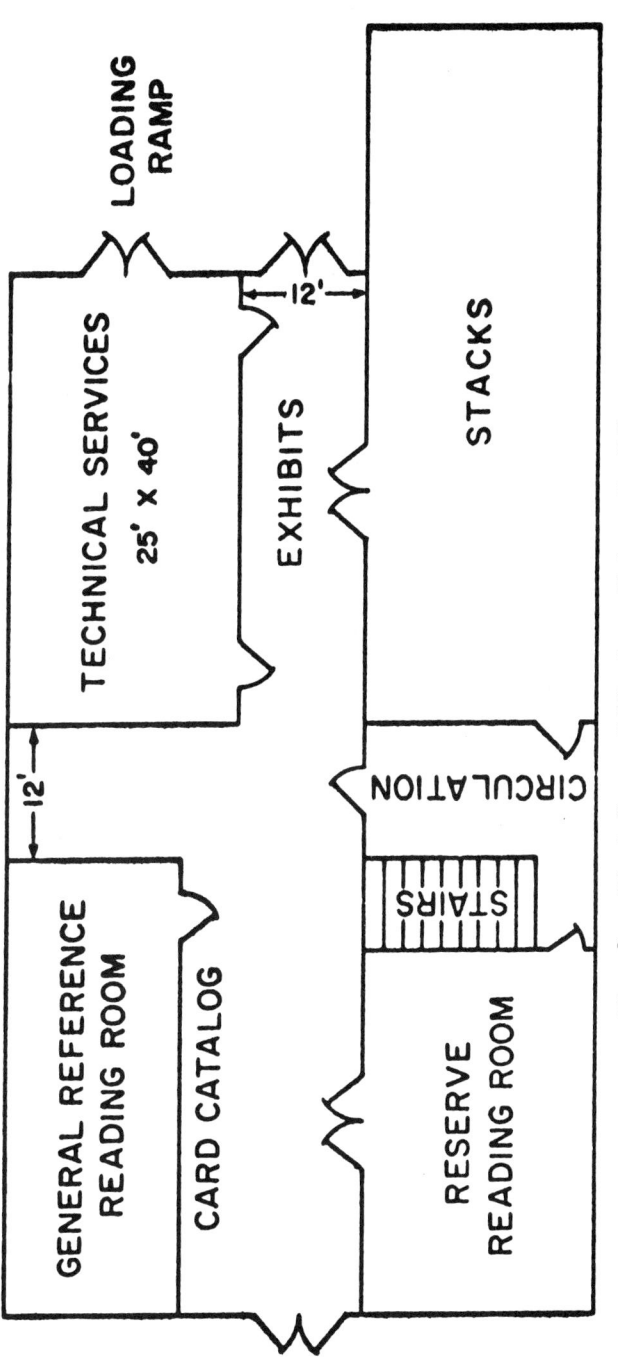

Fig. 2. First floor of Woodrow University Library

78 / Library Management

superintendent of buildings and grounds and from the university's insurance department to use the space in the two exhibit halls (see Fig. 2) for the technical services department. One of the doors on either the north or the east side must always be usable as a fire exit. A new library building is planned for completion in about six years, so no major structural changes to the building can be made.

Here are some facts you need to know about the Woodrow University library building: The first floor is shown in Fig. 2. The second and third floors contain subject reading rooms, a rare books room, and administrative offices. One floor below ground contains a duplicating area and public restrooms, mechanical equipment and stacks. Two levels of stacks are below ground and several above (to roof).

The building was constructed in 1941 with high ceilings and many corridors. Originally there were three entrances into the first floor, but this arrangement caused control problems. Hence, it was necessary to close the north and east entrances. This space is now used only for a few exhibit cases. Each entrance has beautiful floor to ceiling glassed walls covered with decorative grills. The corridors are flooded in the daytime with natural light, have marble walls and terrazzo floors and are heated and air-conditioned. The halls are twelve feet wide; the technical services room is twenty-five feet by forty feet.

*   *   *

If fire regulations permit, how would you reorganize the floor space in Fig. 2 to utilize the available corridors? What changes would you make in the technical services room?

Case 27

MOMENTUM
(Role playing)

The staff of the Taro Public Library frequently put on ambitious programs for the public and cooperated actively in various community endeavors. For example, each year during National Library Week special programs, exhibits, and events were carried out. Recently, in cooperation with the League of Women Voters, three luncheons were sponsored at the library on the subject of how to develop a sense of civic responsibility. The luncheons were catered and served in the library. This meant a lot of work for the staff as they were responsible not only for the speakers and the programs but also for carrying in tables, chairs, and dishes because the library had no kitchen or dining facilities. The luncheons were well attended and considered a big success.

Role for Mrs. Dock:

You are the librarian of the Taro Public Library. Your staff consists of fourteen full-time employees, four part-time adults, and sixteen part-time college students. Your staff works together harmoniously, cooperatively, and efficiently. You have observed that the week following every "big push" of the kind described above, there is always a loss of momentum: little groups talking, long-time goals lost sight of, and only routine essential jobs done. You are not a "slave driver" or a shrew but your staff is never large enough to permit slacking off at any time. The staff seem to work best and most efficiently when engaged in planning a special event. After the event, they do not appear to be physically or nervously tired. The "let down" appears to be merely reaction to the relaxation of pressure or to a change of tempo.

You define "tempo" as the pace at which the staff in an organization gets things done, the speed with which problems and opportunities are identified, the attitudes and alertness to seeing new service opportunities or to improving procedures, the origination of new ideas and the putting of these ideas into operation, and the reaction to change. During the preparation for a special event, the staff saw many things which needed doing and had many ideas for improvement or change; but you observed that after the event they are not thinking so keenly or so productively.

You have regular monthly staff meetings of the entire staff except the pages. You have decided to present this problem at the next meeting but, before you do, you want to talk it over with your two department heads to get their suggestions. That meeting with them is scheduled for this afternoon. You believe that it is possible to get the staff into the swing of things faster by planning ahead for the period following an event, and hence prevent loss of tempo --possibly by having the staff write down, during periods of preparation for events, their ideas for more efficient procedures or operations, the problems which developed, suggestions for innovation or change or new services; then, after the event, checking this list to get new inspiration to avoid a period of "let down."

Role for Mr. Kudzu:

You are twenty-nine years old and have been head of public services in this library for three years. Prior to that you worked as a reference assistant in a large public library. You are open-minded and receptive to innovation and change. You try to operate circulation and reference efficiently and to serve the needs of the community. You are always watching for new ways to serve groups in the community. For example, when you were a member of the expectant parent class at the local hospital, you observed the need for a brochure listing suitable reading materials and sources of information for this group. You and your staff prepared such a brochure for that class and it has been distributed to every class since as well as at the library. Another example, which has been popular with the public, was a reading list for brides which is sent out to every prospective bride as soon as the engagement is announced in the local paper. These lists are also distributed to the dress shops and department stores which have bridal consultants.

During the preparation for every special program, your entire staff is involved and many non-routine activities are necessarily neglected. You, too, are concerned with this "sag" in productive work after each program and would like to plan to avoid it the next time.

Role for Mrs. Guar:

You have been head of technical services in this library for fifteen years and before that you were a cataloger in a small college library. You are forty-five years old. Although your staff is involved only on the periphery of public programs, the attitudes and change of tempo and the sort of "holiday" atmosphere in the public service areas affect the work environment of your staff also. To keep the work in your department moving at an even pace you, too, would like to avoid such let down periods in the future.

Case 28

POPULAR MATERIALS IN A RESEARCH LIBRARY

The collection in each Mayway Corporation library, tailored to fit the specific needs of its patrons, consists of highly technical literature, theses, reports, and journals. In each library a large collection of highly technical books supports the specific research being done in the laboratories, and each library subscribes to foreign language periodicals. No popular or recreational materials are included in the collections, although several of the libraries do subscribe to what might be considered popular business weeklies. Practically all of them have a subscription to the Wall Street Journal.

Mayway Corporation was a pioneer in non-discriminatory personnel policy. Race and religion have never been determining factors for job eligibility. Recently, however, the company has aggressively recruited in Negro colleges. Because several Mayway plants are in the southern half of the United States, the company plans to fill many more of its technical and professional positions with talented Negroes.

Although Midwest D library serves a plant in which very few employees belong to any minority group, Mr. Chase, the librarian, was recently approached by the company's public relations director, who wanted a collection of books on race discrimination and the civil rights movement to be included in each plant library. The public relations director had received tentative approval of the plan after consultation with top management and library supervisors in several of Mayway's locations. All the library directors wanted to see the list of books that were to be considered for inclusion.

The list submitted to the librarians consisted mainly of popular materials which should be in every public library. Included were Baseball Has Done It, by Jackie Robinson, Dick Gregory's Nigger, Freedom Summer, Why We Can't Wait, and several of James Baldwin's books.

No general policy statement accompanied the books, and each librarian was free to decide whether to include the listed books in his library's collection. Mr. Chase has refused to put them in his collection because he believes that if he does, every special interest and minority group will demand equal coverage.

*   *   *

Do you support Mr. Chase's decision about inclusion of this group of books? Has the public relations director any right to interfere with the librarian's responsibility for selection of materials. Should funds from a research budget be spent on popular materials?

Case 29

EDUCATION DIVISION VS. LIBRARY

About three years ago the Kilowatt Electric Company set up an education division in its plant, which employs about 7,000 persons. This division provides in-company educational programs, including management development, programmed learning, closed-circuit television classes, and courses in surveying, mathematics, physics, and electrical engineering. None of the courses carries any college credit. The company also has a fine library staffed by three professionals and seven clerks; this library was started more than twenty years ago. Both the division and the library are under the supervision of the executive vice-president in charge of finance and have equal status in the organization.

Early in the history of the library a company policy was established, specifying that all printed materials requisitioned by any department or office of the company should be ordered through the library. The library staff did all searching for bibliographical information, placed the orders, checked in the materials when they arrived, paid the invoices, and charged items to the department which had done the ordering. The reasons for this policy were: 1) most of the printed materials ordered were for the library; 2) the purchasing agent believed that the library staff were more competent to place orders for printed materials than he was because they knew more about publishing and dealer sources; and 3) the discount pattern was different from the three-bid structure required for purchasing equipment and other items.

Prior to the establishment of the education division, the quantity of printed materials to be ordered for departments was so small that the library staff could easily handle this work. Since its origin three years ago, the division has placed tens of thousands of dollars' worth of orders through the library. Such an increased work load has required adding another half-time clerk to the order staff.

All of these materials ordered through the library are processed in and circulated from the education division. Last month 620 persons borrowed materials. The chief librarian believes that: 1) this activity is an encroachment on the function of the library; 2) the education division is fast becoming a competitor; and 3) some policy decisions should be made by the executive vice-president under whom the two divisions operate. She is preparing arguments to submit to the vice-president in support of her contention that the education division should plan and supervise courses and programs but that all materials supporting the courses should be part of the library collection, should be classified and cataloged, should be intershelved with the rest of the library collection, and should be circulated from the library.

* * *

Do you agree or disagree with the chief librarian's assessment of this situation?

Case 30

SPECIAL FUNDING

The Jamestown High School is one of the least educationally progressive in the state. Although it does offer college preparatory courses, the main emphasis is on athletics and technical programs.

Administrative positions are awarded to older teachers, most of whom are lifelong residents of the community. Younger teachers and newcomers to the community are given heavier teaching loads and extra-curricular assignments. Their opinions on curriculum are heard, but rarely implemented, although most of them have had educational backgrounds superior to those of many of the older faculty.

Mrs. Fields, a professionally trained librarian, has been on the staff of the high school for more than twenty years. Because of her age and her years on the faculty she is considered an important part of the "established" faculty, although she mixes with the younger faculty.

Her main interest in the library is helping students. All freshmen have a series of lessons on the use of the library as part of a required English course. Mrs. Fields enjoys teaching it, and most of the students like and respect her. She makes displays for the bulletin boards to encourage wide reading. The student assistants shelve and help check out materials at the desk.

Last year the library budget was substantially increased by a special grant to be spent on books. Notification of the grant came late in February and the deadline for submitting the book list was the first of April. Mrs. Fields, pleased to have an opportunity to enlarge the collection, immediately started thinking how she might best spend the grant. She decided to enlist the aid of the faculty in selecting books. Although she reserved the right to make the final decisions, she felt inadequate in some subject areas and wanted suggestions. She duplicated a letter to be sent to the teachers, asking for suggestions for books in their subject areas. She asked for a list of titles and publishers and put a due date of March 15 on the letter. Since she was certain that all eighty faculty members would respond to the letter, she concentrated on selecting general reference books.

By the fifteenth of March only two lists had been put in her mailbox. One, a science list, contained about fifty books; the other, from the industrial arts teacher, contained one entry, Hot Rod, a magazine for car enthusiasts.

Mrs. Fields immediately put a notice in the bulletin for the next day requesting "immediate return of the recommended titles." By the end of the week six lists had been turned in, and there were only five school days until the final list was due.

* * *

Comment on Mrs. Field's heavy reliance on the teaching faculty for book selection. What is the librarian's role in deciding what should be purchased? Evidently, she kept no "possible purchase" file.

Case 31

A BRANCH IN A LOW-INCOME NEIGHBORHOOD

The Christmas-Chanukah Festival at the Smith Branch of Big City Public Library had become a well-publicized library tradition. During the six months since Robert Heath had become director of libraries for the city, he had heard about the Smith Branch, which was housed in a neighborhood center and which served as a typical public library for the surrounding area as well as a city-wide library of Judaica. Although he had visited a number of the city's twenty-six branch libraries, he had not yet seen the Smith Branch. And so, when the branch librarian urged him to attend the Christmas-Chanukah Festival, he agreed to go. Knowing that the branch was near the city's central business district in an old, somewhat deteriorated, low-rent neighborhood, he was rather surprised when he arrived at the festival to see many late-model cars parked nearby. He concluded that the festival attracted people from other parts of the city as well as from the neighborhood.

During the social hour which followed the lecture, the branch librarian introduced the director to many of the guests. He observed that most of them seemed to know each other and were long-time friends of the branch librarian. There seemed to be great interest among the group for the displays of Yiddish and Judaic materials, and enthusiasm in discussing the lecture which they had just heard.

In his brief conversation with the guests, Mr. Heath discovered that only a few of them lived in the neighborhood. On his way out of the building he passed some teen-agers coming out of one of the recreation rooms and overheard one of them say to his companions, "Looks like the librarian is entertaining her friends again!"

As he drove home the director puzzled over his observations and experiences of the evening. The program had been a well-prepared, intellectual lecture delivered to a nonresident, well-dressed audience in a low-income neighborhood center. The people had been enthusiastic, appreciative and friendly. But why wasn't the neighborhood better represented in the audience? What, after all, was the function of a branch library in a neighborhood center?

The next morning he asked his secretary to phone Jane Winslow, assistant director in charge of branches, to make an appointment for her to bring him information about the Smith Branch.

"Was the festival at Smith Branch well attended?" she asked him when she arrived for the conference.

"Yes, indeed," Mr. Heath replied. "Miss Singer seems to be doing a superb job of publicizing the branch's special collection of Yiddish and Judaic materials. But I am interested in knowing whether the branch is also serving the neighborhood. Tell me something of its history and how it happened to have this very special kind of collection. Here in the central library we have thirty or more special collections, so why isn't the Yiddish and Judaic collection housed here?"

Mrs. Winslow told him some of the history of the neighborhood and how the Smith Branch had developed. The neighborhood had been at its height between about 1910 and the early 1930's when the population was largely Jewish. In response to the demands of the community, the Smith Branch was established in 1935, and a Jewish librarian (the present Branch librarian, Edna Singer) was appointed to develop a collection to meet the needs of the population in the area. She was twenty-three years old and had recently graduated from one of the nation's best library schools. The people were articulate in telling her what they wanted and used the library heavily. Being young, energetic, and ambitious, Miss Singer joined various clubs and groups in the neighborhood and thereby got acquainted with many of the residents in the community, which at that time had a population of about 25,000. She also rented an apartment in the neighborhood so as to further identify herself with her patrons.

As the buildings in the area aged and deteriorated, families whose income would permit moved out to newer areas of the city or to the suburbs. As Jewish families moved out, various immigrant groups moved in--Italian, Polish, Irish, Albanian, Ukrainian, and Greek. By 1966, the population in this area had shrunk to about 7,500 individuals. The population decline was attributed to decreasing family size among the descendants of immigrant groups and to the gradual reduction of dwelling units as deteriorated buildings were torn down and replaced by businesses or industries or parking lots. The area in 1966 could be described as an old, somewhat deteriorated, low-rent neighborhood which housed a variety of people, most of whom were poor, but it was not considered a slum. Most of the apartments had large, comfortable rooms and were in good repair. Although some of the inhabitants did have problems, those did not stem from the neighborhood. For most of the population, their way of life constituted a distinct and independent working-class subculture. Residential stability was characteristic of the neighborhood. In 1966 only about ten per cent of the population was Jewish; about half were native-born Americans of Italian parentage; about ten per cent was Polish; and the remaining 30 per cent was composed of the other ethnic groups mentioned above, some postwar newcomers who were interested in low rents, broken families subsisting on Aid to Dependent Children, middle-class professionals, and college students.

The educational level ranged from functional illiterates to college graduates, but most of the inhabitants had completed eight years of elementary school. For most it was a peer-group society because most of their relationships were with people of the same sex, age, and lifestyle. The mainstay of the adult peer-group was the family circle.

As the Jewish exodus from the area progressed, the branch librarian discovered that the new residents were much less interested in using the library. Out of her bitter disappointment at the loss of the Jewish clientele, she conceived the idea of preserving the already collected materials as a repository of Yiddish and Judaic materials for the city and of keeping the collection up to date. The organized Jewish groups in the city approved of Miss Singer's idea and set up an endowment for the collection. The director of libraries and the board of trustees accepted the endowment and encouraged the librarian to build up the collection. Miss Singer dedicated herself to caring for this collection and to promoting an interest in it. Her program included a number of lectures and festivals held at the branch library every year.

Although these lectures and festivals were open to residents of the neighborhood, all but a handful of those who came were Jews from other parts of the city; most of them had at one time lived in the area and had used the branch library.

When the Jewish clubs moved out of the neighborhood, Miss Singer continued her memberships and attended meetings in the new locations. The new ethnic groups brought in new organizations, clubs, and churches, but she made no attempt to learn anything about them or to join them. As a result, she gradually disassociated the functions of the library from the needs of the people. Most of the patrons were children and old people from the area.

Miss Winslow concluded her briefing of the director with this comment: "When I took this job five years ago I visited all of our branches and found that the Smith Branch was the best administered. It was efficiently organized and had well-trained and efficient clerical assistants and pages, a comprehensive reference collection, accurate and full records and reports, attractive displays, and that magnificent special collection of Judaic materials. I learned that the special collection was financed chiefly from an endowment provided by Jewish groups in the city. The public library budget supported everything else. My only criticism was that the work of the staff and the collection were not oriented and identified with the needs of the present population. Actually, the population is no longer large enough to justify the city's maintaining a branch library there. All that the area needs now is a reading center of popular materials with reference, children's, and other services from a regional center. As you know, I have tried to organize all the branches in the city around several regional centers. In doing this, we have eliminated or combined many small branches.

"Several weeks after my first visit to Smith Branch," Mrs. Winslow continued, "I proposed to the former director that Miss Singer and the special collection, including its reference books, be moved to the main library and that the Smith Branch become a reading center under the supervision of the Marble Regional Center. He called in the head of special collections to get his reaction to this move and he not only approved but was most enthusiastic about the idea. Because of recent stack renovation and addition he could assign a separate stack area to the collection and give Miss Singer an office in the stacks near the collection.

"With the approval of the director of libraries and the head of special collections, I invited Miss Singer to come in for a conference and presented this idea to her. She was most unhappy about the prospect of a change. She felt that if she moved she would lose status and prestige because she and her collection would be 'buried' in the stacks. Although I told her that she could still have her lectures and festivals and use the main library auditorium, she didn't think that that arrangement would be as satisfactory as having them in the old setting.

"After another conference with the former director, we decided to leave the Smith Branch as it is until Miss Singer retires in 1977. After all, she has been there for many years, and we need some time to recruit staff, to work out community-wide programs in cooperation with the neighborhood center and other groups, and to decide how to divide the collection--some to the regional center, some to the main library, and what should be left for the new Smith Reading Center."

Mr. Heath thanked Mrs. Winslow for the thorough report and asked her to submit within two months detailed plans for phasing out the Smith Branch and for developing the Smith Reading Center. He specifically asked for: 1) recommendations for staff, equipment, space, materials, and budget; 2) programs which would coordinate and cooperate with the neighborhood center, the Community Action Program, and the Head Start Program; 3) lists of adult materials for new literates; 4) plans for using motion pictures and filmstrips; 5) utilization of high school graduates in the neighborhood to be employed under the Economic Opportunity Act to publicize the library; 6) plans for gaining community acceptance of the library; 7) ideas for luring prospective patrons to the library, to motion picture programs shown outside the library during the summer, and to children's story hours held outside the library.

* * *

Did Mr. Heath's predecessor allow this situation to go on too long? Shouldn't he have taken decisive action years ago to remove Miss Singer and her special collection to the main library, so that the branch could be redesigned to meet the needs of the present population? Evaluate Mr. Heath's administrative approach to the problem.

Case 32

MISSION OF RESEARCH LIBRARIES
(Role playing)

Because of its reputation as an outstanding collection of American historical materials, mail requests for information came to the Mallard Historical Society Library from all segments of the population, from grade school children to senior research scholars. The quantity of mail was so great that a junior professional, Miss Irma Indigo, and a typist were assigned full-time to sorting and handling the mail. Requests for access to study certain documents or portions of the collection were answered by sending formal application blanks to be filled out and returned with the names of references.

Many general, "blanket" requests sounded as though they came from grade school children, from high school or college students, or from adults writing speeches. This type of request was usually phrased something like this: "Please send me all the information you have about...." In reply to these letters, Miss Indigo sent one of several form letters explaining that inasmuch as the Library had no circulating collection, no publications could be mailed out. If the writer asked for a few specific facts indicating that he had done considerable work on the subject and just needed a little information which only this collection could provide, Miss Indigo would photocopy up to five pages which contained the information.

If the writer was a grade or high school student, the reply suggested that the sender talk to his school librarian or visit his local public library. If the writer appeared to be an adult, the form letter listed the names and addresses of historical collections in the writer's state, the state's academic institutions, the state library, and large public libraries and suggested the writer contact them.

Many letters asked something like this: "I am a descendant of _____ who was a signer of the Declaration of Independence. Will you please compile a genealogy for me. I was born in _____ on _____, the names of my parents are _____ and their birth dates and place of birth are _____." In reply to such requests, a form letter stated that the staff of the Mallard Society Library was too small and the library budget too limited to do genealogical research but that "a number of persons throughout the nation earn their living doing this work. Normally their charges are from ___ to ___ per hour. Enclosed is a list of the genealogical collections in your state and region. We suggest you write the curators of these collections for the names and addresses of genealogical searchers in the area."

Requests for information which came from serious research scholars, editors, or publishers were referred to one of the senior librarians or curators of special collections for reply.

Many requests were from graduate students writing term papers, master's theses, or doctoral dissertations. If the request displayed a lack of basic knowledge of the subject which could be obtained from standard historical works or indexes, the librarian to whom the request was referred would send a tactfully worded reply suggesting that this information was probably available in his academic library or in other large libraries in his state or region. The reply stated: "After your local library resources have been exhausted, you might wish to come to the Mallard Library to search for specific details which you lack. An application blank requesting access to materials in this collection is enclosed." Typical of this type of letter from graduate students was the following:

I am doing research on _____. (I am not sure of the spelling of his first name nor of his middle initial.) He was born about 1815 in Pennsylvania or Connecticut and emigrated to Indiana about 1845 to teach in a newly established seminary. I believe your library may have information about his parents, where he was born, the schooling he had, what led to his western migration, and any other facts you may be able to give me. I am specifically interested in the impact of his views on the educational development of the state of Indiana.

Some of these requests asked for "original" material, which meant something in handwritten form. In many instances, the librarian included in her reply a mimeographed sheet explaining and defining primary source materials. The nature of some requests sounded as though the writer expected the Mallard staff to do most of his research for him and send him by return mail what would seem to be a full draft of something which he could retype and hand in.

More specific and intelligent requests from senior scholars were answered as fully as possible by a senior librarian or curator. If the writer asked what materials were available on a certain subject, he was referred to or sent one of many printed bibliographies produced by the Mallard staff. If the writer asked for facts which would take many hours to locate, the reply suggested a trip to the Mallard Library to do his own searching. But if the writer needed an isolated fact which could be readily located only in some rare pamphlet or document owned by the Mallard Library, the staff would go "all out" to find it for him.

The Mallard staff believed they were doing a conscientious job of answering requests and making the materials available to those who came to the library. But recently the President of the Mallard Historical Society received several very caustic criticisms of the library's access policies. He has asked the library director to come to his office for a conference to discuss the mission of the library as understood and interpreted by the library staff.

Role for the President, Mallard Historical Society:

In your position, you are understandably sensitive to public opinion and criticism. The charges made in those letters are serious and you need more background to answer them. Copies of some of the letters were sent by the writers to newspapers, historical journals and library periodicals, where they were published. The Mallard Historical Society is supported privately through memberships and endowments and supplemented by some research grant funds. This adverse publicity may discourage future donors as well as affect future membership campaigns as well as membership renewals. The criticisms can be summarized as follows:

A college faculty member who was writing a book on one period of American history charged that he had traveled a long distance to study certain documents in the Mallard Library which were essential to a section of his book. He had asked to see "all" documents pertaining to this period. He asserted that he was given access to seven and learned later that there were fifteen others he should have studied. He did not know of the existence of these fifteen until another book was published which referred to them. He charged that the library staff applied institutional censorship in permitting one historian access to the fifteen documents and not bringing them out for him to study.

Several scholars claim that over the past ten years, access to various archival materials in the Mallard Library was denied or withheld from them by the library staff and consequently seriously affected their work; and, in one instance, prevented the compilation and publication of a volume. The staff member responsible for withholding the documents in both of foregoing examples claimed that the papers in question were not available at the time due to restrictions imposed by the donor.

A doctoral candidate working on his dissertation reported, in an irate letter, that he was denied access to certain papers because they were "reserved" for a cooperative research project sponsored by a famous national institution. Another doctoral student was told he could not see certain papers because they had not been unpacked from the cartons in which they had been received from the donor and, according to library policy, a staff member must examine, sort, list, and file all incoming material before it could be made available for use by the public.

Role for Director, Mallard Historical Society Library:

You have investigated each of the charges cited above. You insist that materials are available impartially to bona fide research scholars and that your staff does not discriminate among them. The contention that materials have been arbitrarily denied or withheld has no basis in fact. In every instance cited, the staff member involved had acted within his authority and any denial of access was in accordance with library policies approved by the Society's board of trustees.

You and your staff believe the mission of a specialized research library is to be a repository of rare and unique resources which contain the materials for new contributions to knowledge. An important function is physical care of the collection and preservation not only for this generation but also for future generations. Accessibility must be regulated within a framework which inhibits destruction or damage from carelessness or loss through theft. It is not a function of this library to be a source of reference for casual or general inquiries.

This library is also a researching library where many members of the staff, as part of their professional responsibilities, undertake the writing, publishing, or editing of books, reports, catalogs, bibliographies, and journals. Whenever their labors are interrupted to spend time answering casual or frivolous user requests, some future researcher will be impeded in his significant work because the Mallard staff didn't produce the necessary bibliography or list or failed to sort and file newly acquired archival material.

The researcher who does not know that certain materials exist or cannot describe his needs in perfect detail has no right to expect staff members to spend untold amounts of time doing the necessary research to identify whether or not they exist.

You and your staff see your mission as supplementing the functions of other libraries. You believe that scholars should exhaust the facilities of local libraries first and that Mallard Library should be one of the last resorts. You believe the function of public, tax-supported libraries is to serve a geographical area as a circulating collection and reference center. The staffs of such libraries are obligated to provide information on any or all subjects and the only limitations on service are normally in terms of policies regarding subjects (for example, legal or medical advice, or crossword puzzle words) or the length of time which can be spent on one search.

You believe the academic library exists to serve its educational complex; again, any legitimate request for reference or research service should be provided. Normally its resources are available also to the general public and to all qualified scholars and researchers. But the academic library is not obligated by function or purpose to serve as a reference source for casual inquiries.

No librarian in any library should be asked or expected to do more than is reasonable or to do research which the user should do for himself. The librarian can assist in the use of various indexes, bibliographies, and catalogs to locate suitable materials and can find and locate suitable materials and can find and locate the materials for the user, but the user must "dig out" what he needs for whatever purpose.

Case 33

SHORT- AND LONG-RANGE PLANNING

Dr. Apple
Professor of Library Science
Elderberry Library School

Dear Dr. Apple:
    Little did I think when I left Elderberry two months ago that I would need to put into practice so soon what I learned in your management and personnel courses! Reluctantly, I have accepted the position as head of the cataloging department at Holly College! I desperately need to talk with you! Mr. Larch, Director of Libraries, has offered to pay my expenses to travel to the campus to discuss my problems with you and my ideas for reorganization of the department. Can you take time to criticize my plans and advise me? If you can, please phone me so we can arrange a time that is most convenient for you. When I see you, I will give you some background about the present state of affairs, and will bring a floor plan, the budget, some work flow-charts I am working on, details about each staff member, and any other information which seems pertinent.

                                          Sincerely,
                                          Mary Heath

    When Mary Heath met with Dr. Apple, she described as follows some of her experiences during her first month on the staff of Holly College Library:

    You will remember, during my last semester in library school, that I decided I wanted a position as cataloger in an academic library and preferred to live on the coast near the ocean and near mountains. Both the position of assistant cataloger in Holly College and the geographic location seemed to be just what I was looking for, so I applied. I didn't have money enough for travel to apply in person and the librarian did not come to campus to interview students; all negotiations were made by mail.

The college is privately supported, non-sectarian, and coeducational, with a liberal arts curriculum which includes teacher education. The undergraduate student body totals about 10,000. In just under two hours' driving time from the campus, I can reach either the mountains or the ocean.

I reported to the Director's office on the date agreed upon for me to start work. Mr. Larch, the Director, told me that the library was print-oriented although there was a small phonorecord and phonotape collection to support music appreciation and literature courses. The collection totals about 105,000 volumes and the library staff about forty full-time persons. He explained the organizational structure of the library and then took me to the catalog department where I met the head of the department, Mr. Bill Partridge. He was thin, slightly built, clean shaven, and dressed in a rumpled white shirt and nondescript tie. He was drinking a cup of coffee and smoking a cigarette. He stared at us with a bewildered look on his face and nervously straightened some of the piles of catalog cards on his desk.

"Bill, this is Miss Heath who received her master's degree from the Elderberry Library School two weeks ago. She will be your assistant cataloger and will start working today." After this brief introduction, Mr. Larch walked out leaving me standing near Mr. Partridge's desk. The latter looked startled and confused and I was embarrassed and ill at ease. I broke the silence, "Didn't Mr. Larch tell you I was supposed to report for duty today?" "He didn't tell me I was going to have an assistant, let alone that he had hired anyone," he stammered.

After another awkward pause, he suggested that he show me around the department and introduce me to the staff. Then I was aware that the whole staff was watching us and listening to all that had been said. The department consisted of one large room and a glassed-in head cataloger's office which Mr. Partridge explained was used by the cataloger of rare books, who needed privacy to do the exacting work of her position. I asked, "Don't you have any private place where you can have conferences?" He replied that there was a conference room on the second floor which could be used if no one else were using it. The catalog department room was cluttered with desks, heavily loaded book trucks, and shelves around the sides of the room which were completely filled with books. There seemed to be no organized work flow. Each person could see what everyone around her was doing as there were no partitions around desks for privacy--not even low bookshelves. The staff consisted of twelve full-time clerks and two part-time students--all women. When we got back to Mr. Partridge's desk near the door, he found a chair for me next to his desk and suggested that he would clear off one side of his desk so I could work there until a desk or table could be found for me.

After the initial shock of my arrival wore off, Mr. Partridge became talkative, gave me some background about the department and staff, and confided some of his problems. We started talking at his desk but were constantly interrupted by his staff asking questions about details of their work. From his answers, I concluded he knew little about cataloging. He finally suggested we go to a nearby coffee shop to talk. The Student Union was next to the library, but he explained the only food service there was from machines and the room was very noisy because it was used so heavily by students. So, we walked across campus to a street which bounded the campus on one side and had a number of eating and drinking places and stores.

I learned that one of the clerks had been in the department for fifteen years, another one for eleven years, and the rest from three months to seven years. The head cataloger retired two years ago. The position was vacant for about two months and then Mr. Larch promoted a young man who had been working part-time in the department for about a year while taking courses for a library science master's degree. After two weeks, the young man told Mr. Larch, "This department is such an incredible mess, I want nothing to do with it. Please transfer me to the vacancy in reference." And he was transferred. (Mr. Partridge told me that the cataloging department had the lowest status of all departments in the library and staff members got out of it and into other departments as fast as they could.) The position was again vacant for a month or two, then a girl was hired from a firm which specialized in placing temporary office employees. Mr. Larch reasoned that although the girl knew nothing about cataloging and library work, she should be able to do clerical work. That appointment was a sad mistake and she lasted only three days. Again the position was vacant.

Mr. Partridge related how he had been appointed ten months ago: "I had been teaching in this city for several years. When I learned about a year ago that team teaching was to be introduced in the schools this academic year, I wanted none of it. Teaching was hard enough for me anyway and this would have been much worse. I have always enjoyed books more than people, so I applied to Mr. Larch and he employed me for this position. He said that even though I had had no library science courses, I was intelligent and had a broad educational background. I didn't know what I was getting into and this job has been very hard for me. I didn't know anything about cataloging, classification, or how to supervise the staff. Furthermore, the staff had always done pretty much what they wanted to do and I didn't know how to handle them. I guess that is why Mr. Larch decided that I needed a professional assistant and employed you."

At noon, he took me to a restaurant for lunch. He seemed very tense, and drank two manhattans before lunch arrived. I didn't know whether his nervousness and uneasiness were due to my sudden appearance on the scene, which perhaps seemed a threat to him, or whether this was characteristic of him all the time. I learned later that the latter was the case.

After lunch, he asked if I would like to see the rest of the library and I said I would. He found a floor plan of the building in a desk drawer and studied it, remarking, "No one ever took me on a tour of the building, so I have never been in some departments." As we walked through, he introduced me to a few persons. Later, he told me that he hadn't introduced me to all the staff members we encountered because he had never met some of them. Incredulous, I asked, "Don't you have staff meetings and department head meetings?" "No meetings of any kind," he said. "How do you coordinate the work of the cataloging department with other departments if you don't communicate?" I inquired. "There isn't much coordination or communication," he replied.

When we got back to the department, he handed me one of the many piles of cards stacked on his desk and asked me to check them with the books on one of the five double-loaded book trucks surrounding the desk. After this process the books left the department and the various slips and cards were routed to the proper places. This seemed to me to be a subprofessional job and not one for the head of the department.

His desk was completely covered with cards, papers, large ash trays full of old butts, and two dirty coffee cups. One of the clerks saw that the little space he had cleared for me to use was quite inadequate so she found an old typing table on wheels, with hinged sides which folded down, and rolled it over to the side of his desk for me. Although it was too low for back comfort, it did give me some work surface.

Evidently Mr. Partridge found me an empathetic listener because during the rest break that afternoon, he talked continuously about himself and his problems. He apologized repeatedly for the state of the department, telling me how difficult it was for him here in this new job because people didn't seem to respond and didn't really understand the work. He seemed reluctant to return to the office, but finally, after an hour's break, he said, "Well, I guess it's time to go back but I just hate to face that desk." I felt sorry for him because he didn't understand what was going on in the department and apparently hadn't tried to learn.

Mr. Larch had told me that employees in the cataloging department worked forty hours a week: 8 a.m.-12, and 1-5 p.m. Monday through Friday. So, the next morning, I was on the job before 8 a.m. I was surprised to see that I was the only staff member there on time--all the others straggled in at various times but all were on duty by 8:45 except Mr. Partridge, who did not arrive until 9:30. Rest breaks were supposed to be fifteen minutes in midmorning and mid-afternoon but Mr. Partridge was gone for at least forty minutes each time and the rest of the staff all took more than fifteen minutes. He left for home about 4:15 that day, claiming he had a headache. I noticed that the rest of the staff soon started leaving too.

On the morning of my third day, Mr. Partridge called in and said he had had a tooth extracted, that he was very uncomfortable and wouldn't be in that day. One of the staff snickered and said, "Well, that's funny. He has false teeth!" That was the last we heard from Mr. Partridge--he never again reported for work. I didn't know what was going on or why he didn't show up. The staff didn't seem to be concerned about his absence but each went on in her own independent way doing, apparently, whatever she was in the mood to do. I continued to do the final checking on the books which kept piling up on the book trucks around his desk.

About a week later someone called Mr. Larch to announce that Mr. Partridge had left town that morning with his belongings and would not be back. He could furnish no forwarding address. This news reached the catalog department via the "grapevine." Gradually, I was getting acquainted with the members of the staff in the department as well as in the rest of the library, and through them I learned more about Mr. Partridge. He was thirty-five years old, unmarried, and had lived in a shabby apartment by himself, except for his cats. He was quiet, unassuming, reserved and shy. He was afraid of responsibility because he didn't want to take the blame for mistakes. He leaned on others to make decisions and let each staff member go her own way. He rarely worked every day in a week and never put in a full eight hours on the days he was there. In the ten months he had been employed, he had used up all his sick and vacation time for about three years.

After learning that Mr. Partridge had left town, I assumed that Mr. Larch would inform me about who was to be in charge of the department and would orient me to my responsibilities. But he did not come near the department, so about a week later I asked for an appointment with him. I told him I had no orientation from Mr. Partridge and asked if he would tell me what I was supposed to be doing and what I was responsible for. His response was, "Just do what Mr. Partridge did." I pointed out that the staff, including me, needed leadership and the whole department required organization. I expressed the hope that a new department head would be appointed soon. And then he asked if I would be the head! I was taken aback. After all, I had only just graduated from library school, had been on the job here less than two weeks, and my only library experience was as a filer in a university library. I had no experience as a supervisor. He suggested I think it over during the weekend and give him my answer the following Monday.

I was prepared to refuse the offer when I saw him Monday morning because I felt that I needed to work under an experienced cataloger rather than be thrust into administration so soon. I explained this to him when I saw him but he wouldn't accept my refusal because he said he felt I was qualified to handle the department. He called in his secretary and dictated a memo to the entire staff announcing my appointment. (I learned later that one of the clerks in the cataloging department had applied for the position immediately after Mr. Partridge's departure and that her application was strongly backed by a member of the board of trustees. Her only qualification was seniority among the clerks in the department.)

That evening I got out the notes, books, and syllabi for my management and personnel courses and started reviewing! The next morning I cleaned out Mr. Partridge's desk so I would have a work station of my own. I hoped to find a procedure manual, a library personnel code, list of staff, some reports, and other documents which would orient me to the organization and operation of the department, but I found none. I did find two books of statistics which had been kept by the former retired librarian--how many books cataloged by Dewey category, how many periodicals, reference books, cards typed, etc. But no entries had been made since she retired.

On top of the desk were many stacks of cards which represented cataloging problems such as disagreements over classification, or two books with the same call number, or mismarked books, or inconsistencies in subject headings. Evidently, Mr. Partridge planned eventually to take care of them. During the next week, I had a personal conference with each member of the staff to learn what her responsibilities and problems were. Here is some of the information I acquired:

There are no job descriptions, no position classification plan, no procedure manuals, no salary scale. Each person was hired on an individual bargaining basis. If one person would accept a lower salary than another person, then the former was employed. When I saw the list of salaries, I was shocked at the inequities. For example, one twenty-five year old typist who has worked in the department two years receives an annual salary within one thousand dollars of Mr. Partridge's listed salary. The typist who has been in the department fifteen years and seems fairly competent is earning less than the twenty-five year old.

None of the staff has been given any real orientation to their jobs or supervision of their work. They help each other when anyone had a problem but it is sort of like the blind helping the blind because they are all uninformed about cataloging rules, filing rules, and classification. They are sharply divided between those who had been here for several years and are interested in their jobs and the young girls who are frivolous, are working only for the pay, and aren't planning on staying here if they can find better jobs. This causes quite a bit of friction between the two groups and I feel I am sort of in the middle because I am the only professionally educated person in the department except the part-time rare book cataloger. I hope I can develop morale in the group and teach each of them what she is to do and how her work fits into the total departmental responsibility and contributes to the library's service goals.

Two filers are expected to spend eight hours a day filing, the girls who sort cards do that all day, and the girl who marks the books is expected to do that full time. A part-time student does all the pasting. All of them are bored with their jobs and I am told the turnover in these jobs is very high. I have already introduced some changes here after talking with the five girls involved. I made a list of jobs that needed to be done in priority order. I told them that two hours at a time on any one of these jobs was long enough, and then to change to another job. Now all five of them work as a team and rotate on sorting and arranging cards, filing, pasting, and marking book spines. I delegated these jobs to them to do in whatever order they wished and gave them the responsibility for seeing that the work got done. They seem much happier. I am trying to motivate them by setting up production goals which they should reach and giving them a chance to exercise their own decision-making. I hope soon to enlarge their responsibilities by assigning to them this final checking that I am doing.

One large storeroom is full of uncataloged books. No one knows how many there are but there must be thousands.

My problems cover most of those involved in planning, organizing, motivating, and controlling: space, backlog, working privacy, communication, supervision, delegation, job classification, division of work, work flow, and others.

* * *

List in order of priority what you would do to reorganize this department if you were Miss Heath. Criticize Mr. Larch's appointees in the catalog department.

Case 34

GIFT APPRAISALS

As curator of the rare book collection of Greenbrier University, Ernest Midway was frequently called upon to place a value on a letter, an autograph, a manuscript, a rare book, or a collection of such items which were given to the University Library. Always, the donor asked for this appraisal in writing so it could be used to claim a deduction on his income taxes for gifts to a tax-exempt institution. On occasion, he was asked by a donor to prepare a special type of document to satisfy Internal Revenue Service examiners.

Until about seven years ago, Mr. Midway would try

to place a true, current, acceptable value on items of minor value. This figure represented the price at which the object could be sold at the time of the appraisal or at the time of the gift. He never attempted to arrive at an appraisal figure for any gift in excess of five hundred dollars but suggested to the donor that this was his responsibility.

An increasing number of requests for appraisals and a very unpleasant experience when Mr. Midway had to prove in court his competence as an expert in appraising rare books, precipitated the adoption of a firm library policy regarding appraisals:

Gift Appraisals

(1) Members of the staff of Greenbrier University do not appraise gifts to the library; they may suggest to donors the desirability of appraisals and may refer donors to such sources as auction records, Book Prices Current, dealers' catalogs, and commercial experts. In addition, they may suggest that the donor should consult a capable tax attorney or accountant.

(2) The appraising for tax purposes of a gift to Greenbrief University Library is the responsibility of the donor since he requires the appraisal. The donor must bear all appraisal costs.

(3) The acceptance by the Library of a gift which has been appraised by a disinterested party does not imply an endorsement of the appraisal by this Library or by any member of the staff.

Since the adoption of the above policy, donors had accepted it without question. Recently, a problem has arisen with one donor, Mr. Hugh Litchi, one of the state's most powerful politicians, who has been a staunch supporter of Greenbrier University for many years and has been influential in obtaining favorable legislation and appropriations for the University in the state legislature.

After his wife's recent death, he decided that at his age (late sixties) it was wise to move from his large home to an apartment. Subsequently, he sorted all of the possessions which he and his wife had accumulated during their more than forty years of marriage. He offered to the Board of Trustees of his alma mater, Greenbrier University, his collection of papers, books, manuscripts, paintings, and sculpture. This "valuable" gift was accepted gratefully by the Board and was publicized widely in the news media of the state.

The gift was received in the University Library two months ago. When the crates were unpacked, all items were listed, books were routed to the Acquisitions Department, and the rest of the items came to the Rare Books Department for disposition. The staff of the Acquisitions Department checked the books against library records to determine whether they were duplicates and to decide which titles should be added to the collection and which should be discarded. According to the library's gift policy, all donors were informed that gifts were accepted with the understanding that the library staff was not obligated to add all titles to the library collection but had the right to dispose of any items not retained for the collection. Many of Mr. Litchi's books were old editions, or for some other reason were undesirable for the university's collection, and so would be discarded or sold.

During his career, Mr. Litchi had served as U.S. Ambassador to an obscure African country. His "papers" consisted chiefly of correspondence relating to his personal political career (which would have some value for future historians to throw light on the state's politics during this period) and carbon copies of letters relating to his less-than-earthshaking months as ambassador. The theme of many of the latter was "Please get me out of this place quickly." The collection of paintings and sculpture were all from this African country and would probably be turned over to the Fine Arts Department. Greenbrier University had no African studies program.

The Director of Greenbrier's Library has just received a memo from the President's office asking for an appraisal of Mr. Litchi's gift, which Mr. Litchi needed for his federal and state income tax returns. The Director called the President and cited the Library's gift appraisal policy. The President would not accept this as an answer to Mr. Litchi and demanded a list of all items in the gift and an appraisal of the value of each item. He said, "It would be an insult to Mr. Litchi, after having given us this valuable gift, to ask him to hire a tax attorney and a commercial appraiser to evaluate his gift. You are all experts and should be fully qualified to do the appraising."

The Director replied, "An appraiser must show that a market exists for the material and must be able to cite instances where similar material has been sold recently for comparable prices. Many of the books are simply old and out-of-date and have no current market value. Neither does a market exist for Mr. Litchi's correspondence, paintings or sculpture. Our only method of appraisal would be to search for a sale of similar material by some individual who may be accepted by the state tax division and the Internal Revenue Service as comparable in status and prestige to Mr. Litchi, and use that figure as a basis. I fear we will not find any such comparable case."

The President still insisted that the library staff come up with an appraisal figure which would be "fair to Mr. Litchi."

The Director telephoned this information to the Acquisitions Librarian and to Mr. Midway. He asked them to think about the problem and to come to his office for a conference the next day. He told them that he had gotten the impression from the President that a true, current, market value would not be acceptable inasmuch as the total collection has little value to the University and such a figure would be very low. The Director does not want to be a party to fraud or deception, nor does he want to involve his staff. He knows full well that any staff member who makes or assists in making an appraisal must be prepared to defend his appraisal in court or to the Internal Revenue Service. This is a delicate political situation as well as a problem of professional ethics.

* * *

Comment on the gift appraisal policy, the president's demands, and the professional ethics involved in this case.

Case 35

A "BARGAIN"

Little space for expansion was available in the stacks of the Linden College Library. The arrival of newly bound periodicals from the bindery usually necessitated extensive shifting to make room for them on the shelves. An addition to the library was included in a campus building program but the present financial status of the college gave the library staff no hope that the addition would be built for many years. Temporary storage space for little used materials had been provided in the basement of a classroom building several years ago but it was quickly filled to capacity.

This liberal arts college library was founded by a

protestant denomination during the third quarter of the nineteenth century. In addition to support from the church, an endowment supplied additional funds. Compared to other academic libraries, the Linden library budget had been more than adequate during the years to build up an above-average college library collection which was especially strong in periodicals and serials. Continuous runs of many titles dated back to the latter part of the eighteenth and early nineteenth centuries.

Inflation, decreased yields from endowment investments, increased costs of labor and equipment, and less support from the church resulted in drastically smaller annual budgets--hence no immediate prospects of any new buildings. The library staff had to "make do" with the present facilities.

The staff had discussed having some of the early serials and periodicals microfilmed and offering the physical volumes for sale or exchange to other libraries; but cost estimates were too high even to consider. When the chief librarian, Dorothy Chat, received the following letter, it appeared to be a happy solution to their problems of space and cost:

Palm City Microfilms, Inc.

Dear Librarian:

We are happy to announce our new exchange program whereby you can exchange, without charge, your bound or unbound serials and periodicals for microfilm. The program offers you three alternatives:

(1) Volume for volume exchange. That is, for each physical volume you wish to exchange, we will give you the same volume in microfilm.

(2) Incomplete sets. In many instances, we will offer you the complete unbroken file on microfilm for your incomplete set.

(3) New titles for your collection. If you have hard to find back files of serials and periodicals which are in demand by other libraries, we will exchange at a ratio of as much as one to four; that is, for each of your physical volumes we will supply microfilm copies of four volumes of any serials or periodical which we have in stock.

This exchange offer represents no money outlay from your library budget. You will not even have to pay any transportation costs because our trucks will pick up your physical volumes and deliver the microfilm reels.

In addition to our exchange program, we have in stock microfilm copies of several hundred titles which are for sale at prices 25 per cent to 40 per cent lower than from any other microfilm publishers. These items are available within thirty days from receipt of your letter.

We are also in the market to purchase complete sets, partial files, or odd numbers of certain serials and periodicals in all fields and languages. We do not handle popular newsstand materials or trade journals. We will gladly send you our current buying list.

Enclosed are two lists: 1) our current buying list of periodicals and serials which we will consider for exchange, and 2) titles available for sale or microfilm.

If you are interested in any of our offers, we will be happy to send one of our experienced consultants, without charge, to come to your library, evaluate your needs, and recommend a program to fit your needs. Please write me the dates which will be most convenient for you and I will try to schedule a visit by one of our consultants at one of these times.

Sincerely,

Neal Shrike
President

To Dorothy Chat this offer seemed like a happy solution to the Linden College Library space problem. Scanning the list of periodicals desired for exchange, she recognized many titles of which Linden Library possessed long runs. Also, in the list of microfilms for sale, she saw a number of titles which her staff would like to add to the collection and for which they would be willing to exchange some seldom-used volumes.

Somehow, though, the offer sounded too good to be true. She wanted to investigate the legality and feasibility of such an exchange, to learn something about the firm and its reputation, and to find out whether any other librarians of her acquaintance had experience with this firm.

At Linden College, any transaction involving college-owned property had to be approved by the president's office and the transaction had to be handled through the office of the treasurer. Any new library policies involving off-campus relationships had to be approved by the faculty library committee. For instance, a number of years ago when exchange relationships between Linden College Library and other libraries were established for exchanging college publications and duplicates, the faculty library committee approved the general policy for exchanges. But this policy would not cover the type of exchange program offered by Palm City Microfilms, Inc. Hence, before the library staff could consider this program, Miss Chat would have to talk to the college treasurer about legality and procedure, and to the faculty library committee about policies.

Miss Chat circulated Xerox copies of Mr. Shrike's letter to the professional members of her staff for their comments and mailed copies to other librarians asking if they had had any experience with this company. As a further check, she sent a copy of the offer to a member of the college's board of trustees who was a prominent banker in the state's capital city, asking whether he could obtain any information about the firm's financial status. Here are the replies she received:

A member of the Linden Library staff commented, "Mr. Shrike does not indicate prices he will charge for the microfilm he has for sale or prices he will pay for physical volumes he wants to buy. This information is basic to any discussion of the offer."

Two librarians reported that they had had no experience with Mr. Shrike or his company and had never heard of them. The acquisitions librarians of two university libraries stated that they had done some business with Mr. Shrike in both exchange and cash operations and had no complaints.

The librarian of a liberal arts college in an adjoining state said, "Mr. Shrike's exchange offer sounded like such a bargain that I accepted his offer to send one of his consultants to our campus. Mr. Shrike came himself, driving a panel truck. He talked to our professional staff to learn our needs, checked our holdings of some titles, and made us an offer. He proposed to supply us with complete runs on microfilm of certain periodicals in exchange for our broken runs of the same titles. He pushed us to agree to the proposal at once so that he could take with him that afternoon the volumes listed in his proposal to us. We were so dazzled by his generous offer that we agreed to his removing the volumes. That was six months ago and to date we have received only a fraction of the microfilms he agreed to send and those were not of standard quality. Repeated letters and remonstrances to him have brought no results. My advice to you is to ignore his offer or, if you do decide to do business with him, to obtain payment or microfilms prior to giving up your materials."

The librarian of a large public library wrote: "We have not done business with Mr. Shrike and suggest that you be very careful about any agreements with him on the basis of unsatisfactory dealings that other librarians have had with him. One library received a bad check from him, others report that he is a crook and a liar and will cheat you sooner or later. Mr. Shrike specializes in small isolated college libraries. I know of one such library which was almost denuded through its gullible librarian."

The acquisitions librarian of a large college library advised, "Those librarians who tell you that their dealings with Palm City Microfilms have been favorable have probably already been 'hoodwinked' by Mr. Shrike and the librarians do not want to admit their mistake. I suspect that Mr. Shrike is disposing of the materials, which he gets from libraries on 'exchange,' to legitimate book dealers for cash and that librarians could do business with these same book dealers at a considerable advantage to themselves rather than letting Mr. Shrike make a profit on the materials. In a recent meeting of acquisitions librarians, I learned that at least sixty libraries have been victimized by Mr. Shrike. The libraries so victimized were evidently blinded by the 'bargain' and thus allowed him to take the original copy before they ever received materials in payment and, in many cases, never did receive the microfilm. If you do business with this firm, I suggest that you insist upon receiving the microfilm to collate them to ascertain their quality before you give up your own volumes."

The banker member of the Linden College Board of Trustees acquired this information: "Through several sources of information available to bankers, I have received detailed reports on Palm City Microfilms and its president, Mr. Shrike. The company has been doing business at the same address for three years in an old rented brick building in a commercial district. Mr. Shrike has been unwilling to furnish financial details relative to his business for banking and trade reference. The company supposedly has an inventory of several thousand dollars in used books and periodicals, with fixed assets estimated in low four figures. Mr. Shrike, the reported owner of Palm City Microfilms, Inc., filed for bankruptcy three different times in the past twelve years, was indicted seven years ago on charges of embezzlement and forgery and served a prison sentence, and frequently changes the name and address of his company to avoid other legal action against him."

* * *

What precautions should librarians take to avoid involvement with unreliable suppliers, etc.?

Case 36

CHURCH AND STATE
(Role playing)

Roles:
  Mr. Hatson, Librarian, Dale Public Library
  Henry Atkins, new member of the Library Board

  Whenever an unsolicited gift subscription to a periodical started arriving in the Dale Public Library, the clerk who checked in periodicals routed the issue to the head librarian, Mr. Hatson. He would examine the issue and decide on its disposition in accordance with the library's selection policies.
  When an issue of Church and State appeared on his desk, he examined it and found that it was a monthly published by Americans United for the Separation of Church and State, a non-profit, tax-exempt organization. Prior to 1968 this organization was called Protestants and Other Americans United for the Separation of Church and State. Never having heard of this organization, Mr. Hatson looked it up and found that its purposes were: 1) to reeducate the public as to the importance of separating church and state for religious freedom; 2) to support the First Amendment to the U.S. Constitution; 3) to study legislation and court decisions regarding church and state; 4) to take remedial actions in the courts when actual violations of church-state separation occurred which could not be eliminated by negotiation; and 5) to resist efforts to join church and state by tax support.
  Mr. Hatson found that the periodical editorially opposed use of public funds for sectarian purposes and presented accounts of litigation and other actions involving Americans United and city and state governments. He learned that Dale had its own local chapter of Americans

110 / Library Management

United and found newspaper accounts of recent highly controversial episodes involving some large city chapters.

Because of the generally negative and highly biased nature of the publication, Mr. Hatson returned the issue to the periodicals clerk with instructions to put it on closed shelves, retain it for one year, and then discard. He based his decision on the library's selection policy. The section concerning religious publications stated that only those periodicals listed in periodical indexes would be offered to the public on open shelves. Six leading religious periodicals were thus displayed on open shelves. In addition, some thirty other religious publications, representing many denominations, were housed on closed shelves but were equally available to the public. Only a limited number of periodicals could be displayed on open shelves because of space limitations. All unsolicited periodicals were kept for a limited time and then discarded. Church and State thus was treated in the same way as the other thirty-odd periodicals on closed shelves.

Henry Atkins, a Dale school teacher, had recently been appointed to the library board. At the board meeting in June, Atkins charged Hatson with censorship for failing to place Church and State on the library's open shelves. He asserted that Hatson had exercised undue influence over the display of library materials by refusing to put out this periodical which was based on "sound factual authority." Hatson replied that Church and State failed this very criterion in that it presented no positive program, but merely attacked and often inaccurately attempted to tear down views to which it was opposed. As far as factual authority was concerned, countered Atkins, no suit had ever been filed attacking the veracity of Church and State. Hatson defended his decision by referring to the board's policy regarding the selection of religious publications for open shelf display from Readers' Guide to Periodical Literature, and that those outside this limitation were to be evaluated at the discretion of the librarian.

In the course of the discussion, Atkins revealed that he was president of the Dale chapter of Americans United.

Case 37

A FIRE

Huckleberry Branch of Metropolitan Library was located in an area designed for a store in a small neighborhood shopping center. The electric clock on the wall behind the charging desk stopped at 4:15 a.m. on Sunday morning because fire cut off electric service at that time. Before the fire reached the library, several stores on one side of the library were fully ablaze. When fire department personnel saw that the fire might spread to the library, they went into it and spread canvas over most of the stacks, the wall shelving, and the furniture to protect them as much as possible.

Firemen determined that the fire had started in a beauty parlor and had spread to stores through a common attic. The roofs of two stores collapsed and the contents of the other two stores were completely destroyed. The library was the last area reached by the fire, which was brought under control while the roof and walls were still standing.

A fireman saw a notice posted on the front door of the library: "In case of emergency, call the branch librarian, Mrs. Janet Hickory, phone number _____; or, the main library information desk, phone number _____." He knew the information desk would not be open at 4 a.m. on Sunday, so he called Mrs. Hickory. By the time she arrived at the scene, the fire was under control and all she could see was smoke in the library. After the firemen removed their hoses and the smoke cleared, she had an opportunity to move in closer and inspect the remains. At first glance it appeared that the entire collection of about 25,000 books (minus those in circulation) had been lost. A closer look showed that most of the juvenile books, practically all of the reference collection, and many other books on the lower shelves had suffered little or no damage. The greatest fire damage had occurred to the books on the upper shelves of stacks and wall shelving. Many books had charred spines and would have to be rebound; others had been damaged by water. Some had fallen off the upper shelves and were both burned and damaged by water on the floor. The action taken by the fire crews in protecting the books with canvas and also in cleaning the water out of the building promptly had undoubtedly helped to minimize losses. Fortunately, the contents of the circulation and registration files, the card catalog, and the shelf list were not damaged. The cases were burned and charred and would require extensive refinishing or might have to be discarded; but the cards inside were undamaged.

Mrs. Hickory's first thought was the necessity of keeping the general public away from the remains to prevent stealing. She phoned the director of libraries to report the fire and to request his advice about personnel to sort the collection, to pack what could be salvaged, and to transport what was left of the collection, the furniture, and the files.

The director asked the city police to station several men at Huckleberry Branch until the salvageable contents could be moved. He phoned the head of maintenance and the supervisor of shelvers, asking them to round up a crew to come to the site as quickly as possible. The man in charge of all library vehicles phoned the director offering the services of several trucks and drivers--he had heard the news over radio and television. Also, staff members came from all over the city to offer their services when they heard of the fire through the news media.

Mrs. Hickory stayed at the site to supervise operations. By the end of the day everything that could possibly be salvaged had been packed in the trucks and the trucks driven to the library garage.

The next day (Monday) the Supervisor of Branches phoned the head of the city real estate management office to request new space for the Huckleberry Branch in the same neighborhood. Later in the day the real estate manager located and rented a recently vacated market building about five blocks from the fire location. The trucks unloaded their contents at this new location on Tuesday.

What a dismal sight Mrs. Hickory and her staff faced! The store building had not been cleaned or redecorated after the last occupants moved out. It needed to be renovated for library use, a partition or two put in, all walls and ceiling painted, and light fixtures installed which would give enough light for reading. Water-soaked books which needed immediate attention had been packed helter skelter in boxes--even mixed with charred books. Smoke-damaged volumes would all have to be cleaned before they were shelved. Books with charred bindings would have to be sent to the bindery. Shelving was lying on the floor as it had been dismantled from the other building. Some of it was warped from the fire and would have to be examined by experts to determine whether it could be repaired and utilized. All of it was dirty from smoke and would have to be washed before any books could be shelved on them; also the units would have to be put together and placed in some logical order on the floor. The furniture and card file cases were dreary; some water-damaged, some charred, and everything covered with smoke residue. One of the first priorities would be an inventory to determine losses in order to file an insurance claim.

* * *

Put yourself in Mrs. Hickory's position. Determine priorities of planning, types of plans, staffing requirements, service to the public, physical facilities, and other problems.

Case 38

A NEW COMMUNITY COLLEGE

A new state-supported community college will open two years from now in Obsidian, a city of 40,000 located at an elevation of about 2,500 feet with mountain ranges on two sides. The nearest college (a teacher-training institution) is located about 150 miles away, across a range of mountains.

For years the residents of this area of the state have clamored for a state-supported community college. Three years ago the Obsidian Chamber of Commerce sponsored a study of the area to ascertain the personnel needs of business, industry, schools, hospitals, agriculture, labor, and the professions. The results of this survey were submitted to the Board of Directors of the State System of Higher Education. The Board decided that the need for a community college did indeed exist in Obsidian. To ascertain types of programs and curricula which should be offered, the Board asked the School of Education of the State University to study the area.

A survey of students presently enrolled in junior and senior high schools of the area was made to determine: 1) how many might be interested in attending this junior college if it were built; and 2) what courses of study they thought they might wish to pursue (terminal or preparation for transfer to a four-year academic institution).

On the basis of the two surveys, the State Board purchased one hundred acres on the edge of the city for a campus, appointed a president and instructed him to plan the campus (with the assistance of an architect), to decide on curricula, and to choose a faculty according to the needs of the curricula. The President to date has selected the following to work with him: a dean of instruction who is to work on curricula, a comptroller in charge of all business functions and physical plant, a dean of students to plan residence halls, and you as librarian to plan the library. The State Board has engaged the services of of an architect to work with the five of you on planning the campus and the buildings to be erected thereon.

By the time you accepted your appointment, the following decisions had been made:

>Estimated student body when college opens two years hence--about 700.
>
>Dormitory accommodations for one-fourth of the student body (it is estimated that three-fourths will live at home).
>
>Terminal programs (two-year) leading to Associate of Arts degree in secretarial and office methods, accounting, computer technicians, vocational agriculture, printing trades, auto mechanics, and restaurant management.
>
>Pre-professional curricula (students will transfer after two years to one of the state's four-year institutions): teaching, nursing, agriculture, engineering, and business administration.
>
>General liberal arts: social sciences, humanities, communications, biological sciences and physical sciences.

You have two years to get ready for the students, faculty, and curricula. You are responsible for planning the building, the library staff, the collection, the services, and the organization of the collection. For the purposes of this case, do not be concerned about cost but incorporate what you consider to be ideal. Assume that you will be allotted a reasonable amount of money to build a functional and practical building, to employ an adequate staff, to acquire a collection suitable for the curricula, and to provide necessary services. In a state-supported institution, you must be practical and economical in spending the taxpayers' money.

What will be your priorities for planning? What do you do first, second, and so on? What decisions must be made for short- and long-range planning? Whom should you consult and work with in the planning? What should be included in a building program? What standards and criteria would be useful in establishing space needs for staff, users, and the collection? How do you decide how many and what kinds of staff should be employed and when and in what order they should be employed? What decisions must be made concerning collection building--will it be print-oriented or multi-media? How will you decide about methods of cataloging and classification--traditional or innovative; card catalog, computer print-out, film cartridge, or other?

Case 39

"BANDAID" WORK

For several years the Superintendent of Schools in the city of Wilson had been under considerable pressure from the public and from teachers to establish libraries in the 128 elementary schools. As a first step toward meeting this demand, I was employed six months ago as Supervisor of Elementary School Libraries. The position of Supervisor of Secondary School Libraries had existed for many years and each of the junior and senior high schools have excellent instructional materials centers. Both of us report to the Assistant Superintendent who is responsible for instruction.

When I was offered the position I was told that I would be responsible for supervising the centralized Learning Resources Center which served all of the elementary schools, for studying the needs of the schools for instructional materials, and for devising both long-range and short-range plans for establishing a library in every school. I was chosen for the position because of my experience as a classroom teacher, elementary school librarian, and supervisor of school media centers in a small city. I knew when I accepted this position that it would be a tough challenge for me.

The Learning Resources Center provided all types of materials for teachers and children in the elementary schools: books, vertical file materials (clippings, pamphlets, flat pictures), periodicals, slides, transparencies, phonotapes, phonorecords, filmstrips, motion pictures, maps, and a professional education collection. In addition, there were collections of objects such as rocks and shells; large display boards showing samples of petroleum products, wheat, coffee, and other geological, agricultural, and botanical items; examples of arts and crafts from other cultures and other peoples; and many other similar teaching materials.

Teachers phoned in their requests, and deliveries and pickups were made daily by trucks. For example, if a teacher was planning a unit on fish, she would receive all of the teaching materials on the subject regardless of format unless she specified some she did not want.

Classroom collections of fifty books were available for one-month loans but were renewable on request. Each collection for fourth grade, for instance, would contain different titles so that if a teacher returned collection number one and requested the next collection (number two), the latter would have titles unique to that collection. These collections were housed in especially built boxes which could be stood on end and converted into bookshelves in the classroom after the top was taken off the box. These collections were checked over and weeded every summer. Worn volumes were rebound or discarded, dirty covers were cleaned, and books with outdated contents were replaced with newer up-to-date books.

When I assumed the position, I found three full-time persons working with the collection at the Center (one cataloger and two clerks who filled requests from the teachers for materials), several typists, and part-time high school student shelvers.

Officially there were no elementary school libraries, but some collections were known to exist. One of the first things I did was to send out a form letter to each elementary school principal, asking whether there was a library collection in the school, how it was housed and organized, who was in charge, and for a brief description of the collection. I was surprised to learn that approximately two-thirds of the schools had some sort of collection which had been accumulated without any help from the staff of the Learning Resources Center. At several schools, the nucleus of the collection had been purchased from Goodwill Industries for five cents per volume. Many of these volumes were discards from public libraries and family homes. New books in the collections were either donations from teachers and parents or had been purchased by the school's PTA. All of the collections were supervised by volunteers: mothers, teachers, or members of the Junior League.

My next step was to visit each of these so-called "libraries." I was very depressed after seeing the miserable rooms in which most of them were housed, the poor quality of the titles, and the volunteer service. The volunteers were dedicated, enthusiastic women but they only spent a few hours a week in the "library" and no one was responsible for supervising or coordinating their work. They were not there long enough to get acquainted with the needs of the children or the curriculum and only a very few of them had any background in children's materials, and those who did had limited background. None of these libraries could ever be effective until each one was supervised by a certified elementary school librarian. In my opinion, most of the contents in each of the collections should be promptly burned and replaced with attractive, readable books suitable for today's children. I would like to see extensive use of paperbacks.

Where many cities had used federal funds to develop individual school libraries, all of the funds for this school system had gone into the centralized collection. I have been told that special funds will be available next year under new programming for establishing seven elementary school libraries in inner-city schools. I have not had time to explore this possibility. No new city funds have been allocated for establishing libraries in individual schools. If I can work out a program of development which is approved by the Superintendent of Schools and the school board, some money for the program will be available; but probably a bond issue will be required to fund the establishment and staffing of really effective libraries.

Since the persons working with the elementary "libraries" have heard of my appointment, I receive many calls to help them. All of them plead for more books and are ignorant of the usual library supplies, so I am now offering library supplies as one of the services of the Center. To give them some books immediately, I have inaugurated a weeding program at the Center. In the past, it has been customary to order forty or more copies of basic titles for which the Center staff believed there would be a demand. Some of these are outdated and need to be discarded, others are still suitable for use by elementary children. When I looked at the book cards for these multiple copies, I discovered many of them had not circulated for a long time. I now have a clerk systematically checking multiple copies on all the shelves and have given her guidelines as to what to do, depending upon how up-to-date the books are and how often they have circulated. She is to leave only about three copies on our shelves and the rest are to be distributed, one copy to a "library" as far as they will go.

This is all that I have accomplished in the first six months on the job. My ultimate goal is a real library in every elementary school with a professional librarian supervising each one--probably only one day a week for a few years. If each librarian had five schools, I would need twenty-five librarians!

What I am doing now with the "libraries" is what I

consider "bandaid" work--providing temporary emergency expedients to give token help (advice, supplies, and distribution of surplus copies) until professional expertise and suitable collections can be furnished through a systematic development program.

*   *   *

If you were in this role, what short- and long-range planning would you do? What would you include in a planning program? How would you "sell" your program to the Superintendent of Schools and to the school board? What would be the next step? If a bond issue is necessary to obtain enough money for your program, what strategies and public relations are required?

Case 40

FACULTY READING LISTS
(Skit)

Characters:

Mr. Mimosa, Research Director of Gannet, Inc.
Mrs. Phoebe, Librarian, School of Business, Toucan University

Mr. M: Hello, this is Bill Mimosa--I am research director for Gannet, Inc., a management consulting firm in your neighboring state. We have just undertaken a project which involves our consulting partners in a survey of a municipal hospital. This is an entirely new field for our firm and our partners have to do considerable study on the general subject of municipal hospitals in particular and of hospital administration and organization in general. You have been recommended to me as the nearest librarian who is competent in this field. Please mail me a list of the best sources on the subject.

Mrs. P: Are you requesting a bibliography which will cover the entire field of hospital administration? If so, I can readily say there is not one.

Mr. M: Our interests are not quite so broad. We want material related directly to these aspects of hospital administration, with emphasis on municipally owned hospitals:

organization	community surveys
financing (bond issues, etc.)	services to the community
purchasing	civil service
capital budgets and operating budgets	personnel administration

First of all, what is the textbook (or textbooks) in the general area?

Mrs. P: To the best of my knowledge there is no good, comprehensive textbook. An old one is by MacEachern. However, it is not presently used. The last edition is probably ten years old. The readings given to students in this school come largely from journals. Without checking further I cannot give you any general text which would be geared to your needs.

Mr. M: I realized that this would require some checking. Would you kindly send us a list of readings used in your relevant courses and also a bibliography which would cover the areas I have indicated. The bibliography should be to the point. You need not cover everything on the subject, just the best.

Mrs. P: We do not distribute the reading lists of our faculty members without permission from them. If you wish I will give your request to the appropriate faculty members.

Mr. M: Don't you have the lists in the library?

Mrs. P: Yes.

Mr. M: Well, just photocopy what you have and send them on. We are in a great hurry. Time is of the essence. You know how consultants are. They need everything yesterday.

Mrs. P: You did not understand my previous statement. We do not distribute lists. To do so would be a violation of our established policies not to betray professional confidences. The lists are the work of the faculty members and distributed only according to their wishes. We will give your request to appropriate faculty members if you wish.

Mr. M: Well, o.k., if that is the only way. But it will probably take them some time to answer and we are in a rush. Will you be able to get your part of the information off today? A handwritten letter will be all right, just so we get it immediately.

Mrs. P: I am sorry. I do not have time to work on bibliographies for outside organizations except for occasional work on a consulting basis or work on a publication. For the most part my time is completely committed to serving the Toucan community.

Mr. M: We usually find librarians quite helpful and willing to give us the information we need. Our company is one of the oldest and best management consulting firms in the country. This is for a hospital and would serve a great many people. It is for a very worthwhile purpose.

Mrs. P: I am well acquainted with the reputation of your firm and can only say that I am sure they are not providing their services free of charge. There is no reason that Toucan University should support a profit-making company with such a service as the one you request. Regardless of all this, I would still say that I cannot undertake your work. It would take, probably, two or three days of time. I do not have that much free time and neither do my staff. Would you like to have your call transferred to a faculty office? Some of them may have consulting time available.

Mr. M: How much do they charge per day?

Mrs. P: You would have to ask them. I should imagine an amount equal to, or more than that charged by the consultants in your firm.

Mr. M: How much do you charge?

Mrs. P: To profit making organizations, $150 per day. To others $100, or less, depending upon the organization.

Mr. M: I shall see what we can do. I do not think the firm will pay a librarian $150. You would not do it for less?

Mrs. P: You misunderstand me. I will not do it at all. My free time is wholly committed for several months.

Mr. M: There is nothing you can do to help us?

Mrs. P: I can do as I suggested before: I can request the faculty members who teach hospital administration to send you a copy of each of their reading lists. Previous experience leads me to believe that one faculty member will refuse but I do not know what reaction you will get from others. I can send you a guide to information sources which I distribute to hospital administration students.

Mr. M: Well, I guess I'll leave it at that. I thought you would be more cooperative. It will take us a long time to do this bibliographic work ourselves because we do not have the sources that you have.

Mrs. P: I suggest that you refer your problem to the Industrial Information Center at Zee University. They offer a research and information service to corporations on a unit-fee basis. They have a most competent staff and will do a very thorough job for you. The Center is self-supporting and charges for service are based on the actual cost of each search. I recommend that you phone the director, Miss Cardinal, and ask her how soon her staff could do this work for you and what she estimates the cost of such a search would be. I will send you a folder describing their services to industry.

Case 41

STAFF CONCERN

State University Library dated back to the middle of the last century. At the time of this problem situation, the library system consisted of nine branches which served departments or professional schools and a large central library built in the last ten years. The total staff numbered more than three hundred, about one hundred of whom had academic appointments. The senior staff consisted of heads and assistant heads of departments in the central library and heads of branches. Some of these staff members were concerned about the overall administration of the library; this group represented all ages from the late twenties to the early sixties. Their length of service on this library staff ranged from three to twenty-five years, with the median length of service ten years. All were seriously interested in the overall development of the library; none was considered a crank, a revolutionary, or as having ulterior motives. Their concern had been building up over several years and had reached a point where they believed this should be communicated to the library administrative staff. When they met with the administrators to present their concerns, the administrators expressed a desire to learn more about the conditions and to try to find solutions. They asked that the concerns be written into a position paper and presented to them formally. The following memorandum resulted:

> To the administrative staff of State University Library:
>
> We, the undersigned senior staff members, wish to convey to you our deep concern about the overall administration of this library system. Although we have not conducted a survey of all senior staff members, we believe this paper represents a consensus of their opinions as well as ours. This knowledge has come from two sources: 1) the informal flow of information gained in day-to-day

operations, and 2) opinions expressed during several meetings of a few senior staff members.

We wish to emphasize that we are acting in good faith and from a sincere dedication to professional service of the highest caliber. We have no interest in blaming any individual or individuals but are concerned about some aspects of the overall administration of the libraries which we believe, if not corrected, will lead to the deterioration of staff morale and library service.

Because you do not provide us with the necessary direction and leadership, we feel handicapped in fulfilling our prime professional obligations which are to provide library materials and bibliographical services. Specifically, we cite the following deficiencies in your administration:

1. You have not communicated to the staff clearly defined objectives, priorities, and policies; in fact, these appear to shift from day to day and situation to situation. Many of your decisions seem to be made to take immediate care of crises instead of being based on overall systemwide goals and policies.

2. You do not appear to take time to give serious operating problems sufficient study. Are you spreading your interests and energies too widely? Or, should you make more use of delegation?

3. You frequently fail to look at the effects of a decision on the whole system. The management technique utilized seems to resolve isolated small problems without relating them to the total system and without looking for causes. Cross-department study is almost non-existent. For example, a decision affecting technical services may not envision the serious consequences upon public services; or, conversely, decisions which result in poor public service may nullify the work of the most capable acquisition and cataloging personnel.

4. Problems brought to you through the usual channels are frequently ignored or you appear to reject any responsibility for facing them.

5. There seem to be conflicts in the delegation of authority and responsibility. We suggest that you study the overall organization, structure, and chain of command.

6. Job applicants should be screened more

carefully. Frequently persons are appointed who are not fully qualified for the vacancies. Is this the result of failure on your part to recognize the need for certain professional skills in given positions or insufficient knowledge about how and where to search for qualified personnel? For example, a recent appointment in the rare books department had neither the necessary language background nor any understanding of the materials she was to work with.

7. We earnestly request the provision of a continuing education program. We cite especially the need for training understudies in supervisory positions so that if the incumbent supervisor is ill or resigns, informed continuity will be insured.

8. We believe many of your responsibilities could be delegated to staff committees which would give you more time for overall thinking and planning and would put more decision-making at lower levels of the organization. For example, a search and screening committee responsible for recommending persons to fill vacancies; a promotions and tenure committee; a grievance committee; a committee to revise the personnel code; and others.

Signed:

_____

_____

* * *

If you were the director of this library, how would you react to this position paper?

Case 42

"THE SHELF"

Southmore High School served a suburb with a population of some 25,000 mostly in the middle socio-economic level. A survey of the community revealed that 85 per cent of the students upon graduating from high school attended college. It was upon these facts that a curriculum and, of course, the library was planned.

From its beginning, the library was considered to be one of the more important and functional departments in the school. The staff, consisting of three professionals and two clerks, served a student body of 2,000. Mr. Smith, a man of fifty, was head librarian. Because he was particularly interested in the technical services area, he did the ordering, cataloging, and processing of materials. Miss Green and Mrs. Young, the other two professional librarians, spent most of their time working with the students and faculty.

The librarians encouraged all faculty members to make recommendations for the purchase of materials. The individual teacher would make an order card, give it to the head of his department for approval and the department head then sent the order card to the library. Only the minimum information was requested. On the order card it was not necessary to indicate the source of the review or the reasons for requesting the book. The head librarian very rarely rejected any of the material requested. If he did reject an order, the cards were simply "misplaced." No selection policy for library materials had ever been officially adopted. There was one on paper if anyone asked, but it was not official.

During the third week in November, Mr. Lucky, a first year teacher in the English Department, filled out an order card for _____. The request was signed by the head of the English Department, who sent it to the library. The book was ordered. When the book arrived, Mr. Smith began to catalog it. As he was examining the book, he began to read it carefully. He decided that the book was not suitable for the library. He placed it on "The Shelf" in the work room. There were approximately twenty other books on "The Shelf" which had been ordered and then not placed on the open shelves.

In the middle of January, Mr. Lucky came to the library to check on the status of the book he had ordered. Mr. Smith told Mr. Lucky the book had been received and that after he had carefully read the book he felt it was not suitable for the library. He then showed Mr. Lucky "The Shelf." Mr. Lucky was furious that Mr. Smith would question his recommendation of a book. After several harsh words to Mr. Smith, Mr. Lucky left the library.

At Southmore High an Advisory Council consulted with and advised the superintendent on practices in or operation of the school affecting students, staff members, or public relations. Members of this Advisory Council also interpreted to those members of the professional staff to whom they were responsible the actions and decisions of the superintendent and the school board. The Council had been set up and organized on the following basis:

Each faculty member had one preparation period per day. All faculty members who had the same preparation period (e.g., first hour) elected one of their group to serve. There were seven faculty members--six elected through period plus one elected by the librarians and the counselors--and the Superintendent. The Superintendent acted as chairman at the meeting. The secretary was selected from among those elected to the Council.

The Council met one evening per month. All faculty members could suggest items for the agenda. Minutes of the meeting were published the following day in the Faculty Bulletin. The recommendations made by the Advisory Council could be accepted or rejected by the Superintendent and the Board. The Board had accepted about one-third of the recommendations made by the Advisory Council.

The regular meeting of the Advisory Council was scheduled for the evening following Mr. Lucky's encounter with Mr. Smith. Mr. Lucky was a member of the Advisory Council. Even though the matter was not listed on the agenda, Mr. Lucky presented his version of the episode with Mr. Smith. He was still angry when he told the group about "The Shelf" and suggested they go down to the library and see it. All members then trooped down to the library and viewed "The Shelf." No member of the library staff was present when the Council visited the library.

After discussion of the matter, the Council (with tentative approval by the Superintendent) wrote a recommendation that appeared in the Faculty Bulletin the next day. The recommendation stated that all orders for library materials originated by faculty members and approved by their department head must be ordered by the head librarian, cataloged, and placed on the open shelves for use by the students.

* * *

Can you defend Mr. Smith's censorship action?

Case 43

SCHOOL REORGANIZATION

The Board of Education of the Andra School System approved an administrative reorganization plan to eliminate the three junior high schools, change the number of grades in the elementary and high schools, and create some middle schools. The system would then include:

Level	Grades	Number
High School	Grades 9-12	2
Middle School	Grades 6-8	7
Elementary School	Grades K-5	14

The Superintendent of Schools believed that this was the time to bring all of the libraries and audio-visual services under the supervision of one person to provide supervision, coordination, cooperation, and better services. Prior to this time, the libraries and the audio-visual services had developed more or less independently in the various schools.

You have just accepted the position of Supervisor of Libraries and Audio-Visual services. Your responsibility is to develop adequate educational media centers in each of the schools. Each of the present elementary schools has a small book collection; the junior high school and the high school have fairly good collections. There are some audio-visual materials in each of the elementary schools but none in the junior and senior high school libraries. The librarian in each of the twenty-three schools will report to you. One of the two high schools is currently under construction and will be ready for use when schools open next September at the same time as the reorganization plan goes into effect. You are to assume your position on February 1.

Assume that you have adequate funds for any reasonable program you wish to develop. Outline your objectives and goals. What long- and short-range planning must you do? What types of plans will be involved? Are there any premises and constraints to be considered? How can you involve the library staff in planning? What kind of organizational structure will you plan? How many and what types of personnel must be employed?

Case 44

STUDY CENTER REQUESTED

"Well, sir, we'd certainly like you to think about this and do anything you can to help us. I know our house isn't alone in wanting the library open later at night. It's just as noisy in the dorms in the evening. Most of us would really appreciate it if you'd do something, Mr. Michael."

"I'll try to do what I can, Tom, but we're shorthanded right now. I agree with you that the library should stay open until 11 p.m., but I just can't make you a promise right now. Give me some time to talk it over with President Howell."

In the past few weeks Mr. Michael, the librarian at a liberal arts college with an enrollment of about 700, had received a number of similar requests for longer hours. Because of increased enrollment, fraternities, sororities and dormitories were filled to capacity. Study conditions were not always satisfactory. The noise reached its peak in the evening hours when most of the students did their studying.

At present the library is open seventy hours a week as follows:

Monday through Friday: 8 a.m.-5 p.m. and 7 p.m.-10 p.m.
Saturday: 8 a.m.-12 noon
Sunday: 2 p.m.-5 p.m. and 7 p.m.-10 p.m.

Any increase in hours of opening would require additional funds in this year's budget to employ more staff and to pay for more heat, light, and janitor service and would require similar additions to all future budgets. To obtain a supplementary budget allotment, Mr. Michael would have to present a formal request to the president which should include supporting evidence showing need for the additional funds.

* * *

What types of planning should Mr. Michael do? Should he request funds for longer hours of opening on the basis of informal individual requests? How could he determine whether the students need longer library hours to study library materials or need just a quiet place to study their own textbooks (dormitory dining room, for instance)? If he found that additional hours of opening are indeed necessary to serve the needs of students and faculty members, how could he determine how many additional hours are needed?

Case 45

INDIVIDUAL RECOGNITION
(Role playing)

At Eucalyptus University Library, it was customary policy for staff members to receive no individual recognition for bibliographies compiled, for news articles or student handbooks written, or for orientation courses developed. The only identification on productions of this sort was the name and address of the library and the name of the director. Through the years, various staff members have occasionally remonstrated against this policy when they were personally involved, but it never became a real issue. Recently, two staff members worked for almost three years on a library orientation moving picture to be shown continuously during freshman week each year. This picture replaced the time-consuming library tours previously conducted. The film showed each of the departments of the central library and each of the branch libraries, gave simple directions about how to check out books and how to use the catalog, and introduced fundamentals of shelf arrangement and classification of books. When the film was completed, the list of credits at the beginning of the film identified the audio-visual personnel who manned the cameras, did the graphics, and edited the final result. But no mention anywhere in the film of the two librarians who had conceptualized the content, interviewed and selected the student actors, made complicated arrangements in the various departments and branches for filming, and wrote the script. The only credits in the film for the library staff stated "Produced with the cooperation of the Director of Libraries, Dr. William Lawrence, and his staff."

This film served as a catalyzing agent for the staff to bring the issue of individual recognition into the open. The issue was brought up at the last staff meeting and an ad hoc committee was appointed to study the problem. The committee has gathered data and has scheduled a conference with the Director to request a policy change.

Planning and Decision-Making Cases / 129

Role for Dr. William Lawrence, Director of Libraries:

You believe that the long-established policy of staff anonymity for any library-sponsored projects is sound because staff members are being paid from the library budget to do these projects which are part of their responsibilities. By having only your name on the bibliography, handbook, or other item produced, any feedback comes through your office, which you believe is good, sound administration utilizing the chain of command. You can then pass on whatever comments (whether praise or censure) to the appropriate department heads for transmission to the staff members involved. If individuals were identified, feedback would no doubt come to them and your office might never be informed. How could individual recognition be given to the professional staff in acquisitions, cataloging, and circulation for their contributions to the total library operation?

Role for Mrs. Elsie Ash, chairman of the ad hoc committee:

You have been head of reference services in this library for a number of years. You firmly believe that individuals who produce creative projects should be personally identified for at least three reasons:

1) To make it possible for users to communicate directly with the responsible person or persons for clarification and for suggestions as to omissions or additions.

2) To encourage high professional standards for whatever is produced. If the person responsible is not identified, she might do a "sloppy" job inasmuch as any criticism would not come to her personally.

3) To boost staff morale and pride in undertaking demanding creative assignments. Although, theoretically, projects are done during working hours, actually many personal off-duty hours are devoted to such projects as preparation of a new personnel code or staff manual, the writing of a new student or faculty handbook, the creation of an effective display, and the production of the freshman orientation film.

You are representing the sentiments and opinions of the staff association in requesting that Dr. Lawrence change the policy regarding individual recognition.

Case 46

RESEARCH LIBRARY PUBLIC SERVICE

The Central University Library, the largest library in the state, was also the only large research library serving the city and the area surrounding the university. (The city supported a good public library system and many school libraries.) Because the university library was a public, tax-supported institution, the general public and industry thought that they should be entitled to its services. When the conflict inherent in differing interpretations of the service function of the university library became apparent, the administration of the library and the university defined priorities of service. The faculty library committee studied the problem and recommended that priority should be given first to faculty, students, and staff of the university; second, to faculty of neighboring colleges and to state officials; third, to graduate students and scholars in the immediate area; and finally, to the general public, industry, high school students, and undergraduates of other institutions. Shortly after the policy statement had been made public, the governor stated in a campaign speech that the libraries and laboratories of the state-supported higher educational institutions should serve business and industry throughout the state. The speech was so widely reported in the press that many more people became aware of the university's facilities. As a result, the number of calls for library service skyrocketed.

Many requests for service from outside the university came by telephone. As the university had no general "information" number, callers who did not request a specific department were connected with the library's reference desk. The number of telephone calls to the reference desk had increased greatly during the previous year. Some of the callers merely wanted general university information, such as where to obtain course catalogs or to find a campus program. The chief of reference was forced to schedule two extra staff members on duty at the desk during peak hours. Because only one person was assigned to desk duty on nights and weekends, telephone calls interfered with service to patrons waiting at the desk, most of whom were students or faculty members of the university. As the number of calls increased, complaints from faculty and students increased too.

The reference chief was told by budget officers that

no money was available to employ more personnel. His problem, then, was to find a way to reduce the number of calls, so that his present staff could handle them. How could calls be screened so that only those which were appropriate to a research library reference department came through?

His first effort toward a solution was to conduct a one-month survey of all incoming calls at the reference desk. The staff member on duty was instructed: 1) to record the time and date that each call was received (morning, afternoon, or evening); 2) to find out the status of the caller (university faculty, student, state official, business, or industry); 3) to learn whether the information desired was a "quick reference" item which could be answered immediately or was a question which required a return call; and 4) to list all directional or general information questions. If the call needed to be returned, the question asked was recorded, as well as the time required to find an answer.

The results of this survey revealed that 48 per cent of the calls were for general university information, such as "The university calendar lists a program this evening in Recital Hall. In what building is that hall located?" "What is the telephone number of Dr. John Jones, who teaches either in physics or mathematics?" Of the remaining 52 per cent of the questions, five per cent were so complicated that staff members should have told the caller to come to the library for the information rather than attempting to reply by telephone; 31 per cent were "quick" reference questions which the staff could answer from the group of books shelved at the reference desk; 16 per cent were questions which required a short search and a return telephone call.

The people who asked the reference questions (that is, those who made 52 per cent of the calls) were: university faculty members, seven per cent; university students, 70 per cent; state officials, one per cent; general public, 15 per cent; and business or industry (including librarians of special libraries), seven per cent.

* * *

Considering the results of the survey, should the library director or the faculty library committee (or both) demand that an "information" telephone number be listed both in the campus and the city telephone directories? This would take care of the 48 per cent of the calls which were for general university information? Evaluate the priorities for service which the faculty library committee recommended.

Case 47

ARBITRARY ARCHITECT

Several years ago a college received from one of its alumni, George Whitley, a large sum of money for building a new library. The only conditions of the gift were that the college was to raise a matching sum, that the building was to be built in a style compatible with the architecture of the buildings surrounding it, and that the interior of the building was to be "nicely" furnished.
The administration was grateful for the gift and immediately started to raise matching funds. After it had done so, planning for the new building was begun. Mr. Whitley was asked to sit on the building committee of the board of trustees. He accepted the appointment, but he came to meetings only a few times and only when the architect was present.
The architect chosen to design the building was a member of the firm which had designed many of the buildings on campus. Since his work was familiar to most of the building committee, general agreement on the style of the exterior and the arrangement of the interior was easily reached. As might have been expected, there were some minor differences of opinion, but most of these were worked out satisfactorily.
Shortly after the planning had been completed the librarian, Mr. Shaw, was asked to go over the final drawings with the architect. When he did so he found that the architect had presented an entirely different design for one of the interior areas. The change greatly increased the size of an open balcony area, decreased the shelving capacity by several thousand volumes, and raised the noise level. To compensate for the loss of the shelving, the architect had increased the length of the building. Mr. Shaw was not at all happy with these changes. The great length of the building would mean many more footsteps for the staff and make control more difficult, and the noise created by this large open balcony would be distracting for patrons and staff alike. The architect's main reason for these changes was an aesthetic one. The architect also told Mr. Shaw that he had asked Mr. Whitley for permission to make the changes and that Mr. Whitley had agreed to them. The donor had never voiced preferences as to architectural style or type of construction; in fact, he had been extremely reticent about making any suggestions for the building.

Mr. Shaw immediately called a meeting of the library building committee to discuss the changes that had been made. Mr. Whitley did not attend this meeting. Mr. Shaw explained why he thought the greatly enlarged balcony would be unsatisfactory, and the building committee was quick to agree. The committee immediately sent a letter of protest to the architect and asked him to submit an alternate design for its approval. The building committee soon heard from the architect, who informed them that his original plan was the only one which was feasible and pleasing.

The librarian felt strongly that the changes would make it impossible for students to work in the library or for the staff to administer the library efficiently.

* * *

Who should have the authority to make final decisions on a library building?

Case 48

CLEARANCE POLICY
(Role playing)

The personnel code of the Metropolitan Public Library system is in the process of being revised. The revision is a project sponsored jointly by the staff association, the Personnel Officer, and the Executive Council (the top administrative officers). Representatives from each of these three groups constitute an ad hoc Personnel Code Revision Committee. One section after another of the Code is being studied by the Committee. Today the following regulation is to be reviewed:

Clearance Policy

1) Articles, letters to the editor, or other forms of writing prepared for publication by a staff member and signed by him as a member of the Metropolitan Public Library staff must be cleared by his Division Chief or Coordinator and the Deputy Director or Director before being submitted to an editor or publisher.

2) Outlines of speeches or written scripts

must also be submitted sufficiently ahead of delivery to permit clearance by the same individuals.

Role for librarian representing professional members of the Staff Association:

You and several of your colleagues believe this rule is a form of censorship as well as an invasion of your rights as responsible members of a profession. Why should you not be allowed to express your expertise or opinions without the intimidation and humiliation of clearance? You believe that librarians should participate actively in professional organizations and contribute often to professional journals; but this policy inhibits the desire to do either one. You want this rule deleted from the revised Personnel Code.

Role for Deputy Director:

As members of the municipal civil service system, the library staff is subject to all the rules and regulations for municipal employees. These rules are incorporated in the appropriate places in the library Personnel Code. This rule is one that was copied from the municipal employees' code; it is part of a broader regulation which enjoins all employees from political activity, even to folding papers and stuffing envelopes. Employees can contribute their efforts to non-partisan community activities such as mental health centers, local control of schools, and intergroup relations. The purpose of these rules is to prevent "crackpots" from sounding off either in writing or in speeches and possibly causing problems for the city administration; they were not intended to discourage professional activities of librarians. In fact, when the rules were written the library staff was probably never even thought of.

Clearance approval by library officers is practically automatic. None of the officers can recall ever disapproving but they have made what they considered constructive criticism to improve content or style. They believe it would be unwise to challenge or delete this rule from the library code unless or until it is deleted from the municipal code.

Case 49

PLANNED EXPANSION

In 1965 Altruria, through concentrated community efforts, had succeeded in completing construction of a new library building. Funds had been raised by several women's clubs in the community, but more than half of the total building costs had come from the bequest of one of the town's citizens. Because the sum from the donor's estate was so large, the library was named for him. His widow, along with the representatives of the women's clubs, was present at the dedication ceremony. Although the building was modest in size and tax funds were limited, the library came to be used extensively, especially by the children in the area. Several of the clubs which had helped raise the money for the library met monthly in a pleasant basement room and used the adjoining kitchen. The Boy Scouts, the Girl Scouts, and 4-H groups also occasionally used the rooms.

In ten years the collection had tripled in size; the 25,000 volumes filled the library to the rafters. The librarian, Janet Wilson, wanted to set up a separate children's room. There was no problem about finding space; the clubroom in the basement was empty most of the time. She consulted a local carpenter and got estimates on shelving; in a few weeks she had estimates from a library furniture supply house for two tables and some small chairs. Although her long-range plan included a part-time employee for the after-school rush hour, she decided that the new furniture and the necessary minor alterations would cause enough increase in the budget for one year. She planned to use volunteer Girl Scouts to help after school at the circulation desk in the downstairs room. Since the few young children who came in during the day would be with their parents, she hoped that they could be trusted to bring books upstairs to the main circulation desk.

Her plans were so simple and the costs were so low for what seemed to be an excellent solution to a vexing problem that she was stunned at the reaction of her board. One of the board members, Mrs. Eliot, was certain that the women's clubs had donated the money for the library primarily to have a permanent meeting room, and that the intent of the bequest was that the meeting room be distinctly separate and not a part of the library. The president of the board, Mr. Hines, was equally sure that the room had been intended for a clubroom only until the library needed it. He added, "The intent of the gift is not important now that we are tax-supported. We have to think first of our users and make the best use of the taxpayers' money. We've known for several years that we must expand. I, for one, applaud Mrs. Wilson's sensible plans."

When the board asked Mrs. Wilson if the library was really so crowded, she told them, "Only last month I had to cancel an order because there wasn't enough shelf space. In 1955 we had a circulation of 13,000 in our old building. Last year our circulation was 60,000 volumes, and our collection has increased from a little over 400 to 25,000 volumes."

Under Mr. Hines' prodding the board finally agreed to have a public meeting to discuss the problem of library expansion and to table the final budget until they could decide definitely in what form the expansion would be. Unlike some public meetings, attendance for discussion of library development was good. Although the board had decided before the meeting to make no comments which could be construed to support any one plan, Mr. Hines did tell the group that the lot adjacent to the library was available for purchase. Several of the audience murmured, "Where's the money going to come from?" Others expressed the view that the clubroom was only for the use of the clubs and organizations, and not for the library. Finally, three alternate plans were formulated:

1. An addition would be made to the present library.
2. The basement would be adapted for use both as a children's room and a meeting room for clubs. The alterations would be made under the direction of the librarian, with the approval of final plans by the board of trustees.
3. A separate civic center would be built.

Mr. Hines, chairman of the meeting, told the group that the library board would meet in a "closed" session later in the month to decide which of the three plans would be most suitable at this time. He tried to make it quite clear to the group that the ultimate responsibility for a decision rested with the board, but that they would be guided by what they had learned at the meeting.

The board asked Mrs. Wilson for the regular schedule of club meetings and the hours proposed for the children's room should the board decide to put it in the basement. Two groups met regularly in the clubroom, one on the last Monday of each month from 2:00 p.m. to 4:00 p.m., and another on the first Thursday from 2:00 p.m. to 5:00 p.m. Mrs. Wilson's proposal for hours in the projected childrens' room was 3:30 p.m. to 6:00 p.m. Monday through Friday, and 9:30 a.m. to 6:00 p.m. on Saturday; the room would be closed during the two afternoons the adult clubs met.

During the interval between the public meeting and the board meeting the trustees tried to sound out opinions from the community. Several letters appeared in the newspaper, some in favor and some opposed to expansion. One man wrote, "It seems strange to have the library board considering, in a very adamant manner, expansion and services which the people obviously do not want or need. It is ridiculous, in my opinion, to provide reading tables for little children. They should be allowed to have a reasonable number of books to take home to read at their convenience, or to have their mothers or elders read to them. Perhaps in the near future the taxpayers will band together in an association to keep the planners at bay."

The laws under which the library operated stated quite clearly that the trustees were to "take charge of, manage, and conduct the affairs of the library" and "to provide suitable room, structures, facilities, furniture, apparatus, and other articles and library appliances necessary for the thorough organization and efficient management of such libraries." The laws also stated that, "the librarian, as the administrative head of the library, shall be responsible only to the board for the operation and management of the library."

* * *

The board has the legal authority to make decisions about space utilization--why did they feel it was necessary to get public approval?

Case 50

WHO CONTROLS LIBRARY SPACE?

This letter is one of many that Catherine Hand, head of the extension division of the State Library Commission, received one day. Miss Hand's stock in trade is problems. The purpose of her division is to provide advisory and field services for local public libraries and state institutional libraries.

> Dear Catherine:
> Problems! I am facing another one of an apparently unending stream. The latest is that the school superintendent now aspires to using my library's basement for school classes.
> He called me last week and asked to talk to the board at its next meeting. I don't know yet definitely what his proposal is, but according to our flourishing 'grapevine' it's nothing good. You know, too, he has a reputation for getting exactly what he wants through all sorts of bargains. Unfortunately, he rarely sticks to his part of the bargain.
> In the plans the basement room was intended for group meetings, and it has been used for just that purpose. In fact, it has been such a popular meeting place that reservations have to be made weeks in advance. We would be strongly criticized if the board announced that the room was no longer available.
> I am afraid some of the board will be swayed by his honeyed plea in the name of education and all the little 'kiddies.' Having classes in the library will cause endless confusion. Classroom use can be very hard physically on a building, too. We've spent a good deal of time and money getting the building in repair, and our bookstock and services have improved and expanded during the past year.
> Perhaps I am anticipating trouble before it arrives, but I am quite worried. My board president has just been in, and she too has heard the rumors. She is as worried as I am. Can you suggest any way that we can handle this problem? Is there any law covering a situation such as this?
>
> Sincerely yours,
> Alice Charter

Miss Hand answered immediately:

> Dear Alice:
> Your board is facing a problem many library boards have faced. Those who did not take a firm

stand against encroachment have almost universally regretted it. A library board has a moral commitment to maintain the best possible library facilities for the taxpayers who have given them money for this particular purpose. They have no commitment whatsoever to provide classrooms or any other facilities for the schools. School boards are appointed or elected for this purpose. If they have failed to provide the necessary needs, that is no concern of the library board.

No one can make a library board do anything it does not wish to do without resorting to the courts. Therefore all that is needed for you to retain the use of your community room for library purposes--which is its legal use--is for a majority of your board to stand firm in their commitment to the library.

Good luck,
Catherine Hand

*   *   *

What are the major considerations in this situation? Discuss the positions indicated in the letters of Alice Charles and Catherine Hand. Is there a course of action which might benefit both the public and school libraries?

Case 51

NO TEXTBOOKS!

Argos is located in a state which is largely rural. The population of about 40,000 is chiefly conservative middle class with no extremes of poverty or wealth. Excellent attendance at PTA meetings and active participation in school activities and projects indicates their interest in the education of their children.

When the one high school in the community became overcrowded, the school board authorized the building of a second high school. Committees consisting of school board members, parents, teachers, and principals visited many new high schools both in and out of the state to observe and learn about the latest features of curricula and buildings and anything else which seemed applicable to the educational objectives of this community.

After discussing various features of other high schools, the committee members decided on a modularly scheduled school with emphasis on individualism, team teaching, cross-over departments, and a media center with four resource units in science, mathematics, social science, and humanities. Several teachers on the committees were impressed with the idea of no textbooks as part of the innovations in teaching approach. In place of textbooks, the students and teachers were expected to rely on the resources of the media center. This idea was promoted vigorously by its proponents and was adopted by teachers in the social sciences and humanities. Teachers in mathematics and science insisted that textbooks were essential for teaching their subjects. In this school system, free textbooks were furnished to the children.

Unfortunately, no librarian was included in any of the committees, nor did anyone foresee or investigate the problems and cost of providing library source materials in social science and the humanities to replace well organized textbooks. The media center became the center of the curriculum; every unit of instruction in humanities and social sciences created an immediate demand by teachers and their students for a wide variety of materials.

Mr. Almond, the librarian in charge of the media center, was employed six months prior to the opening of school to select and order all types of materials for the center. He had had five successful years of school library experience in conventional schools before he was invited to accept this position. He knew the demands of high school students and teachers in schools which utilized textbooks and where the media center provided supplementary materials, but he had had no experience with a no-textbook environment. Neither did the school board or the principal of New High visualize the problems or demands in a school without textbooks in social science and humanities. The budget allocated for the first year of New High seemed generous in comparison with the annual budget for Old High. To this budget allocation was added the item in the budget which was earmarked for the purchase of textbooks in social science and humanities. By combining the textbook money with a good healthy first appropriation, the administration thought they had provided adequately for the media center. However, this budget proved most inadequate because of the very heavy demands. In retrospect, the librarian should have been employed at least one year in advance of school opening instead of six months and the budget should have been much larger.

During the six months prior to school opening, the principal notified Mr. Almond when each faculty member was employed. Mr. Almond then wrote to each teacher asking for a list of all materials he or she would need to teach his courses--books, periodicals, pamphlets, government documents, filmstrips, tape and disc recordings, and displays of objects. The teacher was to star the titles of books in which he would assign one or more chapters for each student in a course to read. These starred titles were purchased in multiple copies. Many of these materials were still on order when school opened.

The initial staff of the media center consisted of seven persons: one professional librarian (Mr. Almond), two clerks in the media center, and a paraprofessional in each of the four research units. Approximately 1,300 students were enrolled in grades 10, 11, and 12 and the faculty totaled fifty-two. Neither the staff nor the collection proved adequate for the immediate intense use of the collection.

The teachers were cooperative in giving Mr. Almond several days advance notice of their assignments but this did not solve the problem of too many students for too few books. At first, the library staff put the materials assigned on open shelves, assuming that the students could be trusted to read the assignment and return the materials to the shelves. But the students usually stole every copy during the first hour or two after the assignment was made. There was no money to replace these stolen copies. After the library staff realized that the open shelf honor plan would not work, the only alternative was to adopt a type of college reserve book system and to ignore copyright laws by "publishing" chapters of books on the ditto machine. The staff found that they could handle 250 students with 50 copies. This system was a heavy drain on the time and energy of the limited staff. Even with this sign-out system there were continuing thefts. By the time the assignment was due, there might be about one-half of the fifty copies still on the shelves!

Prior to the assignment of a paper to be written by a senior class in English on a unit about the eighteenth century British novel, the library staff got together everything they could borrow from other libraries and what was in their collection. In the first two hours after the assignment was made, fifty of the books were stolen.

The faculty and library staff members asked themselves and each other--why did these students steal? They were not underprivileged, the mores of their conservative middle-class background did not sanction such behavior. A high percentage of the student body went on to college--did they steal because they felt the pressure for grades? Members of the faculty and the library staff concluded that they had not been weaned away from the textbook and consequently felt the pressure of holding something in their hands that they could call their own.

* * *

If you were Mr. Almond, how would you handle this problem of thefts?

CHAPTER III

CONTROLLING CASES

Librarians and libraries are subject to four types of control: direct, external or indirect, financial, and internal. Library staffs can do little to alter or change the first two types of control but they can do something about the third and fourth.

Direct control is imposed through laws and legislation, charters, articles of incorporation, boards of trustees, and library committees. Public libraries are part of the hierarchy of government and hence subject to whatever controls exist in the hierarchy. Their boards of trustees have legal responsibility for the library. Academic libraries are subject to control by institutional boards of trustees, administrative officers of the institution, and library committees. Various types of corporation and/or institutional control are exerted on special libraries. School boards and school administrators have authority over the funding and operation of school libraries.

External or indirect controls include standards, certification, accreditation, civil service, unions, building codes and zoning ordinances, wage and hour laws, political interference, conditions of gifts or grants, state aid, and such economic factors as depression and inflation.

Financial controls involve budgets, accounting, audits, cost studies, contracts, and bond issues.

Internal controls include communication, feedback, records and reports, public relations and publicity, patrons, inventory, circulation, surveys, security measure, and performance standards. Internal control is closely related to planning and is necessary to measure what is being accomplished, to compare performance with norms or standards, to identify activities or operations which are not contributing to the attainment of goals, to locate reasons for poor achievement by persons or by units of the library, and to take remedial action. Adequate control may mean making minor changes in direction to adjust to altered conditions, setting new goals, formulating new plans, changing methods or procedures, or reassigning staff.

Case 52

A PENITENTIARY LIBRARY

The Jason Penitentiary is a maximum security institution with an inmate population of about 4,000 men ranging in age from eighteen to seventy years. New inmates are placed in an orientation unit for two to four weeks. During this time they undergo medical, psychological, educational, and vocational testing which determines their classification and work assignments. Many of the men are serving long-term sentences; the average stay is approximately six years. The educational level ranges from illiterates to college graduates, but the average is less than fifth grade. Those who test below third grade are required to go to school until they reach this level; attendance after that is optional. Those who test above the third grade may choose between going to school and working in one of the prison industries or offices. All inmates who do not understand English are enrolled in English language classes until they reach a certain level of proficiency. More than a half of the inmates are enrolled in one of the educational programs: elementary, secondary, vocational, or English language.

The library is considered part of the educational program and is open from 8:00 to 12:00 and 1:00 to 4:00 daily and two evenings a week. The men may come to the library once a week and may borrow five books at a time. A professional librarian administers the library with the help of full-time inmates. The quota of inmates for the library is ten, but usually there are only six to eight.

During the orientation period, inmates are informed about every department of the prison, including the library. The librarian tells each new group about the library's program and resources. As a result of this talk, some inmates request to work in the library. A staff classification committee arbitrarily makes work assignments, but those assigned to the library must be able to type and have enough educational background to be useful to the librarian. Most of them have had some high school, or are high school or college graduates. The librarian must train each one

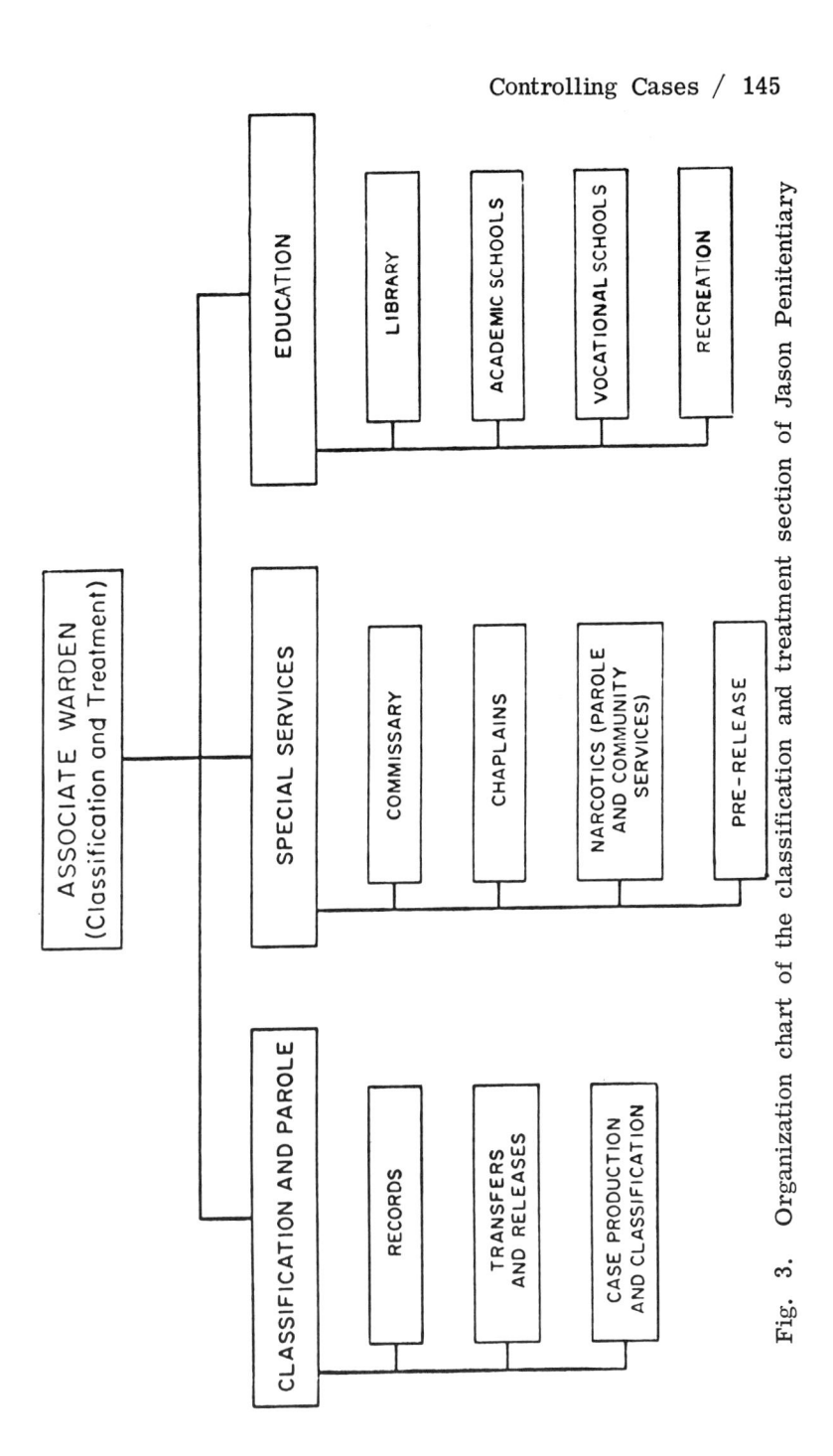

Fig. 3. Organization chart of the classification and treatment section of Jason Penitentiary

for the work he is to do. A few inmates have even had some library experience.

The librarian is responsible not only for the central library but also for other collections in the institution: two hospital collections (one for patients and one for staff), a professional library for the correctional staff (housed in the warden's office), and a vocational shop collection. The books in all of these collections are purchased and cataloged by the library. No books are acquired on such subjects as explosives, gunsmithing, locksmithing, poisons, and medicine, or on highly controversial subjects like religion or politics.

In addition to administering the library and its branches, the librarian: 1) screens all books carried in stock in the commissary which are for sale to inmates; 2) approves all manuscripts written by inmates for publication; 3) is co-leader of a Great Books Program on alternate Saturdays; 4) handles personal book, periodical, and newspaper orders for inmates; and 5) supervises the use of law books.

The librarian's most serious administrative problem involves the law books and legal work done by inmates in the library. According to the penitentiary's administrative manual, space must be provided in the library for all law books. The collection has accumulated from donations given by inmates, friends of inmates, lawyers, and others. This collection is supplemented by loans from the state library. All inmate requests are submitted weekly in one package to the law division of the state library and a truck delivers the volumes. Such requests are limited to five books per inmate per week. In addition to this collection, available to all inmates, space is provided in the library for storing personal copies of legal books belonging to inmates. To help avoid conflicts between prisoners, no inmate is allowed to possess law books in his living quarters. The prison staff has learned that if a man has a volume containing a case in which he is especially interested, another inmate may steal it out of spite, malice, or greed, and either hide the book until the owner gives him something for it or cut out the case and destroy it.

The purpose of the legal collection is to insure each inmate's access to the courts and to attorneys in order to challenge the legality of his conviction and incarceration.

The librarian is responsible for: 1) housing the legal collection in reasonable condition; 2) allowing each inmate access to the collection once a week, or more often if facilities allow; 3) supplying instructions for preparing writs; 4) routing through the associate warden all requests for legal

materials from condemned men or men in segregation; and
5) borrowing legal books from the state library. Also, the
librarian is responsible for enforcing all the rules and regulations governing the use of the collection: permission from
the warden is required for an inmate to have access to the
collection; inmates can consult law books during week days
if they have no work assignments, and during leisure time
on Saturdays and Sundays; no law books can be taken from
the library; and no inmate can assist another inmate in the
preparation of petitions or writs. The office of the supervising parole officer provides clerical assistance and supplies for typing the petitions or writs which the inmates
write for their own cases.

 The use of the law books has increased steadily in
recent years, but especially since the Supreme Court's decision in Escobedo v. Illinois in 1964. This decision voided
Escobedo's murder confession on the grounds that he was
denied his rights to counsel and set the stage for the Court's
1966 decision to apply the rights of silence and counsel to
all police interrogation (Miranda v. Arizona). In the last
few years, use of the law books has increased 1,245 per
cent. Use of the books by inmates in the condemned row
has increased 318 per cent. More than 5,000 writs were
sent to the courts from this prison last year. During the
past month 269 men used the legal collection, made 600
visits to the library, and used 1,017 legal books. Cost of
the legal work is a large item in the library budget: postage and insurance on interlibrary loans, packaging and
wrapping, payment for lost and damaged books, printing of
forms, and correspondence.

 Not only has use increased since the Danny Escobedo
case but the inmates have demanded more and more legal
books. The library budget is not even large enough to cover
necessary materials for the educational program let alone
recreational reading, so no legal books can be purchased
from that budget. The incessant demands of the legal work
have left the librarian little time for orienting new inmates
and staff to the library, giving reader guidance, assisting
the teachers in the academic programs, providing more information and reference service, preparing booklists, developing a listening program, and preparing exhibits.

 Other aspects of the library work have also increased
in recent years: circulation, growth of personal book, periodical, and newspaper ordering for inmates, and reference
services. Although use of the library has increased, the
number of clerks and the size of the library have remained
the same. The staff can no longer handle this workload.

148 / Library Management

Some work must be transferred to other departments in the prison, or the library staff and quarters must be greatly enlarged.

According to the 1966 standards for correctional institutions,[1] an institution of 3,500 inmates or more should have one professional head librarian, one professional assistant librarian, and two full-time paid clerks in addition to inmate clerks. The librarian of the Jason Penitentiary is trying to manage with only inmate clerks. The standards estimate that seats should be provided for five per cent of the population,[2] which in this prison would be 200 seats. Only 25 are available.

In addition to the impossibly heavy regular workload in the library, the librarian spends at least forty hours a month reviewing inmate manuscripts. He is not compensated for this service.

The librarian would like to convince the prison administration to assign to other departments the non-library activities of handling personal book, periodical, and newspaper orders for inmates, approving manuscripts, and supervising the use of law books. The librarian believes that the library will never be able to function as it should in the rehabilitation, education, and recreation programs of the penitentiary as long as he and his staff have to spend so much time and energy on non-library activities. What would you advise him to do?

Notes

1. American Correctional Association. Manual of Correctional Standards (3rd ed.; New York: American Correctional Association, 1966), p. 511.
2. Ibid., p. 515.

Case 53

CONFRONTATION
(Role playing)

Roles:

    Librarian
    Man studying for civil service exam
    Second man

The Mulberry Branch Library is located in a neighborhood with affluent high-rise apartments on one side and ghettos on the other. Because of the two extremes in the economic status of the patrons, problems sometimes arise in the library because of differences in attitudes as to how a library should be administered. The Children's Department is open from 2 to 8 p.m., Monday through Thursday, to provide ample time for children to do their home work in the library in the evenings. On Friday and Sunday, it is open from 2 to 6 p.m. and on Saturday from 9 a.m. to 6 p.m. This schedule is based on a record of use. Normally few children come to the library after 6 p.m. on Friday, Saturday or Sunday. Those who have school work to do on these evenings are allowed to study in the adult reading and reference room. Children are always cautioned that they must not disturb the adults who are reading or studying.

To keep the children off the streets, the library staff provides games, puzzles, recordings, and filmstrips in addition to an excellent collection of books and periodicals. The staff feels very strongly a social service responsibility for the children to keep them interested and occupied in the library as many hours as possible. As a result, the Children's Department is a very busy place during most of the opening hours.

One Saturday evening several children were given permission to do their school work in the adult department. They studied quietly for an hour or so and then became noisy. Many adults were reading or browsing, so a staff member spoke to the children and told them they were distracting the adults. The children quieted down for a while and then again became very noisy.

One of the adult readers stormed up to the librarian in charge and demanded in an angry voice that the children be sent out of the library. He explained that he was studying for a civil service exam he was to take on Monday morning and that he had no quiet place in his apartment to study because he, his wife, and four children shared a two-bedroom apartment. Before he had finished talking another man came over, glared at the first man and belligerently announced to the man and to the librarian, "If you send those children out, I will report this to the local community citizens association, to the authorities in the neighborhood, to the press, and to the library board. These children belong here as long as they want to stay because they have no place to go except the street. They should be allowed to stay."

Case 54

THE SCRIBBLER

Defacing and mutilating library materials have undoubtedly been a problem since libraries originated. In school libraries, the severity of the problem depends upon such variables as demands of assignments, personalities of students, library atmosphere, respect for library staff, and local mores.

Recently, in a large city high school library, the work of a scribbler was discovered in The New Yorker, Ebony, and other magazines. The scribbler appeared to be an exhibitionist who delighted in shocking the next reader or the librarian. Some of his comments pointed up the weaknesses and failures of society in general, and of the high school and its library in particular. Some of the additions to illustrations were anatomical in nature.

Although four professional librarians were on duty throughout the day, it was impossible to police the library and look over the shoulders of each of the several hundred boys and girls who used the library daily. What could be done? How could the scribbler be identified?

In consultation, the staff decided to try this approach. A notice was placed in the school's daily newssheet, which was posted on all bulletin boards in the school, and which also was read over the public address system during the first fifteen-minute period of the day, when all students were in their "home" rooms. The notice read as follows:

> Will the student who has been utilizing his literary and artistic talents on the pages of periodicals in the school library, please identify himself either to one of the librarians or to one of the deans so that he can be referred for the psychological testing and psychiatric treatment he so badly needs.

The following day another notice was included in the daily bulletin. In addition to the above statement, a sentence was added thanking those students who had volunteered to watch for anyone writing in periodicals and to report their findings either to librarians or deans.

The scribbler was never identified, but the scribbling ceased as suddenly as it started.

When this problem and its solution were reported to the coordinator of school libraries for the city system, she debated whether to call this to the attention of all school librarians in the system. Several questions occurred to her: Did the end justify the means? How did this incident affect the attitude of students toward the library and its staff? Would advertising such a problem put ideas into the heads of other students and possibly create a more severe problem in the future? Were the students encouraged to be spies?

Case 55

A SENILE PUBLIC LIBRARY BOARD

Big City has a population of about two million of which 38 per cent are from various minority groups. Of these, the largest is Black (26 per cent); the second largest is Spanish-speaking, who constitute four per cent of the total population. The users of the library system are predominantly a young group, two-thirds being under 25 years of age. Within the city are two universities and several colleges.

In addition to the main headquarters building in the center of the city, there are about 50 branches and many bookmobiles. Only 27 per cent of the staff have BLS or MLS degrees in library science; the rest of the staff were employed on the basis of their scores on the library civil service examinations. The personnel promotion policy favors internal promotion, which results in many "professional" positions being held by staffers whose on-the-job experience is their chief qualification.

The library is governed by a semi-permanent nine-member board, all of whom were appointed by the mayor. The board is composed chiefly of apathetic senior citizens with a disturbing record of absenteeism and an even more disturbing composite philosophy which proclaims that it is more virtuous to hold the line on spending than to serve the needs of the population. The average age of board members is in excess of 65 years; the average number of years which they have served on this board is more than fifteen. Attendance at board meetings is poor--in the last ten years 13 per cent of the regularly scheduled meetings have had to be cancelled for lack of a quorum of five. Evidently most

152 / Library Management

of the members regard this unpaid job as a civic honor rather than a civic duty. Here is some information about the board members:

Member	M-F	Age	Occupation	Years on Board
A (chr)	M	83	Retired business man	31
B	M	62	Labor leader	11
C	M	59	Bank executive	9
D	F	52	Housewife active in volunteer clubwork	6
E	M	77	Protestant minister	40
F	M	71	Retired city employee	3
G	M	72	Retired from boxing club	12
H	M	45	Physician	6
I	M	60	Attorney	20

* * *

Does this absentee, rubber-stamp board provide the best representation of taxpayers' interests? Does it represent community interests, the majority users who are under 25, the minority groups?

Ideally, what should be the size of this library board? Qualifications for membership? How appointed? Age limitations? Length of term.

Should appointment to any public library board be semi-permanent?

Case 56

FUND ACCOUNTING

After having searched many months for a qualified person, the president of a small liberal arts college offered the position of librarian to Miss Dorothy Rust. She was about thirty years of age, had a master's degree in library science, and had good experience in two other college libraries.

To assist Miss Rust in getting acquainted with the college curriculum and library procedures, the president provided a two-week period for the retiring librarian, Mrs. Austin, and Miss Rust to work together. Miss Rust found Mrs. Austin charming, gracious, and kind. She gave a tea in her home for Miss Rust's introduction to faculty members, student leaders, and townspeople involved in cultural activities.

Six months ago a private foundation had given a sizable grant for book purchases. The money had to be spent within twelve months. Mrs. Austin said that about one-third of the money had been spent and that Miss Rust's immediate concern should be selecting materials to be purchased with the rest of the money. It would take a minimum of two months for the invoices to clear the business office after publications were received in the library. This meant that Miss Rust should spend the rest of the money within four months.

Mrs. Austin showed Miss Rust all the financial records, which were filed in a cardboard box. Mrs. Austin explained that the three filing cabinets in the librarian's office had been full for several years, so new filing went into cardboard boxes which she had picked up at a grocery store. The two librarians did not go over the records together because of lack of time. Since the library seemed to be operating smoothly, Miss Rust assumed that the financial accounts were up to date, accurate, and complete. She soon learned, however, that the library was almost totally unorganized, with no written procedures and poor operating procedures.

A week or so after Miss Rust had taken charge, she went to the financial file to study the records and to learn the exact amount remaining in the grant fund. She could find no accounting record of any kind. She asked the assistant librarian if it might be kept in another place. He said that he was certain Mrs. Austin kept no accounts herself but relied on statements from the business office. Miss Rust had found a business office statement that was two months old. When she telephoned the business office for an up-to-date statement, she was told that nothing newer was available because they were behind in their work.

More searching in the files revealed that no procedures had been set up for approving invoices. In addition, invoices sometimes came to the library and sometimes to the business office. If they came to the business office, they were not sent to the library for checking. Miss Rust telephoned for an appointment with the head of the business office to inquire about its procedures and records; she hoped that she could set up library accounting procedures which would conform to business office practices. Mr. Brown showed Miss Rust the ledgers in which all paid invoices were recorded and the cabinets where invoices were filed after payment. He agreed that henceforth all library invoices would be sent to Miss Rust for approval before his staff handled them. They agreed on the method of approval: a rubber stamp containing items that Miss Rust was to check and initial. Miss Rust walked away from this conference feeling that she had made some headway in initiating orderly accounting methods.

Having decided that she had to know the exact balance at all times, she set up a bookkeeping ledger that showed precisely what was left in each fund and each item of her budget. She found the file of requisitions and had her clerk-typist arrange them chronologically and record them in the ledger. Then having obtained Mr. Brown's permission to record all paid invoices that were in his files, she and her clerk discovered that some invoices had been paid two or three times. Mr. Brown was glad to have this brought to his attention and said he would caution his staff to be more careful. But, he added, they were so far behind that sometimes a second or third invoice was received before they got around to paying the first one. Miss Rust pointed out that if invoices were not paid within a given period, discounts were lost. Mr. Brown knew this but appeared to be unable or unwilling to improve his procedures. When Miss Rust inquired about the procedure for obtaining refunds on invoices paid more than once, she was told that a form letter was sent out.

Some invoices which came to the library were second or third reminders for payment of shipments that had been sent six months previously, or even earlier. Miss Rust checked each of these with the business office to find out why they had not been paid. Most of the original invoices were found in an untouched pile of papers.

She had received complaints from faculty members and students that the best newspaper in the state, published in the largest city, was not being received at the library. When she telephoned the newspaper, she was told that the subscription had expired. Then, in looking through the requisitions, she discovered that a renewal had been requisitioned three months earlier. A telephone call to the business office revealed that before they had paid the first invoice, a representative from the paper had come with a copy of the invoice and had threatened to stop the subscription if payment was not made. That person had been paid in cash and had initialed the invoice. Miss Rust reported this information to the newspaper office. When a search of the files revealed no record of such a transaction, the newspaper office asked for the name of the person who had received the cash. The business office could not supply this information, as only initials were on the paid invoice. The newspaper office could not identify the initials as anyone in its employ and insisted that the invoice be paid by check to the main newspaper office before it would renew the subscription.

As she looked over the new ledger, Miss Rust observed that no invoices had yet been received for many requisitions placed three months earlier, although she knew that the books ordered on those requisitions had arrived. Another conference with Mr. Brown and a check of the files revealed that the invoices had come to the business office and that they had been paid without Miss Rust's approval--a complete disregard for the procedure that they had agreed upon. Mr. Brown's only answer was, "Sorry, guess somebody slipped up." Miss Rust was exasperated and shocked by such inefficiency.

* * *

If you had been Miss Rust, would you have gone directly to the president of the college with this problem? Of course, she was new on the faculty and the business manager had been there for more than twenty years. How would you have solved her problem?

Case 57

A GIFT WITH STIPULATIONS

Over the years the librarians at Rockville State College sought gifts from individuals to supplement an inadequate budget. Recently, Melba Conover, a patron of the symphony orchestra, which is located in the state capital about 80 miles away, offered to give the library $25,000 for increasing interest and appreciation in music.

She stipulated two conditions:
1. The money was to be spent on a definite program to foster appreciation among non-musicians, to add materials and personnel to the humanities division of the library, and to create small groups who would listen to music while

156 / Library Management

following the scores, and who would also study the history and development of music.

2. The program was not to be under the direction of George Blair, who had been Head of the Humanities Division for fifteen years.

The second condition of the gift created a problem. Mrs. Conover had hinted strongly that Mr. Blair should be replaced, although this was not a condition of her gift. She thought that Mr. Blair neither gave good service in this department nor had the personal enthusiasm or educational viewpoint necessary for directing the present program.

Robert Magnus, Librarian of Rockville State College, knew that Mr. Blair maintained an excellent collection and administered his division well. However, Mr. Blair had never become involved with the art and music interest groups in the college or the community, and he was not a particularly sociable person, although he maintained good working relations with his staff.

* * *

If you were Robert Magnus, would you accept or reject this gift? Here are details about the institution and its library which may help you in making decisions:

Type of institution: co-educational; state-supported.
Enrollment: 10,500 (7,500 men; 3,000 women).
Curriculum: Agriculture, engineering, veterinary medicine, home economics, arts and sciences (includes small departments of art and music appreciation).
Library: 940,000 volumes; small collection of phonorecords and tapes, two small listening rooms, microfilm and microcard readers. Collections and reading rooms arranged by subjects: humanities, social science, science and technology. (Each subject area is on a separate floor.) Audio-visual services are in the library and under the direction of the librarian.
Librarian: Robert Magnus, age 45; Ph.D. in library science; 20 years experience in college libraries. Planned and built the present library in 1960.
Head of Humanities Division: George Blair, age 50; B.A. in history; M.A. in musicology.

Case 58

A FACULTY LIBRARY COMMITTEE MEMBER

The library committee of Cole College consists of seven faculty members who meet regularly four times a year and who elect a new chairman each year from their group. Appointment to the committee is made upon the recommendation of department chairmen.

The committee usually works well because its members clearly understand that their relation to the library is advisory, not administrative. Discussions at meetings center around budget requests, student and faculty use of the library, library hours, stack privileges, and similar matters. The committee has, on occasion, suggested to the librarian areas in which the collection might be strengthened, but rarely or never recommends single titles for purchase. No committee recommendations, however, are considered binding upon the librarian, whose duty it is to make the final decisions.

For several years, one member of the committee, Thomas Beardsley, has annoyed the librarian. Professor Beardsley frequently inspects the books for duplicate exchange. More often than not, he finds books which, in his opinion, should be kept. Once he sided with a department head who refused to put into effect certain changes that the director had suggested. Professor Beardsley frequently goes to the cataloging department to check on the size of the backlog.

Since Professor Beardsley is chairman of the library committee for this year, the librarian anticipates more trouble than he has had in the past. He has heard rumors that Professor Beardsley believes that the library committee should help the librarian prepare the annual budget and that it should be approved by the committee before the librarian presents it to the president.

* * *

If you were the head librarian, would you take action now to head off Professor Beardsley? If so, what? What are the functions of a faculty library committee?

Case 59

A PILFERAGE RACKET

The Dunn Historical Collection of Metropolitan Public Library contained many rare documents, books, and letters. Recently, when the curator, Albert Crow, was preparing an exhibit of rare books and archival materials to display during the city's 175th anniversary celebration, he spotted an interesting volume appropriately clothed in a dusty, old black binding. It proved to contain British political and religious pamphlets written between 1648 and 1651. Close investigation revealed an inscription in gold on the binding, "Gift of G. III," and a British Museum stamp inside the book. He wrote the British Museum about the book and learned that it was part of a collection of bound volumes of pamphlets and newspapers given to the Museum by King George III. Upon checking the collection after receipt of Mr. Crow's letter, it was discovered that nineteen volumes were missing.

Metropolitan Library records showed that the volume had been given to the Dunn Collection six months ago by a local resident who was an avid rare book collector. A phone call to the donor revealed that he had obtained the volume from a book dealer in New York City who, in turn, had purchased it from an "English" couple. Before returning the volume to the British Museum, Mr. Crow notified the FBI of the theft. The FBI had quite a file on the activities of this couple, who were wanted in seven states and nine cities for thefts of rare items from various public, university, and governmental libraries. Descriptions of the couple and their mode of operation were supplied Mr. Crow by the FBI. No photographs of the couple had ever been obtained. So far, they had eluded every trap set for them. The FBI agents said that the pair were members of a highly organized and profitable national pilferage operation. Historical documents and rare books were stolen from libraries throughout the nation and then sold to rare book and autograph dealers, private collectors, and libraries. Mr. Crow distributed photocopies of this information to all members of the library staff as well as to Metropolitan City's dealers and collectors--just in case the couple should show up in that city.

A few weeks later, a well dressed, attractive woman came to Mr. Crow's office offering to sell four letters which she claimed she inherited with other family papers.

All of the letters had been written by prominent American statesmen in the early 1800's.

Mr. Crow asked the usual routine questions about the letters and examined them for authenticity. The woman said she was offering them for sale because she needed the money. Mr. Crow was interested in acquiring the letters for the collection but the price she was asking was high and he would need the approval of the library director to purchase them. He suggested that she return the following day.

Later in the day Mr. Crow's assistant reported, "Yesterday a spectacled man with a scholar's stoop came to the reading room and asked to see some pamphlets on early history of the state. I took him to the stacks and showed him the boxes in which pamphlets on this subject were kept. He selected some of them and spent several hours in the reading room industriously taking notes before returning them to the desk. This morning, he came back, chose more boxes of pamphlets, and again took more notes. When I returned from lunch, I found he had left. I checked the boxes to see whether the pamphlets had been filed in correct order in the boxes and discovered that all of ours were missing and had been replaced with others which looked like ours but were not on the same subject." Mr. Crow examined the substitute pamphlets and found them to be worthless.

The appearance of the woman selling rare letters and the thefts on the same day made Mr. Crow and his assistant wonder if this might be the couple wanted by the FBI because they answered the general description furnished them. They reported the incident and their suspicions to the director of the library who, in turn, called the FBI. An agent came at once to the library and instructed Mr. Crow to meet Mrs. Towhee as scheduled the following day. The man arrived early the next morning in the director's office and demanded he be allowed to use restricted areas of the library "for research." These areas had been denied to him the previous day by the staff of the Historical Collection. The director granted the permission. An FBI agent and a library staff member observed him all the time he was in the restricted areas. They saw him hide in his clothing: an eighteenth century diary, a journal of an 1835-36 expedition to the Rocky Mountains, and a rare 1776 treatise on wagons. The FBI agents searched and arrested him as he left the library. Another agent followed Mrs. Towhee to her apartment when she left the library and arrested her after a search of the apartment. In the apartment, agents found seven suitcases full of historical papers, and priceless documents stolen from various libraries. They also found about one hundred forged documents among the legitimate papers. The approximate value of all documents was estimated at $500,000. The two were arraigned on a charge of transporting stolen documents across state lines and on three mail fraud warrants. They were convicted in Federal Court and each was sentenced to ten years in Federal prison. They also faced separate indictments from seven states on charges of theft from libraries.

The arrest and trial of Mr. and Mrs. Towhee led the FBI to the master mind of the pilferage operation--a rare book dealer, Mr. Gadwall, in New York City, and another one of his traveling thieves, Mr. Ibis. Mr. Gadwall knew the rare book market; he would spot valuable items in libraries, planned itineraries for Mr. Ibis and the Towhees, and told them which items to steal from which libraries. He also taught them tricks of thievery; he provided the men with capacious top coats which had large inside pockets in which stolen books and manuscripts could be concealed. He taught Mrs. Towhee how to walk normally even though she was holding stolen volumes between her legs and how to conceal single sheets and pamphlets in her clothing. Also, she was taught approaches to sell items and was supplied with names and addresses of rare book collectors and librarians.

Mr. Gadwall paid the three thieves on the basis of the value of what they stole; then he sold the items for whatever higher price the market would bear. He removed all embossing stamps by heating a large spoon and using a bowl as a flat iron to smooth out the embossing. Frequently he sent Mr. Ibis to London with quantities of valuable stolen items disguised between commonplace bindings. Some of these he sold to certain book dealers. Others, which contained library stamps of ownership, were taken to a skillful binder who removed the stamped portions of pages, matched the paper with old paper from his stock (either exactly or by imitating aging of the paper with chemicals and heat). Then he wove the paper into the mutilated page replacing the sections removed. If printing had been on the removed section, it was replaced from old types, imprinted by hand with ink mixed to match the old ink. Mr. Ibis would then return to the United States with the "restored" volumes for Mr. Gadwall to sell.

This experience with the Towhees and the information about the operation of the theft ring made the staff of Metropolitan Public Library keenly aware of the vulnerability of the total collection to organized theft. The question of security was on the agenda for the next meeting of the administrative council, which was composed of the heads of all departments and divisions. The chief of public services reported "staggering" book losses in recent years. For example, during the last two years, the Metropolitan Library System had lost the equivalent of the entire book stock of five branch libraries. Book losses, through non-return, theft and mutilation, had cost the library about $500,000 per year for the past two years, or 7.1 per cent of the total library budget. The last inventory taken of non-fiction books showed a loss of 48,000 volumes per year. In addition, messengers were sent after another 71,000 volumes which were never returned.

To combat this loss problem, the council came up with three recommendations: 1) that the staff increase their vigilance; 2) that the staff observe and study the problem in order to identify when losses were heaviest in the various library agencies; and 3) that a Security Unit be established which would be staffed by retired investigators and former members of the city's Police Department.

* * *

Can you suggest other security measures?

Case 60

HARASSMENT AT STONECHAT BRANCH

The whole summer of 1974 had been one of harassment and tension for the staff of the Stonechat Branch of a large city public library. The staff consisted of Mrs. Floyd (librarian), Mrs. Julian (children's librarian), Miss Elder (part-time circulation assistant), and high school pages. Here are a few examples of incidents which occurred.

From two to twelve black boys and girls would come in for water at the drinking fountain and then saunter around the library disturbing and annoying both staff and readers by turning over chairs, running around and flipping periodicals onto the floor, and noisily opening and closing catalog drawers.

Saturday afternoons were usually very quiet during the

summer, so only one staff member and a page were normally scheduled to work. On one of these afternoons, Mrs. Floyd was busy helping some patrons at the desk and an inexperienced page was shelving books some distance away. About ten teenagers (who were clearly not patrons) came in and dispersed throughout the library. Several gathered around the desk and monopolized Mrs. Floyd by asking many questions. Others went into the children's area and knocked over a shelf of books--which drew Mrs. Floyd away from the desk. While she was thus engaged, one boy quickly and silently went behind the desk and emptied the cash drawer while another searched the workroom and found both Mrs. Floyd's and the page's purses and took all the money in each. The gang then ran out of the library shouting triumphantly. Mrs. Floyd reported this incident to the Director of Libraries Monday morning.

The following Wednesday evening a group of teenage youths came in. Mrs. Floyd recognized them as the same group which had caused the disturbance Saturday afternoon. She asked them either to sit down quietly and read or leave. They became verbally abusive. She called the police from the desk while the boys were milling around. Mrs. Floyd went to the workroom to lock it and found one young man ransacking the desks and files. By this time she was very angry and tried to stop him, hoping to hold him until the police came. He pulled away, pushed her back so that she fell on the floor, and ran out of the library. By the time the police arrived, none of the boys was in sight.

Several nights later, Mrs. Julian, the children's librarian, Miss Elder, and a page were working. Six boys came in and walked among the reading tables talking to students who were studying. Mrs. Julian asked the boys to leave unless they wished to read. The leader was offended and began to feint slaps at her face. When she did not flinch, he tapped her on the cheek. She went to the desk to call the police and he disconnected the phone. Then he picked up a large periodical and threw it at her, hitting her on the shoulder. Then, they all made a hasty exit, laughing as they went.

A favorite maneuver, repeated many times, was for a group to come just before closing time (9 p.m.), sit at tables near the circulation desk, mumble and stare, and refuse to budge when closing time was announced.

Despite all the scuffling, whistling, horseplay, thefts, and other harassment, the staff managed to keep a semblance of order during the summer and patrons continued to use the collection about as much as they had in previous years. On several occasions it had been necessary to call the police but only one time did they see the offenders. Because the police had been so slow in answering the calls, the staff had decided to try to manage the discipline themselves if at all possible. They were reasonably successful until early September when two incidents convinced the branch staff as well as the administrative staff of the library system that some drastic changes would have to be made.

The supervisor of branches, Mrs. Maru, came to Stonechat Branch one day early in September for one of her regularly scheduled routine visits. When she left (about 5 p.m.), she walked out the back door to the parking lot carrying her purse loosely on her left arm. Mrs. Floyd was on her right, walking out to the car with her as a gesture of courtesy. They noticed three boys, who appeared to be about fourteen or fifteen years old, loitering near the building but did not pay much attention to them. Suddenly the women were accosted--one boy forced his way between the two women and pushed them apart, another grabbed Mrs. Floyd's right arm and pulled her farther to the right, and the third boy slid his right arm under Mrs. Maru's left arm and wrenched the purse off her arm; in the process, she lost her balance and fell to her knees on the pavement. Then all three boys ran as fast as they could. The two women screamed and a patron just getting out of his car saw what happened and pursued the boys. When he was about to overtake them, they dropped the purse; he retrieved it, picked up the contents which had been strewn along the path of flight, and returned the purse to Mrs. Maru. The latter was examining her bruised and bleeding knees and torn hose, and was shaking all over from shock. At Mrs. Floyd's insistence, she went into the library, administered first aid to her knees, and lay on a cot for a while before going back out to her car.

By the time she reached her home, her knees were very painful; and, during the night, she experienced increasing pain in her left shoulder, arm, and hand; one finger was swollen to twice its normal size. The next morning she consulted a physician who found the muscles in her arm and shoulder had been badly wrenched and told her they would be painful for several days but that no permanent damage had been done. The swollen finger had been dislocated about a year previously and the yanking of the purse handle from her hand had aggravated the old injury.

The second incident which made evident the necessity for some drastic changes in handling harassment occurred two days later. Several times during the afternoon a gang

of local teen-aged youths drifted in and out of the library
making as much noise as possible under pretense of looking
at magazines. The staff could not recall that any of the
gang had ever checked out any library material; they ignored these deliberate bids for attention and continued with
their normal work routines. When Mrs. Floyd heard the
small chairs in the children's area being bumped about,
she investigated. The gang leader, a stocky black youth,
and some of his friends were sitting on the table and were
in the process of turning the chairs around so they could
put their feet on them. With restraint, Mrs. Floyd said,
"Aren't you fellows a little large to be in the children's
area?" One of them replied quickly, "We're helping this
little girl get her lessons," and they all laughed tauntingly.
Others of the gang drifted in and stood around.

    Mrs. Floyd watched and listened for a few minutes
and again reminded them that they did not belong on that
side of the library. She also told them that the library
staff were glad to have teenagers use the library but sitting
on the tables with feet in chairs was not proper use. That
elicited a hilarious hoot from one and mutters back and
forth from the others. Mrs. Floyd stood there quietly and
those who were standing drifted toward the door. The
leader tried to get the child to leave but when she would
not, he brought up the rear of the apparent retreat.

    By this time Mrs. Floyd had returned to the desk.
As the youth passed her she said quietly, but angrily, "I
don't want you to come back in here again." At his im-
pudent question of "Why?" she told him that he had been in
dozens of times causing disturbances. This brought on a
tirade of vile, abusive, threatening language and the announcement that he would come in whenever he chose. He
came behind the desk, pushed his forefinger repeatedly to
within an inch of her nose, dared her to call the police,
and continued to spit out filthy names at her. She finally
said defiantly, "Just why don't you hit me if that's the way
you feel?" However, he just kept up the name calling.
Since some of the gang had gone outside, she decided that
she would try to lock them out and him in and call the police. She went to get the key.

    When she came back out of the office he followed
her. At the door he grabbed her arms and slung her away
from the door. Before she knew what she was doing, she
slapped him--hard. Of course that gave him the excuse he
wanted. He punched her chest and arms with his fists
while his gang looked on with obvious enjoyment. She did
not fall to the floor, but fell against a radiator. She

turned to his friends and asked if they were not going to stop him. They thought that was hilarious and answered, "You hit him first." She took the blows without a whimper, but was so stupified at all the filthy talk and general savage behavior that she could only shake her head in pity. This increased his anger. A white teenager came to see what was going on and she persuaded him and the page to stand back, because she knew the gang wanted to cause a riot. The leader kept daring her to call the police, but she thought they would mob anyone who did, so she just "took it." Finally a younger boy on the steps persuaded the leader to leave.

    Mrs. Floyd went back to the office, took some aspirin, and started to write a report of the incident to send to the Director of Libraries. About twenty minutes later Mrs. Elder came in to tell Mrs. Floyd that a woman wanted to talk to her. A crowd of about fifteen persons were standing there--six to ten of the gang, some other large young men, and some women and children.

    The leader's aunt accused Mrs. Floyd of mistreating a child (he was supposed to be only sixteen years of age, but he had the physique of a man). He had also told her that Mrs. Floyd had said, "Niggers don't have no sense." Mrs. Floyd asked who heard her say it and two youths volunteered that they had. She saw that he could get "proof" of anything he chose to report, so she decided to depend on any sense of fairness which the woman had. The woman listened resentfully, for she did not want to believe that the staff had been fair to black children. She closed the session by turning angrily to him and saying, "If you're not in here, they can't do anything to you, so you just stay away!" They left with mutterings of "show them" and curses. Mrs. Floyd was relieved and pleased that the woman had enforced the order which Mrs. Floyd had earlier not succeeded in enforcing.

    The next morning Mrs. Floyd called the Director of Libraries to report the incident and asked for police protection for the library until the gang of boys was apprehended. He inquired about the injuries and insisted that she see a physician. Although her body ached all over, her chest and arms were black and blue and her shoulder swollen and bruised, the physician could find no permanent damage.

    A special meeting of the Board of Trustees was called for the purpose of considering what action should be taken concerning the incidents at Stonechat Branch involving the safety of the staff there. The Board decided that the two most important factors involved were maintenance of public service and the safety of the library's employees. In order to provide for both, the trustees curtailed hours at the branch so that the full staff could be on duty when the library was open.

The Director informed the city's Urban League, the Human Relations Commission, and the Community Action Commission of the harassment during the summer. The Urban League offered to conduct an investigation. The head of the Human Relations Commission suggested that he organize a program to try to change the attitudes of these groups of young people, and the Community Action Commission promised cooperation in handling discipline in the library.

* * *

Evaluate the handling of these incidents and the decisions of the trustees.

Case 61

CITY HALL

The government of Jordan, a city of about 500,000 population, had an unsavory political reputation. The structure of the city government was such that the mayor and city council had little control over the various boards except that board members were appointed by the mayor. Many municipal functions were handled by semi-independent agencies, such as the Park and Recreation Commission, the Sewer and Water Board, and the Public Library Board. The "old regulars" among the politicians wanted to run every appointed board as well as everything else in the city government.

The Jordan Library Board consisted of eleven appointed members who served nine-year terms that overlapped so that the terms of not more than two members of the board expired in any one year. In practice, though, the board was essentially self-perpetuating because either the same individuals were reappointed upon expiration of their terms or their relatives or close friends were appointed. The members represented the wealthy "upper crust," old-line families of the city: one physician, two lawyers, one dentist, one banker, three businessmen and three housewives. The board did not fully represent the population of the city; there were no representatives from labor, ethnic groups, the clergy, women's clubs, parent-teacher organizations, or the schools.

The board members had other interests; they served on other boards and had little time to fulfill their responsibilities as library board members. One member had been on the board for twenty-one years but had not attended a meeting for years. Board service was a status symbol. Rarely did board members use any of the library's collections or services. They were more interested in maintaining their public image than in acting as spokesmen for the library to the people of the city. Their meetings, often disorderly and noisy, were rarely conducted according to parliamentary rules. An inordinate amount of time at the meetings was spent on trivia, so that there was little time for long-term planning. They lacked concern for staff morale and welfare; they confused policy and administration and would not listen to the successive directors of the libraries who tried to point out that they were a policy-making body and that the director of libraries and his administrative staff were supposed to be responsible for administration and should be allowed to do it without interference. The various directors pointed out to them that it was the board's job to justify the library budgets to the people of the city as well as to the politicians.

The library consisted of a main building in the center of the city, nine branches throughout the city, and several bookmobiles. The collection totaled about 500,000 volumes. The library had never been adequately supported, and as a consequence, the collection was not as large or as well selected as would be expected in a city of that size. Low salaries had resulted in the promotion of many staff members through civil service examination rather than the employment of library school graduates. The "old guard" among the staff rather resented anyone being employed in an administrative position who had not grown up in the city or the state. The library system had become virtually petrified.

In the past five years the library had had three directors. The board, having found no person on the staff qualified to be promoted to director, had each time employed someone from outside the state. A city hall spokesman had suggested that the job should be given to a citizen of the state, but board members had pointed out that since this was the largest public library in the state, a librarian coming from a smaller system would not be prepared to handle such a large staff and budget. The first of the three directors was a woman and the second and third were men. The first two had been exceptionally well qualified by education and experience to head this library system. They had had good ideas for improving the system and each had succeeded in making some changes, but they had not stayed long because of the political climate, the indifferent board, and staff dissension. Both of the former directors had found it impossible to run the library on a professional, non-political basis.

  The third director, Patrick Keenan, also well qualified, was employed thirteen months ago after an extensive nationwide search. Several of Mr. Keenan's professional friends had warned him before he accepted the position that he was not equal to this "big league" political situation. He had successfully handled two public library administrative positions, however, and was confident he could handle this one. Patrick Keenan's friends characterized him as aggressive, ambitious, egotistical, and very sure of himself.

  Soon after accepting the position he boasted to some of his friends at a national library meeting that he was going to "shake up" some "entrenched" members of the staff, get rid of some "dead wood," and reorganize the whole system. Unfortunately this statement got back to his staff. His predecessors had also recognized the need for drastic reorganization and staff changes but, having believed that they must prepare the staff for change, had tried to do so by involving the staff. Since such methods had been used, change had been slow. Keenan soon learned that because all city employees were under a city civil service commission, he did not have a free hand in hiring and firing employees.

  Mr. Keenan was appalled at the backlog of orders and cataloging he found. Also, many time-consuming "old-fashioned" procedures and methods were being used throughout the system. Most of the department heads had been in their positions for a long time, were comfortably in a "rut," and believed that they were doing an adequate job. Keenan realized that modern ideas must be introduced to bring the library services up to current standards. The branches were in even worse shape than the main library. He decided to work according to a long-range plan, carefully considering each future move.

  To begin with, he closed two branches. Circulation at these two libraries had been steadily dropping for several years, and the buildings badly needed repair. Although the board approved this move as an economy measure, it did not back up Mr. Keenan when city hall, the newspapers, and the residents of the areas involved strenuously objected to the closing. Keenan was forced to reopen the branches.

To improve staff and services in the branches, he reassigned the head of reference (who had been in his position twenty-five years) as librarian in the largest branch. In his place a chief of adult services responsible for reference, extension, and circulation was employed. The heads of cataloging and acquisitions were transferred to branches and were replaced by a chief of technical services. A new position, assistant director in charge of personnel, was created. For each of these three new positions, Mr. Keenan searched the nation for qualified people and found two men and one woman whom he employed. All of them were in their thirties and had had excellent education and experience. Keenan had to request special consideration by the city civil service board to waive certain requirements for one job in order to employ the person of his choice. A member of the city council was quoted in the newspaper as objecting strenuously to this action.

To improve public relations, Keenan asked the board to pay dues for him in several local civic organizations. In the past, only a very few staff members attended or participated in professional library organizations. Believing that the staff needed upgrading, Keenan proposed to the board that it help defray the expenses for a certain percentage of the staff to attend various state and national library meetings. Policies and rules were worked out to make the opportunity equally available to all professional members of the staff. A certain percentage could go at any one time; they would be given the time off and the equivalent of round-trip coach air fare. Each staff member would have to pay the rest of his expenses himself.

All of these changes were too much for many old employees. They resented being stirred out of their "ruts" by a new young administrator. The staff association prepared a letter to Mr. Keenan; it was signed by fifty-eight of the seventy-five members of the association:

> Mr. Patrick Keenan, Director
> Jordan Public Library
>
> Dear Mr. Keenan:
> You have made great strides toward improving the library. In making such changes we realize you must take some drastic steps, sometimes unpleasant to the staff. We are not opposed to changes that are carefully planned and executed;

but we do object to abrupt changes without any warning. For example, although the city civil service makes the firing of permanent staff members difficult, no protection is provided against our being transferred to positions for which we have little experience or training and/or to positions of lesser importance which will eventually lead towards demotion. The number of transfers already made has caused the staff to be apprehensive about the stability of their jobs and, as a result, has lowered the morale of the staff. We work in an atmosphere of fear and distrust, resulting in great part from the sudden and unexplained shifting of staff members to new positions.

We realize that the ultimate decisions in administering the library are left to the discretion of the director. However, in situations directly affecting the staff, we believe that the staff should be included in the planning. In the past, staff opinion has not been given serious consideration; on the contrary, when our opinions have been expressed, they have been disregarded.

We respectfully request that the staff be included in your deliberations concerning future changes.

The Jordan Public Library Staff Association

Mr. Keenan acknowledged the letter and made a few attempts to include some of the staff in decision-making, but he lacked the patience to utilize the democratic process. He considered the staff association a social organization. Consequently, he continued to irritate the staff by making more changes and became increasingly unpopular. The "grapevine" was used to the fullest by malcontents who wanted to "get even" with him for some of his decisions. News of this discontent reached a member of the city council, Mr. Thomas, who saw a chance to get his name in the newspapers and to boost his political potential for future elections. Probably other politicians were also involved in what followed.

In a long letter addressed to the chairman of the library board, Mr. Thomas accused Patrick Keenan of malfeasance in the conduct of his office and said the library board probably should consider his dismissal. Mr. Thomas sent copies of his letter to the mayor, the members of the city council and the library board, and to the news media.

He told a reporter that he felt obligated to make the information public. His name, then, appeared in large-type headlines in all the newspapers for as long as the charges made news. He claimed that his statements were based on facts supplied him by library employees.

Board members, angry because Thomas had released the letter to the news media, claimed that he had done so for his own political advantage. According to the city charter, only the city council as a group could bring charges of neglect of duty or gross misconduct against any person appointed to a position not covered by civil service. Thomas countered by saying that he had not brought charges against Keenan but simply had provided information to the library board for action.

His charges included: 1) Keenan's poor judgment in closing two branch libraries; 2) the director's attitude toward fringe benefits for the staff at taxpayers' expense (helping to defray the cost of attending professional meetings); 3) the appointment of staff not on the civil service lists; 4) the high cost of entertaining important library visitors; and 5) the lack of consideration for old-time staff members by shifting them to new positions suddenly and without explanation.

Board members took the charges as a personal affront to their integrity and honesty. One board member contended that by making the charges public through the news media, Thomas intended to reflect unfavorably on the board. Another board member, who was actively campaigning for election to a city office on another political party ticket, considered the charges an attempt to discredit him and cost him votes in the upcoming election. The staff members who gave the information on which Thomas based his charges remained anonymous. The president of the board instructed Thomas to bring his informers to a board meeting, where they could make their charges.

Keenan advised the board to take a firm stand against Thomas because he represented city hall interference in library affairs. He told its members that the city charter provided that the library board and only the library board was to control and provide for the administration of the city's libraries. When Thomas, as a member of the city council, listened to discontented staff members and bypassed the board in making the charges public, he interfered in the administration of the library. Keenan told the board that it should react quickly and strongly in indicating its resentment to such interference, that the city charter specified that the librarian was responsible solely to the board, and the board, in turn, must protect the librarian.

* * *

Should the board ignore the charges of Mr. Thomas, which were clearly a form of political interference? If you were Mr. Keenan what action would you take?

Case 62

OVERDUES

The Niper Regional Library system, which serves three counties, represents a merger of five small libraries. It has a seven-member library board, three members of which had served as trustees in their counties before the merger. A large part of the region is served by a successful, popular bookmobile operation. Since the collection of the regional system is not yet as large as it should be, the bookmobile librarians are always concerned when patrons keep books longer than the usual loan period. One of the worst offenders had been Mrs. Georgia Dunn, wife of a board member.

The first notice for overdues is a postcard requesting the return of the charged-out materials. The second notice reads in part as follows:

> Our records show that the books listed below are charged out to you. We sent you a notice on _____ requesting their return. We have not received any response from you. It is the policy of the Niper Regional Library system to serve all patrons on an equal basis. Unless all materials are returned promptly we cannot do so. Please return the books immediately.
>
> Sincerely yours,
>
> James Windsor
> Circulation Librarian
>
> cc: Mrs. Claudia Moore
> Director, Niper Regional Library system

Several days after a second notice had been sent to Mrs. Dunn, Mrs. Moore received an answer. Mrs. Dunn was furious that such a "rude" letter had been sent to her.

She informed Mrs. Moore that this matter would come up for discussion at the next board meeting. In her letter Mrs. Dunn admitted that she had received notices in the past but stated that she had always returned the books. She refused to admit that the books had been overdue through any fault of hers.

When Mrs. Moore checked with the head of circulation she found that although Mrs. Dunn was a habitual offender, she had never before been sent a second notice because she had returned the materials before the deadline. All the records showed that Mrs. Dunn had not yet returned the requested books. Mrs. Moore immediately wrote Mrs. Dunn a letter in which she said:

> Everyone makes mistakes occasionally, and of course the staff of the Niper Public Library is no exception. To make sure that the letter you received was not in error, I personally checked our records in the circulation department. The materials are still charged out to you.
>
> The staff of the circulation department is anxious to follow the procedures set forth by the library administration and approved by the library board. One of the most important steps in the operational program is to see that all materials purchased by all taxpayers are returned promptly, so that they are readily available to any taxpayer who might wish to see them.

A few days later Mrs. Moore received another letter from Mrs. Dunn. The letter said:

> This is not the first time I have received notices from the library, although it is the first time I have ever received such a rude and threatening letter. Please check your records again. I am certain I have returned all the books you allege I have. Since you have made so many mistakes in the past, you have undoubtedly made another.

* * *

Should the wife of a library head member be extended special privileges? Do you consider the second notice "rude and threatening"? Are circulation rules and regulations a responsibility of the head?

Case 63

CENSORSHIP

After a long and heated campaign, the state librarian of a very conservative area succeeded in starting a federally funded bookmobile demonstration project. One of the bookmobile's regular stops was in the playground of a large consolidated school.

One day a teacher in the school heard a tenth grade girl snickering as she glanced through a book. When the teacher investigated, she discovered that the student was reading Catcher in the Rye. The teacher immediately took both student and book to the superintendent who, in turn, went to the bookmobile librarian and told her that he was horrified that she would allow such a book to fall into the hands of a child. The librarian explained that Catcher in the Rye appeared on many lists of recommended books. She also tried to explain to the irate superintendent that the bookmobile served all groups in the population, not just students, and that it was a public library, not a school library. Furthermore, she saw no reason why a tenth grade student should not read the book. The superintendent left the bookmobile with the book in his hand. As he left he said to the librarian, "I'll see to it that this gets to the right people."

Several days later the director of the bookmobile program received an angry letter from the superintendent, who said that he would allow the bookmobile to stop in the playground only if Catcher in the Rye was removed from the collection. If the librarian agreed to remove this offensive book from the collection, then, and only then, would the bookmobile be allowed to resume its service to the school.

The project director consulted with the bookmobile librarian; they talked to the state school library supervisor, the state librarian, several lawyers, and various elected and appointed government officials. All of them believed that the book should not be removed from the shelves. The bookmobile librarian wanted to continue to serve the community, since there was no local library.

The director wrote to the superintendent and told him that the bookmobile would no longer stop in the playground, since neither he nor the librarian would remove Catcher in the Rye from the bookmobile's collection.

* * *

Censorship is one form of external or indirect control. Do you agree with the decision of the project director?

Case 64

CONTROL OF SPECIAL APPROPRIATION

Last year a small privately endowed liberal arts college applied for accreditation to a regional accrediting agency. A team appointed by the accrediting association visited the college for several days and subsequently sent a copy of its report to the board of trustees. This report included a list of items which would have to be corrected before the college would be approved for accreditation and the suggestion that the college reapply for accreditation as soon as the deficiencies had been removed. The college hopes to be ready to file another application in two years.

One item on the list of deficiencies involved the library: "The collection must be greatly strengthened in reference books, back files of journals, and government documents." The president recently announced in a general faculty meeting that he had allocated special funds to correct some of the deficiencies and specified that the money was to be spent in the next two years to get ready for the second application to the accrediting association. The librarian, a member of the faculty with the rank of associate professor, attended the faculty meeting, as is her custom, and learned that $40,000 had been allocated to the building up of the reference, journal, and government document holdings of the library. The announcement did not state whether the librarian or the faculty would control this sum of money. In the past, about two-thirds of the library budget for books and periodicals has been divided equally among full-time faculty members, and the library staff has been responsible for the remaining third.

The librarian is a genial, intelligent, forthright woman of about thirty-five with high professional ideals. She holds a master's degree from an accredited library school and worked for twelve years in the reference department of a university library; she has been in her present position less than a year. She was rather appalled when she first learned that two-thirds of the book and periodical budget was controlled by the faculty. At the university where she formerly worked, all departmental allotments were abolished several years ago and the library staff had full responsibility for the collection. Faculty cooperation and recommendations were encouraged, of course. She hopes to abolish the faculty allotment system at this college as soon as she has become better acquainted with the faculty members and has built up some rapport with them.

In studying the collection, she has found that certain subject fields need strengthening and that others include much unused material. This imbalance is apparent both in the general collection and in the reference area. She is not yet prepared to start a campaign to change the allotment system, but because of the president's announcement, she knows that she must meet with him before other faculty members present their pleas. She does not want to antagonize the faculty by making changes too suddenly. On the other hand, most members of the faculty are more interested in additional books for their reserved reading shelves and for collateral class reading materials than in reference books. She has not yet learned of any faculty member who is doing serious research, although a few are engaged in writing. Their main interest is teaching. Because of her experience in a good reference department and her study of the holdings in this library, she knows what is needed for the collection, will spend the money wisely, and is determined to get exclusive control of the $40,000.

In the chain of command, the librarian reports to the president. She must act quickly to persuade the president to give her control of the money. She is familiar with research findings relative to faculty selection vs. library staff selection.

* * *

What arguments can the librarian use with the president to convince him that she should control the expenditures of this special appropriation?

Case 65

THE SEALED ENVELOPE

Shortly after the death of Cecil Faxon, a prominent government career employee, his widow presented some of his papers to the Bertram University Library. The files contained mostly technical memoranda, which were made available to students and scholars for study. The widow also presented to the manuscript collection a large sealed envelope containing correspondence between her deceased husband and people still living. These letters she donated with the understanding that the envelope was to be kept sealed for ten years. The librarian signed the agreement.

    About eight years later, during the course of a presidential campaign, sensational charges were made that Cecil Faxon had been a "spy." The case immediately became a subject of national discussion. One day an FBI agent appeared at the library and, asking to study Faxon's papers, was given access to the files. These he found rather dull and uninformative. The curator of manuscripts notified the director of libraries that an agent was in the building. The director requested that the man stop by his office when he had finished his work. When the agent came in, the director told him that he felt obligated to mention the existence of a packet of correspondence which was not available because of the library's agreement with Mrs. Faxon. The agent asked to see the outside of the envelope and wrote a description of it in his notes. He seemed completely satisfied and left.

    Various requests to see the contents of the packet, including a request from a prominent senator, were received during the next few months. All requests were declined with the explanation that the Bertram University Library had an agreement with the donor which under no circumstances could be broken.

    One day the director received a subpoena <u>duces tecum</u> ordering him to appear before a federal grand jury investigating international subversion and to bring the sealed packet. The director informed the president of the university, who called in the university's attorney. After learning details of the problem, the attorney sought out the widow and discussed the matter with her. She agreed at once that the package should be made available to the grand jury, saying that she knew her husband was not a spy and that she would be willing for the authorities to examine any of the papers. The seal on the envelope was broken in the presence of the jury, the contents were itemized, and copies were made available to the jury.

    Since that episode, when sealed files are accepted in this library, some appropriate safeguard making the material available to duly constituted government agencies with investigative powers is written into the agreement.

* * *

Under what terms should gifts be accepted which have restrictions on their use?

Case 66

HOW MUCH AUTONOMY SHOULD A BRANCH LIBRARIAN HAVE?

As soon as Roger Barnes had completed his course work and had received a professional degree in library science, he was offered and accepted the position as librarian in the Industrial Engineering and Management Department library of a large university. Mr. Barnes already had worked in several departments in the main university library as a student assistant and in clerical positions. On the first day of his new job he was met by the director of branch libraries, who opened the door for him, handed him the key, and pointed to a desk. "That's it," she said. "It's sink or swim, Roger."

With no other orientation, Mr. Barnes was plunged into his first professional position. At that time the Industrial Engineering and Management Department library was really no more than a name. Because of a merger between the Industrial Engineering and Industrial Management departments the collections of both departmental libraries were to be integrated. The library was occupying temporary quarters; within a year a new building for the School of Engineering would be completed and the library would be moved into it. The two collections had been hastily moved into these temporary quarters and arranged by a crew of workmen directed by the chairmen of the library committees from the two departments.

The libraries of both departments had traditionally been under faculty control, and their collections reflected the interests of the faculty members who had spent the most time and effort in suggesting books for purchase. Neither library had ever had a professionally trained or even an experienced librarian because the faculty committee could see no need for any special training to administer and maintain records, to handle binding, and to circulate materials. Consequently, the job of "librarian" had usually been awarded to the deserving, but never the able. At one time in the recent past the head of the Industrial Management library had been a sub-professional librarian who had introduced some order and accuracy into its records and its catalog. This was not the case in Industrial Engineering.

Mr. Barnes was faced with an enormous collection of unbound periodicals, an outstanding book order file, which still contained slips for books that had long been on the shelves, and a card catalog from Industrial Engineering which was in such bad order and so crowded that more-knowing patrons searched the shelves rather than use it.

Within a few weeks Mr. Barnes discovered that almost every graduate student in both departments had a key to the library. (He had learned earlier that it was the policy to issue library keys to all faculty members.) All graduate students who had been issued keys were to turn them in when they left the university. But no control existed to insure that this was done, and so many students had apparently turned their keys over to a friend. He decided to issue no more keys to graduate students, but because the academic year was well advanced he could not put the new policy into effect until fall. Each morning when he came to work he found that his desk was covered with call slips on which the information was rarely complete and the names of the borrowers were frequently illegible. Everything circulated overnight. Books, bound and unbound journals, reference materials, and even rare books left the library. Despite the fact that everyone seemed to think such procedure normal, he had been faced several times by an irate faculty member demanding a copy of something which could not be located because of an incomplete or illegible call slip. Many items without any circulation record were missing, so that he had to canvass every office and laboratory in hope that the missing items would turn up. It was not easy to search for these missing books even on the shelves in the library itself because the shelving arrangement was in three sequences.

One of his early reforms had been to keep the library open longer. Under the direction of an experienced student assistant, the library now remained open until nine every night. Although the student assistant had been ordered to expel all non-key holders before the library was locked up at night, many graduate students spent the night in the library, typing papers or studying for exams. On several occasions the non-key holding graduate students refused to leave unless they were bodily removed. The student assistant, who could not or did not care to do this, left them there.

Within a few months Mr. Barnes had established sufficient rapport with the faculty to develop a lending code and a system of rules for use of the library when it was closed as well as when it was open. He established a liberal circulation policy, but it restricted bound journals to one-week circulation and made them subject to immediate recall upon demand. His policy further provided that unbound journals could circulate only by special permission and that books could be checked out for two weeks and even for a semester by graduate students and the faculty, but they were subject also to recall upon demand. Reserve books, however, could circulate only overnight. After the code had been typed, he circulated a copy to the faculty for their comments. Most of them approved it without reservation or change, although some thought that unbound periodicals should circulate with less restriction.

Since no duplicating equipment was available in the library, he called the main library to see how he might get copies of the new regulations reproduced. The clerk who talked to him told him that he would need the approval of the director of branch libraries.

The next day when he telephoned the director to get her approval, he was amazed to hear her say, "You can't do that. All branch libraries have to abide by the loan rules of the main library. You can't circulate journals. I want you to leave things just as they are. Don't change a thing."

After he had recovered somewhat from this surprise, he wondered what he could do. To render any service under present conditions was almost impossible. He thought, "What if I post these rules here in the library complex? What would happen if I did?

*   *   *

What alternative courses of action are available to Mr. Barnes?

Case 67

MISUSE OF SEABROOK COLLEGE LIBRARY

For the past several years the library staff of Seabrook College has become increasingly concerned about the loss of library materials. The library serves about seven hundred students, half of whom reside on campus, and fifty-two faculty members. The collection consists of about 35,000 volumes, pamphlets, tapes and phonograph records, and elementary and secondary curriculum materials for education students. Except for reserve books, the entire collection is on open shelves.

Staff members believe that many books are taken from the library without being charged out. A complete inventory of the entire collection has not been taken for ten years, but many unsuccessful searches for specific titles have convinced the staff that losses are significant. When the housekeeping staff clean dormitory rooms at the end of each semester, they find many books which have not been charged out. At times, groups of books in a specific subject area, several titles by one author, and even the entire collection in a given field are missing from the shelves, yet no checkout record can be found. Some of these books are found in dormitory searches or by students' landlords, or are returned to the book return box outside the library.

Even though the reserve collection is housed in closed stacks and students must request and sign for titles at the desk, approximately sixty volumes have disappeared from the reserve department during the past year. Some students allege that they have returned the books; others claim that the signature on the card is forged and they know nothing about the book. In any case, these books are missing and are in demand for class assignments. So, despite a closed reserve system, many reserve books disappear from the shelves. This frequently happens when an instructor makes assignments in a specific book or places several copies of a book on reserve. Eventually many of these books return, but they are not available when most needed. As many as half of the copies of some books on reserve, along with their charge cards, are permanently lost, thus making it impossible to trace them. For example, during the past year Commager's <u>Documents of American History</u> has been replaced three times.

The staff discovered that one reason why books disappeared from the reserve shelves was that two student assistants were giving books to their friends without charging them out. These students were fired. Perhaps others are doing the same thing.

Reference books are not supposed to circulate, yet they too disappear. Of thirteen sets of encyclopedias purchased in the last five years, only eight complete sets are now on the shelves. At one time during the last academic

year only one set was complete. From some sets as many as a fourth of the volumes are missing.
Other valuable reference works disappear from the shelves each year. One has been replaced three times within the past two years. Some new reference books disappear within several days after processing and are never seen again. Last year a thorough, systematic inventory was taken of the reference collection. Approximately 30 per cent of the collection was missing.
The curriculum collection contains all types of teaching materials furnished by publishers: textbooks, workbooks, supplementary readers, teachers' manuals, and sample tests. These circulate just as the books in the open stacks. A rough count recently revealed that approximately 25 per cent of that collection had disappeared since the last count two years ago. Even though the tapes and phonograph records are charged out at the reserve desk, losses there are also heavy.
At Seabrook College the attitude among the students seems to be "every man for himself" or "get everything you can get when you can get it and don't worry about anybody else."

* * *

Can you suggest security measures which might be adopted at Seabrook?

Case 68

TOO MUCH ADVICE

The plans for the Hadley Medical Foundation building provided for housing two libraries, neither of which had ever employed a professional librarian. Seven months before the building was due to be completed, I, a professional librarian, was employed to organize and administer the joint library. One library served a school of nursing, the other served medical school students and the staff of a teaching hospital. The existing libraries were a city block apart. The nursing library totaled about 2,029 volumes plus an uncounted number of bound journals. It was very crowded. The medical library totaled about 9,737 volumes and many bound and unbound journals, yearbooks, and reports. I decided to make my headquarters in the medical library because there was enough room for me to work until the new building was completed.

My problem was to combine the two collections before moving, at the same time keeping the libraries open forty-five hours a week and the collections available for use. Requests for service increased markedly as soon as I arrived because, for the first time, the students and staff had a librarian who knew how to help them.

The administration of the foundation provided an adequate budget for supplies, equipment, and clerical assistance. I had requested to employ my own clerks but did not succeed in filling the positions for two months and then had to train them. The assistant in the medical library was a reject from another department of the hospital who had worked in that library for two years. When she learned that she could not sit all day at a desk reading but would be required to assume some responsibility for checking, filing, and processing, she resigned. That meant I had one more to train.

I decided not to bring the nursing library over all at once, but to have the books brought over one subject at a time, as fast as we could take care of them. The secretary in the nursing school office was most accommodating in agreeing to send over the books according to a schedule I worked out.

The medical library was classified by the Boston Medical School Library scheme and the nursing library by the National League for Nursing scheme which was originally drawn from several sources including the Boston Medical Library system. The two were not actually incompatible. Both schemes presented some difficulties because they were a bit outdated. The Boston scheme was last revised in 1955 and the Nursing one in 1953. Experienced medical librarians disagreed as to which was best for a small medical-nursing library. Some favored the Boston, others favored the Cunningham classification, but most believed that the National Library of Medicine classification system was the one to adopt. Although it is intended for large collections, it will never be outdated. One medical librarian suggested it would be wise to recatalog the entire library in the NLM classification.

The faculties of the nursing and medical schools and the hospital staff said that my staff and I had insufficient time to recatalog the two collections. They recommended that we retain the nursing books in the National League of Nursing scheme and that all other books be recataloged into the Boston Medical Library scheme. They agreed that this was a matter of expediency and that I should postpone a decision as to recataloging in the National Library of Medicine scheme until I have more staff. But plans call for a greatly expanded collection in the next few years. From the suggested budget I estimate that in three years the collection will exceed 20,000 volumes.

* * *

Who should make the decision about what classification system to use--the faculties and staff or the librarian? On what basis can outsiders determine the advantages and disadvantages of the three classification systems?

Case 69

THE TUPELO FAMILY

For two generations the Tupelo family had been active in politics in the city of Laurel. The present head of the family was the city prosecuting attorney. His wife was very active in the Democratic party and was chairman of the county organization for many years. During her chairmanship she was influential in securing the election of the present mayor seven years ago. One of her "rewards" for this effort was appointment to the county library board as the mayor's personal representative. She liked to "run" various county activities and had been trying to get an appointment to the library board for a number of years.

The board of the Laurel County Library was composed of eleven members--the chairman of the Board of County Commissioners and four members appointed by that Board, the Mayor of Laurel, four members appointed by the City Council, and the county Superintendent of Schools. The chief librarian, of course, was an ex-officio member and secretary of the board.

The Tupelo's only son, Lex, was a secondary school teacher certified to teach English and public speaking. He had been teaching in the Laurel schools for five years at the time his mother was appointed to the library board. His father had wanted him to be a lawyer, but one semester in law school convinced Lex that he was not interested in that profession; so, he returned to teaching. He did not dislike teaching but neither was he enthusiastic about it. Opportunities for promotion were infrequent in the public school system. Lex was ambitious and wanted to move ahead faster. His parents were also ambitious for him.

Three months after Mrs. Tupelo was appointed to the library board, the librarian in charge of public relations and publicity resigned to accept another position. Mrs. Tupelo told Lex about it. The salary was higher than Lex was earning and he thought the job had more prestige and status than that of a teacher. The job specification called for a master's degree in library science, a minimum of three years of library experience, and an ability to speak in public and to write news stories. Mrs. Tupelo talked to the chief librarian, Mr. Corbin, about the job description, suggesting that a teacher of public speaking and English would be qualified to fill this position. Mr. Corbin explained the responsibilities and duties of the position and stated that it must be filled by a librarian. Mrs. Tupelo next went to the Mayor and other politically influential persons in Laurel and asked for their assistance in securing this position for her son. A few days later the chairman of the library board called on Mr. Corbin and told him that if he appointed Lex Tupelo to the vacant library position, the Mayor could assure Mr. Corbin that the county commissioners would transfer to the library budget about $40,000 of uncommitted funds. Mr. Corbin protested that Lex did not have the necessary qualifications for the position. The chairman said, "I thought you would be happy that I was able to get this money for the building renovations you have been requesting for several years. Surely being overly particular about one position is not worth losing all this money." Mr. Corbin was furious to be put in such a situation but he held his tongue. He did point out though, that appointing a relative of a board member constituted nepotism. The chairman said it did not and quoted the following excerpt from the staff personnel manual on nepotism:

> Nepotism: Relatives of library employees cannot be appointed to any position on the staff. This rule applies to all levels--custodial, secretarial, clerical, professional, and specialists.

The chairman claimed that the rule involved relatives of library staff members and did not include relatives of board members. Mr. Corbin replied that even though board members were not specifically mentioned, appointing Lex would constitute bestowal of patronage by reason of relationship rather than merit, because Lex did not meet the job specifications.

At the next library board meeting, the appointment of Lex Tupelo to the position of "Adult Education Specialist" was approved. During the next six years Lex proceeded to build an "empire" of his own within the library. He started discussion groups for every age level from junior high school to senior citizens; one for high school students on how to select a college; a great books series for adults; one for inmates of a boys' reformatory which was located in the county; play reading for senior citizens; and many others. He started speed reading classes and film programs in the main library and all the branches. He co-sponsored programs of all kinds with the Chamber of Commerce, the Better Business Bureau, the county medical society, the American Cancer Society, and others. Arts and crafts classes were held in the main library and the products of these classes were exhibited frequently. These burgeoning activities encroached on the space of other departments in the main library and also took over activities which normally belonged in branch libraries or in such departments as Young Adult, Fine Arts, and Audio-Visual. Although Mr. Corbin refused to increase the budget for the Adult Education Department, Lex managed to find money from outside sources. His colleagues charged that he was too independent and cocky, and "a law unto himself"; they found him to be "an uncooperative prima donna" and hard to work with.

Lex had been in this position for six years. Two months ago Mr. Corbin announced he would retire at the end of this fiscal year. Lex applied for the position.

A search and screening committee of the board was appointed to find a replacement for Mr. Corbin. Mrs. Tupelo was a member of this committee. Their first action was to draw up a list of qualifications for the position:

> The chief librarian of the Laurel Public Library must have a bachelor's degree, have five years of experience as head, assistant head, or business manager of a large library system or as the manager or executive officer of a large organization engaged in public or community service. The examination of the candidate will consist of an evaluation of his personal and professional qualifications, and an interview which would deal with administrative problems. If an applicant is not a librarian, he should, prior to the interview,

familiarize himself with some problems concerning library administration and management.

When the library's professional staff learned of this job specification they speculated that the position was going to be someone's political reward or had been written to fit Lex's qualifications. In a letter to the board, signed by every professional librarian on the staff, the staff protested these qualifications; they demanded that the head librarian have a master's degree in library science and at least five years of administrative library experience. Furthermore, they requested that two library staff members be appointed to the Search and Screening Committee to represent the interests of the staff. Copies of the protest and the request were supplied to all of the local newspapers and to the radio and television stations.

* * *

Has the library staff any means of exerting pressure to prevent a political appointment by the board?

Case 70

SERVICE TO HIGH SCHOOL STUDENTS

On February 1 Mrs. Martha Hunt, librarian of the Tyler County Public Library, posted a notice at the circulation desk that junior and senior high school students could no longer use the non-circulating reference materials or reading room of the library, but that they could still check out books and materials for home use. One of the students affected by the new ruling was the son of the editor of the daily newspaper.

In an interview on February 3, Mrs. Hunt told a reporter that the main purpose of the Tyler County Public Library was to serve mature adults. The library was neither a social club nor a meeting place for teen-agers. During the past year she and her staff had been distracted by the noise and disturbances caused by teen-agers and their demands on the library's collection. Mrs. Hunt added that many valuable reference books and periodicals had been mutilated. She blamed this destruction on students.

The reporter also talked to several board members,

but none of them could remember whether the decision to ban the students from the reference room had been discussed at the last board meeting. He learned that the chairman of the board had personally told Mrs. Hunt that it was all right with him to keep out the students or to do anything else that she thought was necessary to keep peace and quiet in the library and to protect the books and materials.

The next Saturday, staff members had difficulty pushing through a large crowd of students who were carrying signs and an effigy of Mrs. Hunt. The picketing continued all day, and during the following week a small group of high school students marched every afternoon after school and while the library was open in the evening.

The picket line at the library received much publicity. Even the wire services distributed the story. For the first time in the long history of the institution, Mrs. Hunt and the Tyler County Public Library were news.

In a second interview Mrs. Hunt was asked if she could properly refuse service to students, since the city and county schools helped to support the library. Mrs. Hunt said that as far as she knew the school boards had contributed only a few hundred dollars in the past year, and that the support of the public library was not a regular item in the school budgets.

Both the county and city school superintendents immediately contacted the editor of the paper to set the story straight. The city school budget provided $2,000 annually for books to be used in the children's room of the public library; the county school budget provided the salary of a children's librarian who worked in the public library and with the county schools.

Papers all over the state continued to publicize the Tyler County library. Reporters interviewed the state librarian and librarians in neighboring communities. None of them agreed with Mrs. Hunt's statement that the library's sole function was to serve adults. The state librarian threatened the loss of state aid to the Tyler County Public Library unless service to students was restored.

On February 16 the board of trustees met in an executive session. A pre-meeting press release mailed to the editor of the daily newspaper stated that the main purpose of the meeting was to discuss the three-way situation involving the public library, the public school administrators, and the students.

This meeting resulted in a series of meetings between the library board and the county and town school superintendents. The board also announced that a new reference area for student use, which was to be established in the basement of the library, would be open after school, in the evening, and on Saturday. No starting date for this service was announced.

A week later, at the first meeting, the library board and the school superintendents agreed to set up an advisory committee to make rules affecting student use of the public library. No mention of student participation on the committee was made. A second committee was created to study libraries in the area and their availability to students. The superintendents agreed that they would have the principals in their systems ask all teachers to check their assignments against available library resources.

No dates were set for the completion of this task, and no future meetings of the advisory committee were planned.

* * *

Is "peace and quiet" a valid goal for public libraries? Was Mrs. Hunt's hasty and arbitrary decision based on facts in regard to mutilation of reference books and periodicals? Can the use of a public library be restricted to specific groups in a community? What decisions must now be made to solve this problem?

Case 71

QUESTIONABLE PRACTICES

Six acquisition librarians from as many academic libraries were seated around a circular table eating dinner during an ALA annual conference. As usual at such gatherings, they were talking about their experiences and comparing notes. Alan Flam brought up the problem of buying reprints of out-of-print books and voiced his dissatisfaction with one reprint publisher whom he accused of unethical practices:

"The You Reprint Company announces in its catalog expensive sets costing from $5,000 to $12,000 with statements 'to be printed.....' with a date about a year later than the date of the catalog. I sent in a prepayment order for a set costing $9,000 and two years later had not yet received it. In another instance, he held a prepaid order for three years before notifying me that the title would not be published and refunding what I had paid. I have learned that in announcing titles like this with a future date he is 'fishing for bait' and has no intention of reprinting the title unless he gets thirty to fifty orders from librarians. Unless he can get that number of orders he cannot justify the expense of reprinting. I do not believe it is ethical to tie up library funds in this manner. I suppose he has all these prepayments out at interest. But the more important point is that the money isn't being spent for the material we need and the faculty are hounding me about why it hasn't arrived. If a set is unavailable, I need to use the money for other priorities. This type of thing makes for poor public relations with the faculty who need the title. I am blamed for tying up departmental funds and for carrying over this encumbrance each year. If a title is listed in the You Reprint catalog for two years and he still doesn't have enough orders, he isn't going to get any more."

Another acquisition librarian at the table remarked, "I agree that this is unethical and I am so fed up with that company that I refuse to send them a prepaid order. If a title has already been reprinted and is in stock, then I will order but I won't order anything 'to be reprinted....' I think the Vee Reprint Company handles the situation much better. He sends a list asking if you would be interested in buying this title if it is reprinted. In this way he finds out whether it would be profitable to reprint and notifies all respondents whether or not the title will be reprinted. It seems to me the honest thing for the You Reprint Company to do would be to say 'intend to reprint if enough orders warrant the reprinting' but not ask for prepaid orders."

Alan Flam interrupted, "Another thing that makes me provoked with You Reprint is that after waiting a year or more, I cancel the order and he customarily sends me a credit memo instead of refunding the money. This means that funds are tied up indefinitely unless there is another item in his catalog which we need."

A third acquisitions librarian pointed out, "These reprint publishers are doing us a real service by reprinting these books but often they don't have the money to reprint so they need cash in hand to finance their operations. It is the only way for librarians to get the books because it is not a mass market and we are financing the operation on a pay-as-you-go basis. We have to hope that the firm will not fold up before we get our materials."

More discussion followed, with candid revelations of names, titles, and instances. Later the conversation turned to the problems of importing books from Asia and from Eastern Europe.

Acquisitions librarian number four told how he had gotten "burned" by one of these dealers.

"In the United States there are only about six dealers handling books from Croslavia in Eastern Europe. In our university we are developing a major Croslavia area so I have the responsibility of searching for and buying many retrospective titles in this area. I have to acquire them from these dealers. One dealer, who has connections with the government of Croslavia, receives all of his stock by mail. Twice a year he puts out a catalog and gives prices for all items listed. His prices are more than double what he paid for each title. Acquisitions librarians normally check his catalogs as soon as they come out so that by the time the catalog is two months old he has received all or most of the orders he will receive for the titles listed. If he gets ten orders for one title, he considers this a demand and ups the price--not five or ten per cent, but 300-400 per cent.

'Our Croslavia Department desperately needed a several-volume set of political speeches and my staff had been watching dealers' catalogs for it for several years. When this set was published in Croslavia several years ago they cost fifty cents (in U.S. currency) per volume. When we spotted it in this man's catalog for twenty-nine dollars we sent in an order for it at once. He wrote back that the set was out of print and the price had gone up to three hundred dollars. I reported to our Croslavia Department and told them this was a most unreasonable price and recommended that we cancel the order and wait for the title to appear in another dealer's catalog. The chairman of the department said they needed the set 'as of yesterday' so go ahead and order it since my staff had not found it listed in any other dealer's catalog. So, I ordered the set and the very day the volumes came in, another dealer of Croslavia books called on me. He operated from his home and he acquired his stock by making frequent trips to Croslavia and bringing back with him those volumes which he thought he could sell. He would also buy parts of sets or partially completed sets but would not offer them for sale until he had actually completed a set.

'He saw this recently acquired set on a book truck on his way to my office. He asked me where we had gotten these as they were fairly scarce in the U.S. and I told him this was the only set available. He was a bit abrupt in his reply and said there must be at least twenty sets for sale in the U.S. and that he had two in his home. I accused him of kidding me but he said he wasn't and that you had to know where to get them. He inquired how much we had paid for the set and when I told him three hundred dollars, he wanted to know why we had paid so much. He said he was asking forty-five dollars a set for the two sets he had in stock. I was really 'burned up' that I had been gypped by the first dealer. I could not return the set because we had already put our mark of ownership in them."

The other acquisitions librarians laughed as they exchanged knowing glances and admitted they too had made some unwise purchases from this same dealer. The suggestion was made that they ought to communicate more often with each other to keep informed about various dealers and their practices.

*   *   *

Outline a communication network which would give these acquisitions librarians the information they need about dealers.

CHAPTER IV

IN-BASKET CASES*

The In-Basket method is a special case study tool which incorporates elements of the traditional case study, while embodying refinements to allow greater flexibility, realism, involvement, and subsequent ease in behavior transfer to a job. It provides significant bits of information designed around typical situations. Information voids, irrelevant facts, conflicting information, time pressure, and carefully defined objectives force the participant to take actions based on incomplete, but nevertheless realistic, inputs. This technique is sometimes classified as a business game. The primary purpose is to stimulate involvement so that the participant can test his normal managerial methods or experiment with newly learned management skills in a controlled situation.

The name "in-basket" comes from the tray or basket which administrators generally have on their desks for incoming and outgoing correspondence. The in-basket case is a collection of items which have presumably accumulated on the desk of an executive and are awaiting his attention. Although not a complete replica of a work situation, the in-basket case: 1) presents realistic problems in such a way as to elicit responses which fall within the realm of administrative behavior; and 2) provides a controlled situation structured around a model of an organization. This approach involves the representation of a manager's administrative workload on a typical day. How the participant handles the problems posed in the situation provides a basis for evaluating his potential in coping with administrative aspects of a managerial position; for identifying areas in which his skills

---

*A detailed discussion of the history, development, and uses of in-basket tests, exercises, and cases is presented in: Lowell, M. H., The Case Method in Teaching Library Management (Metuchen, N.J.: The Scarecrow Press, Inc., 1968, pp. 33-38.

need to be developed; and for measuring his ability to apply management principles to a realistic decision-making situation.

In this chapter are five library in-basket cases. An attempt has been made to include typical problems varying in importance, immediacy, and complexity which face library administrators in different types of libraries. These problems include: fiscal and budget problems, professional ethics, community relationships, building facilities, security of staff and buildings, personnel problems, public relations situations, personal professional relationships, organizational difficulties, and trivia.

INSTRUCTIONS FOR PARTICIPANTS

You are to pretend to be the administrator in each case and to deal with the set of items provided. You bring to the new job your own background of knowledge and experience and your own personality. Deal with the problems as though you were really the incumbent of this administrative position. You must act on the items found in the in-basket of this executive: memoranda, contracts, reports, requisitions, letters, expense vouchers, personal notes, invitations, telegrams, interlibrary loan requests, telephone messages, drafts for approval, advertisements, announcements of in-service or continuing education courses, papers to be signed, and various other communications which have come by mail, messenger, or telephone.

Read and analyze each item and take whatever action you think seems appropriate, or avoid action if that appears to be advisable. No item can be ignored and no decision postponed. You cannot take any work with you from the office. You must act on each item within the time allotted. Utilize principles of good management involving planning, organizing, motivating, and controlling.

Read all the items and write what you would do and why you would do it. Write down every decision or plan: memoranda to your secretary, to others, and to yourself; draft or write letters for your secretary to type; outline plans or agenda for meetings; delegate action to others; sign papers or indicate approval where necessary; request more information; and record telephone conversations. Avoid making any assumptions that are not supported by the information provided in the case.

Decisions must be made as to which items call for immediate action which can be routed or delegated to other staff or line employees for decision and action, which require consideration by other people before you can act, and which can be ignored. Consideration must be given to such factors as: chains of command, public relations, staff morale, library objectives and goals, short- and long-range plans, policies, rules, procedures, and politics.

Case 72

INTERNATIONAL LEAGUE LIBRARY

Assume that you are Peter Stefan, Director, International League Library. Here is your appointment calendar for today, November 17:

9:00-10:00: weekly meeting of division chiefs in the office of the director of the department of cultural affairs
11:30-11:45: greet visitors from the University of South Africa (the associate director will show them around library until time to leave for luncheon in their honor)
12:30-2:00: luncheon for South African visitors
2:30: Dr. Hans Myer
3:00: Jerry Bush
3:30: William Rank
4:00: Mrs. Fairfield

It is now 2:30 and you have just returned to your office. The memorandum from your secretary which is prominently displayed on your desk creates a sudden change in your plans (Item 1). You will have to leave your office by 4:30 in order to go home, pack, and get to the airport by 9:00 p.m. You will be in Geneva, Switzerland, for about ten days so you must clear your desk before you go.

Background Data:

The International League operates through a large number of agencies and institutions throughout the world, all upholding the objectives of achieving peace, justice, and security; of promoting, by cooperative action, economic, social, and cultural development; and, of strengthening collaboration among the member states.

The league library was created to collect, process, and organize materials for and from the nation members; to prepare and publish indexes, bibliographies, and other publications; to provide reference and bibliographical service to the staff and offices of the League, to government

officials, scholars, and others from the nations belonging to
the League. Although individuals engaged in research on
the university level are permitted to use the library facilities, they cannot borrow materials. Service to the general
public had to be curtailed several years ago because of the
demand from personnel of member countries who have first
priority. Reference questions come from all over the world
at the rate of more than 10,000 per year--by mail, telephone, and cable, and in person. Interlibrary loans average
about 450 a month. These loans are usually from libraries
in the immediate area so that materials can be quickly returned if they are needed. Materials in demand never leave
the library. A limited photoduplication and microfilming
service is available to the staff, offices, and member nations. Microfilm and microcard readers are provided in the
library. The library is open from 9:00 to 5:00 p.m. daily
except Sunday.

The collection totals about 250,000 volumes of books,
3,500 maps, 26,000 photographs, and large holdings of national gazettes, government documents, musical scores,
microfilms, and microcards. Approximately 3,000 serials
are received currently. Holdings are strong in publications
of international agencies, international law, economics and
banking, social and child welfare, history, and bibliography.
Many languages are represented in the collection. A strong
exchange program covers both official governmental exchanges
and unilateral exchanges with learned societies, universities,
and other institutions. This library is a depository for all
publications from international organizations and official publications from members.

The library staff consists of nineteen professional librarians, and twenty-two other full-time staff members
(translators, subject specialists, or clerks). Mr. Stefan
reports to the head of the department of cultural affairs.
The heads of three library departments report to Mr. Stefan:
bibliography, documentation, and publications; public services; and technical procedures. The following outline gives
a breakdown within departments and the personnel involved
in this case:

    Director: Peter Stefan
    Director's secretary: Claudia
    Bibliography, documentation, and publications (also
       associate director): Mrs. Patricia Heath
    Public Services: Mrs. Madeline Fairfield
       Information
       Loans
       Photographs and photoduplication: Paul Daniel

Dear Mr. Stefan:

This letter expresses appreciation for assistance that I recently received in the photographic section of your library from Mr. Paul Daniel.

A few weeks ago, time was sweeping me inexorably toward the deadline for presenting a program on United States-Chinese History. I felt the need for a suitable vehicle to transport the audience mentally into an unfamiliar environment. In fact, I was almost too late in sensing the need for visual aids in my presentation.

Thanks to Mr. Daniel, however, I met my deadline with pictures capturing the historical detail which I intended to present and the particular mood which I hoped to evoke. In short, Mr. Daniel's kindly and patient attention to every detail of my needs and his knowledge of the library's holdings enabled me to portray graphically that which words had failed to describe.

With appreciation, I am very sincerely yours,

Naldo Macklin

ITEM - 6

Medical News
Sixty East Montgomery Street, Big Town

Director   November 14
International League Library

Dear Sir:

Your library has been so helpful in the past when we needed pictures, I hope you can furnish us some of the following which we need for a feature story on wild game dishes. We will not include any pictures of people shooting or carrying home wild game, or of fish.

    Caveman or primitive eating or preparing wild game
    Greek and Roman ditto. Include feasts
    Medieval ditto
    Renaissance ditto
    National wild game, such as Latin American iguana and armadillo steaks
    U. S. buffalo, venison, partridge, pheasant. Include barbecues.
    Exotica: hippo burgers, elephant steak, snake, wild pig cooked whole with apple in mouth (possibly English)

Very truly yours,
Dana Todd

ITEM - 7

International League
Memorandum
To: Mr. Stefan November 14
From: William Rank, Head, Indexing section

On November 19 clerks will start typing the list of periodicals which will be included in the forthcoming supplement to the Index to African Literature. I have asked Claudia to make an appointment in the next day or two so that I can discuss with you: the form of the list of periodicals for the supplement, the sample pages which the publisher has sent for our approval, and several other details.

The lengthy correspondence relative to this supplement is filed in your office. Briefly, here is the situation to date. In 1970, you remember, we signed an agreement with Index Publishers, Inc. to publish the Index to African Literature, 1940-1970. Last August we signed an extension of this agreement to publish the supplement covering the years 1971-1975. In September we sent the publisher the official title of the supplement, a description of the supplement for their advertising flyer, a representative sequence of 60 cards to serve as models for them to determine the dimensions of their copyboard in preparation for photographing our card file, and some suggestions for new sources for their mailing lists.

Last month I estimated that my staff couldn't have the index cards ready for photographing until March 31 next year because we still have to: 1) check the alphabetizing; 2) coordinate author and subject headings of entries; and 3) insert a considerable number of cross references. At that time I estimated there were about 45,000 cards to be photographed, but since then one of my staff has made a closer estimate and believes the number of entries will not exceed 35,000.

ITEM - 8

PAKISTAN-AMERICAN CULTURAL INSTITUTE

November 13

Dear Director Stefan:
On behalf of this Institute, it gives me great pleasure to invite you to a reception honoring Mr. Ahmad Jammu, Minister of Education, and three members of his staff.

We do hope it will be possible for you to attend the reception, which will be held at the Institute on November 25 from five to seven.

RSVP: 723-5512

Sincerely,
Abdul Karim
Secretary

ITEM - 9

International League
Memorandum
To: Mr. Stefan   November 16
From: Claudia

Here are copies of the photographs taken last week in the Council Room during the visit of the group of administrators from Singapore. Do you want to dictate a note to accompany them? Should they be sent air mail all together, or a separate communication and picture to each person?

ITEM - 10

DEPARTMENT OF STATE
Washington

Mr. Peter Stefan, Director   November 13
International League Library

Dear Mr. Stefan:
A group of twenty libraries from as many different countries has been chosen to come to the United States to study library buildings and organization. They will arrive in Washington on November 28 and will spend the next three months in this country. After a week of orientation here in this department, they will then visit libraries all over the nation according to an itinerary we are working out for them. For their first library visit, we would like them to spend a week in your library starting about December 6-8. Will this be acceptable to you, and if so, will you make the necessary arrangements?

Enclosed is a list of these distinguished librarians.

Cordially,
John T. Warden

ITEM - 11

743 Lockwood Avenue
Chicago, Illinois
November 14

Mr. Peter Stefan, Director
International League Library

Dear Mr. Stefan:
 For my high school social studies course, I am writing a theme about literacy in Iceland. Will you please send me some books and pamphlets on this subject and a bibliography of periodical articles?

Sincerely,
Joe Graves

ITEM - 12

International League
Memorandum
To: Mr. Stefan   November 16
From: Mrs. Madeline Fairfield, Head, Public Services

 I have an appointment scheduled with you for 4:00 p.m., November 17, to discuss two personnel problems. In case you wish to review the background, I am supplying herewith some background data. More information about each person is available in the personnel office.

Miss Rama Singh:

 Miss Singh's contract expires on December 31 of this year. No provision for further extension has been made. Her visa will permit her to remain in this country one more year for library practice work. At the end of that time, she will return to India to utilize her library education there. Her knowledge of several Indian languages is invaluable in reference and bibliography. And, I believe, what she is learning in this library will be valuable to her as a librarian in her native country. She is a most willing employee, even under the difficult and demanding situation within the reference and bibliography unit. She is pleasant, adaptable to any kind of work, quick to comprehend, and therefore, in my opinion, a most desirable person to keep on our staff.

You remember we called this appointment to the attention of the League's personnel office about five weeks ago but no action has been reported to me. If Miss Singh's contract cannot be extended, she must soon make travel arrangements to return home.

Mr. Jose Francisco:

You will recall that I reported to you a month ago that Mr. Francisco's performance was unsatisfactory. His probationary period will end on February 1. I suggest that you take up his case with the personnel office and recommend that they ask for his resignation. If he refuses to resign, I recommend that he be disengaged from the library, leaving to the discretion of the personnel office the decision concerning transfer to some other department or section of the League.

He has not accepted the job requirements of the position. An employee in the services area must respond not only with attitudes of service and selflessness but also with initiative to lead and supervise the personnel under him. His unit should operate smoothly and responsibly because it is an important key to good library service. He has been incompetent and disagreeable, and has created a poor morale situation in his unit.

Replacement for Mr. Francisco:

If it appears that the personnel office will remove him from the library staff, I suggest we start searching for a replacement. The job requires the following:
  (1) Supervisory responsibility of personnel in the maintenance of the stacks: obtaining and reshelving books, reading shelves, and keeping the collection orderly and clean
  (2) Receiving, sorting, and distributing the mail
  (3) Recording periodicals in the Kardex
  (4) Sorting and arranging documents received from international agencies
  (5) Preparing shipments to the United States Book Exchange and to the bindery

ITEM - 13

779 River Street
Pocatello, Idaho
November 13

Mr. Peter Stefan, Director
International League Library

Dear Sir:
    My wife and I are planning a trip to Mexico this summer. We would be most grateful if you would personally recommend to us some good travel guidebooks.

Sincerely,
Joe Kokes

ITEM - 14

UNIVERSITY OF LINCOLN
Department of Geography

Chief Librarian   November 14
International League

Dear Sir:
    This department is engaged in a research contract concerning basic physical environment studies. One of the tasks is the compilation of a source file for physical environmental data and information which must include coverage for all land areas of the world. Particular emphasis is being placed on the extent, accessibility, reliability, means, and methods for retrieval of the information from established repositories.
    Below is a list of the types of information which I am interested in during the initial stages of the project:
    soil and surface maps
    disease maps and atlases
    geological atlases, structure maps, and indexes
    insect distribution maps
    bibliographies of pedological and geological maps
    topographic and relief maps and indexes
    bibliographies of biotic realm subjects
    air photos and indexes
    climatic station data, atlases, bibliographies, and
        maps
    ground photos and indexes

weather maps
landform maps, atlases, and bibliographies
manned and unmanned satellite photography
vegetation maps, atlases, and bibliographies
general atlases
land use maps and atlases
stream, river, or lake data and maps
coastal station data and maps
groundwater data and maps
hydrology maps, atlases and bibliographies
geophysical activities
astrophysical activities
general physical geography manuals, handbooks, etc.

         Sincerely,
         George M. Bartholomew
         Research Geographer

Case 73

TECHNICAL INFORMATION CENTER

The director of the Technical Information Center of Aerospace Research Laboratory, Mrs. Margaret Nelson, arrived at her office on September 10 at 8:30 a.m. Her secretary handed her a telegram from the U.S. Navy, Bureau of Personnel:

> We regret to inform you that your son, Ensign Robert Nelson, was seriously burned while engaged in a training exercise on board his ship. He has been flown to Bethesda Naval Hospital for treatment.

Mrs. Nelson put in a long distance call to the hospital and learned that her son was in critical condition and had asked for her. She requested her secretary to check on flights to Washington and to make a reservation on the next available flight; and then turned her attention to the work on her desk. A few minutes later her secretary came in to inform Mrs. Nelson that she had a reservation on a 2:00 p.m. flight. Mrs. Nelson made a quick calculation of time and estimated that she would have to leave the office by 11:00 a.m. That gave her two hours to clear her desk and make the necessary arrangements for her absence, which she thought might be a week or longer.

Background Data:

The Aerospace Research Laboratory is a privately owned industrial corporation which also handles contracts for the federal government. The laboratory's responsibilities involve basic and applied research; systems and manufacturing development of testing, reliability, and quality control; technical support activities such as personnel and computing; and field engineering and training in maintenance and operation.

The entire laboratory is under tight security regulations. Applicants for employment must be cleared by the FBI; all employees must wear badges with their pictures on them; everyone entering the plant must be cleared by guards at check points; strangers must register at a guard's station, be vouched for by an employee, wear an identification badge while in the plant, and return the badge when checking out. Arrangements for overtime work must be made in advance so that the guards will know that the presence of personnel during normal closing hours has been approved.

The primary purpose of the Technical Information Center is to serve the scientists and engineers so well that they do not "reinvent the wheel." The staff stress the service aspect of their work. Service is restricted to employees, consultants, and other libraries. The collection includes materials in the following subjects: physics, chemistry, mathematics, electronics, meteorology, ordnance, metallurgy, optics, mechanics, aeronautics, aerospace, bioastronautics, oceanography, and engineering.

The collection totals about 60,000 books, 16,000 bound journals, and 250,000 technical reports. The latter include research, development, test, and evaluation reports; proposals, studies, brochures, and related materials in original form as well as Defense Documentation Center reproductions and NASA microfiches. About one-third of the technical report collection is composed of confidential documents; both this collection and the staff working with it are housed in a fireproof vault which is locked when the library is closed. More than 3,000 periodical subscriptions are received currently. Special reference files are available for electronic devices, test equipment, specifications and standards, and manufacturers' catalogs. All circulation, periodical sorting, serials records, and ordering are automated.

Of the forty-six staff members, fifteen are professional librarians, and the rest are subject specialists, translators, or clerks. The clerks belong to unions and the positions are graded. Mrs. Nelson reports to the Director of Research, Information, and Publications. Five department heads report to Mrs. Nelson: order, catalog, circulation, reference, and translations. There is no assistant or associate director. Mrs. Nelson has a full-time secretary who is assisted by a clerk. All personnel matters are handled by the laboratory's personnel division.

The following personnel are involved in this case:

    Director: Mrs. Margaret Nelson
    Director's secretary: Nadine
    Order Department (head): Mr. Lewis Bloom
    Catalog Department (head): Miss Abby Seward

Circulation Department (head): Harris Relson
Reference Department (head): Mrs. Rita Temp
Translations Department (head): Miss Elnora White

ITEM - 1

To: Mrs. Nelson September 7
From: Harris Relson, Head, Circulation

 Because of our urgent need for more space, you recently asked Mrs. Temp and me to study the problem of weeding out materials which we do not need. We had a joint staff meeting of all professional and graded employees in the two departments to discuss the problem. I was elected to report to you our recommendations. Attached to this note is the report, written in such a way that, if it meets with your approval, all you have to do is to sign it and have it duplicated for distribution to the staff.

Suggested Memorandum:

  To: Library staff, Technical Information Center
  From: Margaret Nelson
  In re: Disposition of library material

  Books and periodicals which are excess to the needs of this Center should be sent to Reclamation according to the prescribed procedures for disposition of surplus property. Our need for many copies of a publication while it is current often results in added copies of books becoming excess to our needs while they are still quite new. Items to be withdrawn from the collection should be selected by members of the reference staff and sent to the cataloging department where an abbreviated author and title list should be typed. Next, the head of the order department should review the list and add a recommended price for each item based on original cost, publication date, current condition, and possible usefulness to another agency. The order librarian may withdraw titles from the list if he is aware of an active current requirement for these particular titles.
  The titles should then be delivered to Reclamation where they will be made available for inspection by representatives of the state agency for

surplus property. Representatives of tax supported schools and libraries or other tax supported agencies eligible to receive surplus property can screen the publications looking for items of potential use to them. The transfer of the material, at the estimated cost, will be made through the state agency for surplus property.

ITEM - 2

NOTICE OF TERMINATION DATE

To: Mrs. Margaret Nelson   September 8

    Belinda Isaacs   has presented the Medical Department with a certificate from her doctor verifying pregnancy. In accordance with established corporation policy, she may work up to   11   30   . Please advise her of this date. Month   Day   Year

It is your responsibility as this employee's supervisor to be sure that she does not work beyond the above date. Please sign the original copy of this notice and return it to the personnel office. Keep the second copy to attach to the employee's file.

                                          Leon Timothy   M. D.
                                        Corporation physician

Approved by:
Margaret Nelson
Technical Information Center

ITEM - 3

To: Mrs. Nelson   September 9
From: Nadine

    The Director of Research, Information, and Publications called to request your presence at a meeting in his office at 2:00 p.m., September 11, to plan a briefing for the new president. Also, he would like samples of all titles published by the Technical Information Center as well as by the Aerospace Research Laboratory in the library conference room for the new president to review.

ITEM - 4

STAFF CLUB
Aerospace Research Laboratory

September 9

If your department wishes to hold a party during the holiday season, please arrange to have a representative attend a drawing in the Club on Monday, September 20, at 2:00 p.m. in the cafeteria. The drawing will be conducted on the basis of numbers equaling the number of departments represented. The department drawing Number 1 will have first choice of date and room desired; Number 2 will choose second, etc. Requests received after the drawing will be confirmed on an "as available" basis only. It is suggested that representatives have alternate dates in mind in the event their primary date is selected by another department. The Club will be available for these holiday activities during the Thanksgiving to New Year period.

Staff Club Board of Directors

ITEM - 5

Overtime Authorization

September 9

For: Technical Information Center employees who are
(check) _x_ monthly paid, _x_ weekly paid
Week ending September 30

5 people for 40 hours--total

Employee	Mon.	Tue.	Wed.	Thur.	Fri.	Sat.	Sun.	Total overtime hours	Total std. & overtime hours
Connie Vitt						8	8		48
Margaret Brett						8	8		48
Lillian Hill						8	8		48
Alice Stein						8	8		48
Staff: Doris Lane						8	8		48

212 / Library Management

Reason for overtime:
  Connie to work on classified and unclassified descriptive backlog of 2700.
  Margaret to accession and search 104 books.
  Lillian to LC search and descriptive catalog 145 books.
  Alice to keypunch some corrections in circulation system.
  Doris Lane to direct work of above employees, to process green sheets, to work on subject headings proposed and to subject catalog internals.

MONITOR APPOINTED: Doris Lane, Building A, Room 100, Saturday, Sept. 9

Requested by: Authorization:
Margaret Nelson   _____
Technical Information Center

ITEM - 6

To: Mrs. Nelson   September 8
From: Harris Relson

     May I confer with you soon to review item by item the draft of new chapters of the Office Procedures Manual pertaining to change-over of the accountability system? After you approve the new chapters, I will have to meet with the Business Methods Committee to get their approval.

ITEM - 7

The Aerospace Seminar Announces a Lecture
on
"HYDRODYNAMIC STABILITY"
by
Arthur Blue
Professor, Mechanical Engineering
Lincoln University

Time: Friday, September 21 at 10:00 a.m.
Place: Building 216
No tickets required

     The physical aspects of several kinds of hydrodynamic

instability will be discussed, and illustrated in motion pictures. The general approach in analysis of these instabilities will be reviewed, and the current success levels of linear and non-linear theories discussed.

ITEM - 8

Request for Visit or Access Approval
(not to be used for temporary or permanent personnel assignments)

September 8

To: Patrick French, Security Division, Aerospace Research Laboratory
From: Missiles Industries, Inc.

It is requested that the following person(s) be granted visit/access approval:

Last name, first, middle initial	U.S. citizen	Alien	Date of birth	Type clearance	Clearance Number	Date of clearance
Smith, Nancy B. Ht.: 5'6" Wt.: 115 Eyes: hazel Hair: blonde	x		6-5-45	Q	CB-10023	8/26/74

Name of facility to be visited For inclusive dates:
Technical Information Center September 11-12

For the purpose of:
Using mathematics books in Technical Information Center

To confer with the following person(s):
Harris Relson

214 / Library Management

Specific information to which access is requested:
Unclassified books and reports. Request non-controlled badge.

Prior arrangements have/have not been made as follows:
Renewal

Approval is granted with limitations indicated below:

Margaret Nelson

ITEM - 9

To: Class A Exhibitors--Family Day September 6
From: Allen Baker, Tours Committee Chairman
Re: Family Day

  Judging from personal observation, and from comments received from numerous sources, Family Day can be considered an unqualified success. The tours committee believes that this success can be attributed in a large part to the efforts of the individual exhibitors.
  Please accept our sincere thanks for your part in this outstanding display of Aerospace Research Laboratory's skills and accomplishments. If there are others in your organization who deserve to share in the credit for this, please pass on to them this expression of our appreciation.

ITEM - 10

Mrs. Margaret Nelson, Director September 5
Technical Information Center
Aerospace Research Laboratory

Dear Mrs. Nelson:
  I am a sophomore at Benedict College and am writing a term paper on cryogenics. This college library has little on the subject. The father of one of my friends works at your Laboratory and told me you have a fine library. Will you please send me the best publications on the subject?

         Very truly yours,
         Dennis Forrest
         Kelly Hall, Room 435

ITEM - 11

Mrs. Margaret Nelson, Director September 8
Technical Information Center
Aerospace Research Laboratory

Dear Margaret:
As chairman of the nominating committee for Special Libraries Association, I would like to propose your name for president-elect in the next election. You are ideally qualified for this position; you know the organization so well through your years of membership and participation in many committees both locally and nationally, and your membership on the board of directors the past five years.
I sincerely hope you will accept this nomination.

With kindest personal regards,
Hazel D. Olmstead

ITEM - 12

To: Mrs. Margaret Nelson September 7
From: Mrs. Rita Temp, Reference
Re: National Aeronautics, Inc. violation of our Interlibrary Loan Policy.

The staff of this reference department have been struggling with this problem for more than a year. I am sorry to take your time for it but the situation has gotten to the point of requiring some administrative decision and action. Please advise me. The problem involves Miss Viola Peterson, Librarian at National Aeronautics. Our Interlibrary Loan Policy is based on the ALA Interlibrary Loan Code. In referencing certain of our procedures (and violations of them) I will first call your attention to the ALA guideline that interlibrary loan service is supposed to be restricted to requests which cannot be filled by any other means. The staff of the borrowing library is supposed to screen carefully all applications for loans and reject those which do not conform to the code.
Miss Peterson screens none of her requests for books. Furthermore, she does not seem to use any of the public, university, and special libraries near their plant; we get everything. As you know, the men of the plants who have access to select their books from our collection, use our collection constantly. These men also select books for other men at the plant who do not have access.

216 / Library Management

There is no violation for journals or reports. National Aeronautics men select and copy some journal articles for themselves, and Miss Peterson brings her citations, searches for them, and copies them in our library. She often requires reference help but it requires less time than it used to when she sent the reference list to us, we clarified the references, copied them, and took them to her.

A second violation occurs in connection with Part II, Section D of the Code concerning conditions of interlibrary loans. The Code specifies that the safety of borrowed materials is the responsibility of the borrowing library from the date of arrival in that library to the date the materials are received back by the lending library. Miss Peterson has failed to administer this policy and will not accept the responsibility for the safety of borrowed materials. When we call her about overdue books charged to the men in that organization or to the library, she refuses to do anything about getting them back to us.

I am appending a print-out of overdues which indicates the extent of the violations.

ITEM - 13

To: Mrs. Nelson   September 9
From: Abby Seward, Head, Cataloging Department

My two professional assistants who catalog technical reports are concerned about their increasing backlog and have discussed the problem with me. We would like to confer with you to consider some solutions we have considered. Final decisions will involve other departments of this library. As you know, one assistant is in charge of unclassified reports and supervises four clerks; the other does classified reports and has six clerks.

At present the backlog numbers 3,395 and is growing daily. Demands for these reports are heavy and we circulate them upon demand even if not cataloged. We receive all reports in certain subject areas from AEC and NASA. We average about 325 classified and 150 unclassified reports per week; but some weeks we receive as many as 800.

Here are some solutions which occur to us:
1. Take library off distribution lists of AEC and NASA, or reduce number of subjects.
2. Do limited cataloging by short title.
3. Rely on STAR Index for subject retrieval for those reports indexed and stop subject headings on catalog cards for those reports.

4. Stamp a date on unclassified reports for which catalogers think we may not have a demand, file by report number on shelves, and do not catalog. If not used for one year, discard without cataloging.
5. Schedule staff for overtime work to get more cataloging done. This would require an increase in wage and salary budget to pay the required time and a half for overtime.
6. Buy some Flexowriters for producing catalog cards.
7. Hire more staff.

Case 74

SHAWN PUBLIC LIBRARY

"Whatever is the matter, Rita? You're as pale as a ghost. Do sit down. Can I do anything for you?" asked Lois Justin. Rita dropped limply into a chair, burst into tears, and blurted out, "The traffic police just called to say that Mr. Whitney was killed in an automobile accident this morning while driving to work."

The shock of the news was so great that neither woman said anything. Rita was secretary to the librarian of the Shawn Public Library, Mr. Alfred Whitney, and Mrs. Lois Justin was the assistant librarian. The ringing of the telephone in Rita's office broke the stunned silence. Rita's office was located between Mr. Whitney's and Mrs. Justin's offices, with connecting doors. When she came back into Mrs. Justin's office, Rita commented that because of Mr. Whitney's absence for the past week to attend a library conference his calendar for the day was full of appointments and his desk had many items demanding immediate attention. It was now 10:00 a.m. on December 1. Mr. Whitney normally got to his office soon after 8:00 but had no appointments until after 9:00. Today four people had appointments between 9:00 and 10:00 and all were now waiting in the outer office.

Mrs. Justin's first thought was to inform the president of the board of trustees. When talking to him on the phone, the president asked Mrs. Justin to serve as acting librarian for an indefinite period. After Mrs. Justin reported this conversation to Rita, they both went to Mr. Whitney's office, gathered up the appointment calendar and the following materials which were either in his "action file" or had been received in the past week during his absence, and took them to Mrs. Justin's office. Rita reminded Mrs. Justin that the regularly scheduled meeting of coordinators and department heads was scheduled for 1:00 p.m.

The library system consists of a main library, nineteen branches, and four bookmobiles. About four hundred employees work in the system.

ITEM - 1

TELEPHONE MESSAGE - 10:00 a.m. - URGENT (Message taken by Rita)

The maintenance engineer, Mr. Brown, reports serious damage to the lawn and shrubs around the building and wants to know what can be done to stop it. This morning he noticed several adults and children prowling around the foundation of the building and prodding the ground with sticks and umbrellas as though they were looking for something. Because the ground is damp, the grass has been badly trampled, topsoil near the bushes has been scratched away, some branches on the foundation plantings have been broken, and the air-conditioning unit has been badly scratched and dented. Mr. Brown asked the intruders to get off the lawn and pointed to damage they were doing. He asked what they were doing--they replied that they were looking for the buried treasure outside the library which was part of a contest being sponsored by the Popeye Fan television program. Mr. Brown asks that you call the television station as soon as possible and protest.

ITEM - 2

UNIVERSITY OF ZACHARY
Library School

Mr. Alfred Whitney, Librarian November 20
Shawn Public Library

Dear Mr. Whitney:
  I am a faculty member in this library school teaching children's literature, story telling, and services to children and young adults. I am interested in getting back into a library situation for the months of July and August. Should there be a place in one of your branch libraries for a children's librarian or a general assistant, I would appreciate being considered.
  On the following sheet you will find personal data giving my educational background, library school record, and experience as a children's librarian and children's services coordinator. I have been teaching for three years and feel the need to renew contacts with the public and books in a library. I would be particularly interested in working in

a section of your city with the disadvantaged.

Sincerely,
Elsie Nigel

ITEM - 3

To: Mr. Whitney
From: Betty Dwight, President, Staff Association
In re: Personnel Code

    I would like to suggest that the Staff Association, the Personnel Director, and the Administrative Council consider revising the Personnel Code. It has not been updated for five years. The need for this revision became evident last month when several members of the Staff Association wanted to go to the library conference and there were some differences of opinion as to interpretation of the rules concerning who could go, whether time would be allowed, and what expenses would be covered by the library budget. When several of us were looking at the Code for this purpose, we noticed a number of other items which also need revising.

ITEM - 4

DAUGHTERS OF THE AMERICAN REVOLUTION
Shawn Chapter

Dear Mr. Whitney:
    Recently I was using some of the books in the genealogy collection which this chapter deposited in the library many years ago. I noticed that this collection is not listed in your card catalog like the other books in the library, nor is it being protected by the electronic book protective system you are installing in your more valuable books.
    I asked the librarian in the History and Literature Section why our valuable books were not being protected and she said the reason was that this collection had never been officially donated to the library, but was merely loaned as a deposit. She explained that the library staff could not legally use public funds for the treatment of property which is not owned.
    I took this problem up with this chapter at our last meeting and we voted to give the collection to the library. This is official notice of the donation.

Will you please catalog them so that they will be listed in the card catalog, install Sentronic protection in them, and take care of them as you do other valuable books you own?

> Respectfully,
> Mrs. Lewis Selwyn
> Regent

ITEM - 5

To: Mr. Whitney November 29
From: Helen Manuel, Coordinator of Branches
In re: disturbance at Quintin Branch

Because you may get a telephone call or an office appointment about this as soon as you return, here is a report on a recent incident at Quintin Branch:

As you know, Mr. Sidney, the branch librarian at Quintin, has only been there six weeks and never before had responsibility for handling the public. One afternoon last week during the after-school rush when there was lots of motion and activity among the children, two girls, about 12 and 14 years old, were observed scuffling with each other near the charging desk. Mr. Sidney saw the older girl pulling at the coat of the younger girl and the younger resisting, but decided it was a friendly bout. Neither of the clerks at the charging desk seemed to notice or pay any attention to the situation because it was being done in complete silence. The situation was misinterpreted by the staff because of the silence. If the younger girl had screamed or said anything which would have indicated that she was being annoyed, one of the staff would have interceded at once. The older girl left the library and the younger one sat down at a reading table.

No one on the staff observed when the younger girl left the library. About an hour later an irate man entered the library with the younger girl, who was disheveled, crying, and bleeding around the mouth. He went to the charging desk and said he wanted to register a complaint. The clerk asked him to talk to Mr. Sidney, who was on duty at the reference desk. Mr. Sidney invited him to sit in a chair next to the reference desk. The man wanted to know why the police had not been called when his daughter was beaten up by the older girl. Mr. Sidney explained that children frequently got into quarrels and that he could not call the police every time one child touched another. He learned from the father that when the two girls were scuffling, the older one was trying to pull the younger one outside. When the younger one eventually left the library, the older one was waiting for her and beat her up. The father said the older girl was overly aggressive and made a practice of beating up younger girls. When the father left, Mr. Sidney thought the father understood that the library staff could not be held accountable for incidents which took place outside the library and of which they knew nothing. He had explained that if the incident had occurred inside the library, a staff member would certainly have interceded and taken some kind of action.

Soon after the father left, a uniformed police officer came in and asked for Mr. Sidney. The father had reported the incident to the police and the officer wanted the name of the aggressor. The clerical staff knew her name from her library card and reported it to the officer. Upon investigation it was found that the card she was using had been stolen. This was the only name the clerical staff could identify with the girl. Mr. Sidney then questioned students studying in the library and they furnished the girl's name. When her name was looked up in the library files, they found she had had a card some time ago but had many delinquent charges against it. Her address was given to the officer and the case was taken to court the next day.

The girl's mother called my office and discussed the incident for about three-quarters of an hour and said that she was also going to talk with you. Since you were out of town, she could not reach you but she may try this week.

Mr. Sidney, Mrs. Justin, and I have had a conference over the incident and Mrs. Justin and I have suggested to him that whenever an irate, upset person has a complaint, the staff member in charge should show obvious concern and interest, remove the person from the public area into an office or empty room, listen to the entire story no matter how long it takes, nod sympathetically, and ask diplomatic questions to get more information but in no way indicate that he is taking sides. We explained to him that usually people just want to be heard and that by the time the patron has told all, he has gotten most of the anger over with and goes away calmed down and mollified.

Would it be a good idea to devote some staff meetings to the psychology of handling problem patrons?

ITEM - 6

To: Mr. Whitney
From: Craig Grover, Coordinator, Technical Services
In re: traffic in Binding, Repair, and Preparation Section

As you know, physical facilities in the Binding, Repair, and Preparation Section are far from ideal. The space is limited and the staff work in very crowded conditions. This department is supposed to be closed to traffic, but it is not. For the past two weeks I have had one of my staff keep a record of the number of people who came through this department. The tabulation shows that between 25 and 30 people walk through this department every day. This traffic disturbs everyone and reduces the work output. Our backlog gets larger every day.

Will you please request that the staff use the public corridors as a passage rather than this department?

ITEM - 7

To: Division Heads
From: Mrs. Lois Justin, Assistant Librarian
Subject: Reference workshop

On Monday, January 27, 1967, a Reference Workshop will be conducted in the auditorium of the main library from 9:00 a.m. to 11:30 a.m. It is planned to be of practical value for library assistants. Please register with the personnel office by January 18 the names of any staff members planning to attend.

Each registrant will receive a brief list of reference books to examine before the workshop. In addition, the use of the card catalog, the Dewey Decimal system, and the Readers' Guide in reference work will be discussed. After the meeting each participant will be given a list of reference questions to be worked on in his branch or agency and to be returned to the personnel office.

Anyone who has not had a basic reference course in recent years may attend if he can be spared from his regular assignment.

224 / Library Management

ITEM - 8

IMMEDIATE ACTION PLEASE

To: Mr. Whitney
From: Floyd Green, Government and Business

      This department desperately needs more help for December!
      You may remember that our last newsletter sent out by the public relations office publicized the services of the Government and Business Department. The availability of out-of-town city directories for addressing Christmas greetings was mentioned. I didn't think the public read the newsletter but I was so wrong. The day after the newsletter came out, this department received 212 telephone calls for directory information and we have had more than one hundred calls each day since then! My staff can't handle all these calls and the normal workload too.

ITEM - 9

COUNCIL ON WORLD AFFAIRS
Shawn, - - -

Mr. Alfred Whitney, Librarian
Shawn Public Library

Dear Mr. Whitney:
      A group of about fifteen Japanese gentlemen will be in Shawn on December 5 and want to spend the day in your library. They came to the United States to attend a publishers' conference and are now touring the country for three months. The Council on World Affairs is sponsoring and planning their visit while in Shawn.
      They would like a tour of your main building and of several branches; also, they would like to meet you and to talk to some of your professional staff.
      I know I can count on your usual gracious hospitality and enthusiastic cooperation.

                              Sincerely,
                              H. G. Blakely, President
                              Council on World Affairs

ITEM - 10

To: Mr. Whitney
From: Rita
In re: FBI agent

November 28

Mr. Jack Sean, a FBI agent, came to the office today to talk with you about some stolen Shawn Public Library materials which the FBI had retrieved from a couple picked up in Detroit. This couple had been stealing archival and rare materials from libraries all over the country. A list of these materials was being prepared and he will have a copy of the list when he calls on you on December 1 (I made an appointment with him for you). I tried to persuade him to talk to some other staff member but he insisted he must talk to you.

ITEM - 11

To: Mr. Whitney
From: Dorcas Cameron, Personnel

Mrs. Ella Garth has worked as a clerk in the circulation department for twenty-five years. Because of the automated procedures recently introduced in that department, her services can no longer be utilized there. I have offered to transfer her to Tobias Branch where she could do the same type of work she has been doing in circulation. She has refused the transfer because she would have to work different hours and also some evening hours. She contends that the transfer would force her to change her car pool arrangements and this would cause great difficulty and hardship.
What do you advise I do now? Do you want to see her folder? Do you want to talk to her?

ITEM - 12

ROY PUBLIC LIBRARY
Somewhere, USA

Dear Librarian: November 23
We at the Roy Public Library are in the process of rewriting our staff manual. In so doing we are reviewing what have been our problem areas in the past. Our staff

believes that a staff manual is an important source of information. We want it to be all-inclusive so that it will answer all staff questions. By comparing other staff manuals we think we may attain this goal.

Does your library have a staff manual? If it does, we would appreciate your forwarding a copy to us. We, in turn, will forward a copy of ours to you when it is completed.

Sincerely,
Vernon Wade
Librarian

ITEM - 13

MURPHY, REGAN, AND OSMUND
Attorneys

Mr. Alfred Whitney, Librarian
Shawn Public Library

Dear Mr. Whitney:

We are happy to inform you that the late Noah Travis bequeathed to the Shawn Public Library his entire record collection consisting of approximately 27,000 phonograph records and tape recordings which he had collected throughout his lifetime. The collection is composed of many rare 78 rpm records (as well as 33-1/3) and varying speed tape recordings. This collection at present occupies about fifteen three-foot sections of shelves. As you may know, Mr. Travis devoted much time and thought to this collection and it is considered unique and valuable. The collection includes oral history (recordings of prominent people, important events); sounds of insects, animals, machines, and cities; authors reading from their own works; folk tales from many countries; and music. The musical records include early New Orleans jazz, folk music from many countries, and electronic music.

The only stipulation Mr. Travis made in donating this collection was that it be housed in a new department to be known as the "Travis Archives of Recorded Sound." To help support this new department, Mr. Travis left a trust fund of $75,000. The income from this fund is to be turned over to the library annually and spent on additions to the collection.

Will you please write a letter to us indicating your acceptance of the gift.

>Very truly yours,
>Harold D. Murphy, Attorney

ITEM - 14

To: Mr. Whitney--URGENT
From: Myron Trent, Business Manager
In re: security at Yardley Branch

I am concerned about security in Yardley Branch and would like to discuss it with you soon.

Because the branch is located in a stable middle-class neighborhood, we have never had serious problems of vandalism there and hence have made no provision for night watchmen or a police check. However, the police have always included this branch in their regular surveillance. We may need more of a security check than this.

Two weeks ago, when the branch librarian opened the library for the day, she smelled smoke and discovered a small fire had been set and started some time during the night. Fortunately, the fire smoldered and never took hold. The smoke was not dense enough to damage anything; but the librarian is worried about the situation. She could not discover how the intruder (or intruders) got in. An inside job?

This morning when she walked through the stacks she found an effigy suspended in the stack aisles. Again, no evidence of forcible entry. Why? Pranksters?

Case 75

TYSON HOSPITAL MEDICAL LIBRARY

Today is June 2. It is 8:30 a.m. Mrs. Lois Sutton, Librarian of the Tyson Hospital Medical Library, has just arrived at her desk. She must make decisions regarding all the items in her in-basket before 10:30 a.m. At that time she must leave for the airport and will be gone for a week attending the annual meeting of the Medical Library Association where she will deliver a paper.
Assume that you are Mrs. Sutton. What action would you take on each item?

Background data:

The Tyson Hospital Medical Library serves both Tyson Memorial Hospital and the University of Tyson Medical School. The 400-bed general hospital is the largest tax-supported hospital in the county. Eight years ago it affiliated as a teaching facility with the University's medical school.
The medical school and the hospital are old and respected institutions. On four separate occasions, plans have been made to build new facilities for both. However, plans have been scrapped each time because of fiscal difficulties. Five years ago funds were raised by the alumni association of the medical school to start construction on several new classroom buildings and federal funds were made available. Matching funds have been earmarked by the medical school to contribute to the construction of a new building for Tyson Memorial Hospital. Although the county administration has been generally favorable to the idea of a new hospital, actual plans have been slow. It is likely that a new hospital will be constructed within five years.
A doctor's library, supported by voluntary contributions from the medical staff, has been in the hospital for many years. Until the hospital became affiliated with the medical school, the collection was maintained by a clerk and the cataloging was done by a part-time professional cataloger. After the hospital became part of the teaching facilities of the medical school, the library needed to be

reorganized and its collection enlarged so that it could be used by the residents and interns. A full-time professional librarian was hired six years ago. She resigned last year and Mrs. Lois Sutton, another professional librarian, replaced her. Mrs. Sutton's salary comes partly from city tax funds and partly from the budget of the medical school.

Since the hospital affiliated with the medical school, the book budget has come partially from the medical school and partially from contributions of staff doctors. Journal subscriptions are paid from the medical school budget, and equipment and supplies from the hospital budget. Separate requisition forms must be used for each. Some purchase requisitions are approved by the new general administrator of the hospital, John Ahearne, others go to the purchasing department of the medical school after they have been approved by the dean.

The library is used by the staff doctors, the teaching staff of the medical school, medical students, the staff of the hospital, and doctors in the city. Generally, its collections do not circulate to the public, although exception is sometimes made for high school and college students who may be writing papers. Since it is supported by tax monies, it could be used by any resident of the county. This fact is not generally publicized.

The library is housed on two floors and a balcony overlooking the main room. All current issues of journals are stored on open shelves in the main reading room and on the balcony overlooking it. Most of the book collection is kept in three crowded rooms in the basement, all of which open onto a public corridor. (These rooms can be reached from the main room by a narrow staircase. Most materials, however, are carried there on the public elevators.) Some of the heavily used reference works are in the main reading room. The Xerox machine is in one of the basement rooms, although payment for its use must be made at the desk in the main reading room.

Besides Mrs. Sutton, the staff at present includes a part-time professional cataloger, two part-time clerks, and several medical students who keep the library open in the evenings until 9:00 p.m. There are about 50,000 volumes in the collection and the library has current subscriptions to about 500 periodicals.

230 / Library Management

ITEM - 1

NUCLEAR LABORATORIES
Shire, United Kingdom

Tyson Hospital Medical Library May 15

Dear Sir:
Would you please send me copies of reports on the Fission Product Inhalation Project. I am particularly interested in details of the experimental methods for carrying out animal inhalation studies.

Yours faithfully,
George Applegate
Health Physics Research Section

ITEM - 2

TYSON MEDICAL SCHOOL
Interdepartmental Communication

To: Mrs. Lois Sutton, Librarian   From: John Ahearne
Dept: Library   Dept: Administration
Subject: Nursing Statistics   Date: June 1

Will you please find for me statistics on how many nurses are engaged actively in their profession? How many nurses we need? Any predictions about womanpower shortage? I need these figures this afternoon.

ITEM - 3

TYSON MEDICAL SCHOOL
Interdepartmental Communication

To: Mrs. Lois Sutton   From: Dr. Lyle Madison,
Dept: Library   Chairman
Subject: Library service   Dept: Obstetrics
                                     Date: May 31

Whose library is this? Recently several of my students have complained that the books that they needed to use have been checked out. I realize that this is about par for a library; I can never get what I want either! However,

several of the interns have reported to me that the obstetrical books they wanted to borrow from the library are being read by the maids.
If you do not prevent such loans, I suggest strongly that you should. Certainly the use of this kind of material by the maids is highly questionable and it is deplorable that the professional staff cannot have what it needs immediately.
Is there anything that we can do to avoid this in the future?

ITEM - 4

SPECIAL LIBRARIES ASSOCIATION
State Capital Chapter

To: Distribution
From: Mrs. June Fry
Subject: MORE NEWS, PLEASE!

It's time for me to gather News of Our Colleagues for the issue of the Bulletin scheduled for publication before the chapter meeting of June 15. Please do send me news of your professional or civic activities, meetings, etc. Short notes about your library (staff, scope, organization, or unusual services) are most welcome.
Thanks very much for your continuing contributions!
JF:bc

ITEM - 5

TYSON MEDICAL SCHOOL
Interdepartmental Communication

To: Mrs. Sutton, Librarian   From: John Ahearne
Dept: Library   Dept: Administration
Subject: annual solicitation for funds   Date: May 29

Here is the draft for our annual "charity." What a way to have to get funds. You have my sympathy. May I have your comments on the letter.
P.S. I couldn't find a copy of such a letter in the files. Excuse me.

(proposed draft of letter to be sent)

TYSON MEMORIAL HOSPITAL

Dear Doctor:
One of the strengths of the Tyson Memorial Hospital is its outstanding staff of doctors dedicated to tireless and unselfish services to the community. Another strength is our fine professional library.

In order that our library continue to render high quality service to you and to help you keep abreast in your specialty, it is necessary that large sums of money be spent to maintain and enlarge its collection. All of you at some time during the year make use of the library and most of you are well acquainted with Mrs. Sutton, our capable librarian.

She and I wish to ask you to make your yearly contribution to the Tyson Memorial Hospital Library in the name of science and service. Due to your past generosity, this library has become one of the most respected ones in the state. Without your financial support it would be greatly handicapped in its growth.

An envelope is enclosed for your use. Last year you gave $_____ dollars. We sincerely hope that you feel that you can be equally generous this year.

Sincerely yours,
John Ahearne, Administrator
Lois Sutton, Librarian

ITEM - 6

ZEE LABORATORIES INC.

Mrs. Lois Sutton
Medical Librarian
Tyson Hospital Medical Library

Dear Mrs. Sutton:
Thank you very much for sending in your request card for rescheduling the film, The Long Term Use of Anticoagulants. We hope this change of dates has not inconvenienced you.

Sincerely,
Robert McGarrell

In-Basket Cases / 233

ITEM - 7

TYSON MEDICAL SCHOOL
Interdepartmental Communication

To: Mrs. Lois Sutton
Dept: Library
Subject: volunteer help

From: Dr. Chambers
Dept: Radiology
Date: May 28

My wife, who is president of the Ladies Auxiliary of the Tyson Memorial Hospital, has suggested that perhaps you would welcome volunteer help in the operation of the library. I have commented several times to her how short of help you seem to be and what fine service you are still able to give.
As you know, each year the wives of the medical staff like to take on a new project. Would you be interested in having the library be their new project? Many of the ladies are great readers and would like very much to work in the hospital library a few hours a week.

ITEM - 8

A REVIEW OF DIABETES

Postgraduate Course
offered by
AMERICAN DIABETES ASSOCIATION
in cooperation with
TYSON MEDICAL SCHOOL
August 1, 2, 3

(fill out attached application form and mail to - - - -)

ITEM - 9

TYSON MEDICAL SCHOOL
Interdepartmental Communication

To: Mrs. Lois Sutton
Dept: Library
Subject: advertising library
service

From: Dr. Karl Merber,
Chairman
Dept: Surgery
Date: May 30

As I was looking through some of my old correspondence I found a copy of the letter sent out last year soliciting funds for the library. It must be that time again and so I am enclosing my annual contribution now, although I haven't received a letter from you yet.

I want to compliment you on your fine service. All the doctors on my staff are very happy with your collection of periodicals, and the good reference service you have given. We all think the library is a great addition to the hospital facilities.

Would it help your fund raising drive if I gave your library a little publicity? As you probably know (since you always send me copies of my newspaper pictures), I lecture extensively around the state and in the city. I wonder how many doctors are aware of the fine service they could get from you. If you'd like me to put in a "plug" for the library I'd be glad to. In fact I probably will anyway. You're too modest.

Encl.

ITEM - 10

Inter-Office Memorandum
To: All department heads
From: Ross Vincent
Subject: Notification to employees of salary changes

Tyson Hospital has not had a system to advise an employee of a change in his or her salary rate. It is evident from the inquiries made to the payroll section that we should adopt a procedure to correct this, and I would like your advice on the method to be used. Please write me your suggestions. Three possibilities are:

(1) The annual salary rate can be printed on the employee's payroll information sheet which he receives with each paycheck or bank deposit slip. This would provide him with the information at the time he receives the first check after a payroll change is made.

(2) We could adopt a simple form and send it either to the employee or to his department head, advising of the change and the effective date thereof.

(3) We could provide the information on all changes to each department head, who would then personally advise the employee.

ITEM - 11

TYSON MEDICAL SCHOOL
Interdepartmental Communication

To: Mrs. Lois Sutton
Dept: Library
Subject: Bequest

From: Dr. John Tyson Powers,
Dean
Dept: Office of the Dean
Date: May 27

At a recent board of trustees meeting I was informed that a distant relative of the Tyson family has made another bequest to the school. It is a 2,500-volume collection of rare pamphlets and books on dermatology.
It is a beautiful collection although some of it is very fragile. However, the donor has specifically stipulated that the collection is not for use, must be housed in a lighted cabinet which is furnished, and must be kept on permanent display.
The trustees voted unanimously to accept the bequest and it will be delivered to you as soon as you have determined where it will best fit in the main reading room.
Will you let this office know when the library is ready to accept this gift. We should probably plan some publicity and an acceptance ceremony. I would appreciate any of your suggestions.

ITEM - 12

TYSON MEDICAL SCHOOL
Interdepartmental Communication

To: Mrs. Lois Sutton
Dept: Library
Subject: Moving

From: John Ahearne
Dept: Administration
Date: May 30

As you know, we are asked daily to accommodate more patients. The demand for more beds comes from both the county and the medical school. To do so we are trying to move all the radiology department to the basement. This is the only floor in the building which is capable of housing safely some of the new equipment. By consolidating the radiology department we will free several rooms which can be converted to four-bed wards.
Although I know you are crowded in your quarters, I would like very much for you to consider two possibilities:

236 / Library Management

    1. Consolidating the radiology department library with your collection.
    2. Vacating one small basement room to be used as a reception room for the radiology department.

The room to be vacated is the one in which you now store bound books which I understand from the staff are rarely used and which also houses the Xerox machine.

We would provide the labor to move the books into storage for you. We could also arrange to cancel your rental contract with Xerox with no loss to the library budget. As you know, there is a Xerox machine in the Records and Admissions office. They have agreed to allow you to use their machine when it is not in use.

Although the staff is unanimous in its high opinion of the library, it is also adamant in its desire for more patient room. I do not like to ask you to give up space inasmuch as I have heard how difficult it was for you to obtain the basement space. However, I am sure you will agree that little-used books cannot compete for space with the ill. You will of course still retain the use of the other two rooms.

This move will be discussed at the staff meeting next Thursday. Would you like to be there?

ITEM - 13

TYSON MEDICAL SCHOOL
Interdepartmental Communication

To: Mrs. Lois Sutton   From: Dr. Bob Clare
Dept: Library   Dept: Surgery
Subject: Bibliography   Date: June 2

    I need a bibliography on adrenalectomy for breast cancer. I don't want anything older than two years and I will need it by 2:00 p.m. I'll send the departmental secretary to pick it up. Thank you.

ITEM - 14

CHEROKEE JUNIOR COLLEGE
Dean's Office

Mrs. Lois Sutton
Tyson Memorial Hospital

Dear Mrs. Sutton:

In the next month Cherokee College is having a series of speeches on vocational and professional opportunities for young women in the world today.

Many of our students will leave Cherokee to go on with their education at State University. Because so many girls are undecided about their major subject, we feel that this is the time to give guidance and counsel.

We here have heard much about you from the father of one of our students, Dr. Tyson. Would you be willing to tell our students a little about the challenges and rewards of being a medical librarian? We would expect you to speak about twenty minutes. Any illustrative material or literature is always welcome.

I will await a favorable answer from you.

Sincerely yours,
Agatha Mann, Dean

ITEM - 15

TYSON MEDICAL SCHOOL
Interdepartmental Communication

To: Mrs. Lois Sutton From: George Riordan
Dept: Library Dept: Internal Medicine
Subject: Library hours Date: May 25

Could you find some way to keep the library open and with a librarian in it on Sunday evenings. A lot of my students complain that it is closed then. It would be a great help for them. It's very difficult to cram study hours in the day of a busy medical student.

Cordially,
George

Case 76

MAY COUNTY LIBRARY SYSTEM

You, Harris Bender, administrative assistant to George Hoskins, Director of the May County Library System, are scheduled to leave on your vacation at 5:00 p.m. today, Friday, June 9. A few minutes ago Mr. Hoskins came into your office with his in-basket, placed it on your desk, and asked you to take action on every item in it. He had just received a telegram informing him of the death of his mother and was leaving at once. He does not expect to be back for a week. It is now 3:00 p.m.

Background Data:

Five years ago an old and famous city library became May County Library. The collection totals about 1,000,000 volumes and the total staff numbers more than 150. The county is served by the main library, 16 branches and 4 bookmobiles.

Items from the following staff members are in today's accumulation of mail and messages:

Director's secretary: Eleanor
Children's Services, Coordinator: Agnes Scott
Adult Services, Coordinator: Beatrice Shelley
Bookmobile Services: David Beason
Readers' Advisor (in Adult Services): Fern North
Technical Services, head: Eileen Egbert
Maintenance: Carl Kuhn
West Side Branch: Wanda Clemens
Assistant Branch Librarian: Dana Baldwin

ITEM - 1

To: Mr. Hoskins June 9
From: Eleanor

Beatrice Julian of the Catalog Department had an

238

emergency appendectomy last night. She is at Methodist Hospital. Want to send flowers or something?

ITEM - 2

Mr. George Hoskins, Director June 7
May County Library System

Dear Mr. Hoskins:
You will remember that I worked in the reference department of the May County Library System from 1963 to 1966. At present I am reference librarian of Agatha College library. I am applying for a position in the University of Elliot library and need references from former employers.
Will you please write a letter of recommendation for me? I will be most grateful if you will.

Sincerely,
Brenda Wade

ITEM - 3

MAY COUNTY LIBRARY SYSTEM
Interoffice Memo

To: George Hoskins, Director June 7
From: Agnes Scott, Coordinator, Children's Services
Subject: Discipline--patrons

The problem of disciplining children is increasing daily in our department. It may be the spring weather or the current parental attitude toward discipline in general and the total disregard for considerate behavior in public buildings. Some of my staff are very distressed and one has suggested that she may leave unless I allow her to forbid the most serious offenders entrance into the children's room. It seems to me, of course, that we all must maintain discipline, but not to the extent that we jeopardize our friendly relationships with parents and children.
However, yesterday Miss Young was rather severely bitten by a pre-school child. She immediately sent him out of the room and one of the pages remained with him until his mother arrived to take him home. Miss Young told the mother never to bring the child into the library again.

240 / Library Management

Will you back up Miss Young and me in this decision? I would like to hear your thoughts. I can arrange to come to your office at your convenience.

ITEM - 4

MAY COUNTY LIBRARY SYSTEM
Interoffice Memo

To: Mr. George Hoskins   June 7
From: Beatrice Shelley, Coordinator, Adult Services
Subject: Fee for meeting rooms

Early last week you told me you would take up the subject of rental fees for the meeting rooms at the next board meeting. However, I have now received the yearly requests from several groups, among them the Borrowed Time Club, the Tennyson Society, the Nineteenth Century Club, and the Happy Hour Club. All of these groups, as you know, are made up of what we now call "senior citizens" and all of them claim to operate on limited budgets. Dues must be kept low and consequently the difference between the present $3.00 fee for a meeting and the $5.00 fee that we talked about is a large one for them.

It makes a difference to our budget too, since each one of these groups rents a room once a month throughout the entire year. I have to let them know our decision by the end of the week because they wish to make other arrangements if we cannot accommodate them.

My first thought was to let them have the space at the old price, but when I hear Carl and the other janitors muttering about union scale I get nervous.

I would appreciate hearing your decision as soon as possible--maybe tomorrow.

ITEM - 5

MAY COUNTY LIBRARY SYSTEM
Interoffice Memo

To: Mr. George Hoskins   June 7
From: David Beason, Head, Bookmobile Services
Subject: Dismissal of Don Lane, driver

Mr. Lane has been absent without permission for

eight working days. I recommend termination of his employment as of May 22.

ITEM - 6

CONFIDENTIAL

To: Mr. Hoskins June 6
From: Dana Baldwin, Assistant Branch Librarian
In re: leave of absence

As you know, I have been employed for five months in the May County Library as Assistant Branch Librarian. For personal reasons, I need to take six working days leave of absence late this month to attend a religious retreat out of state. Six weeks ago I presented a written request for this leave to my supervisor, the branch librarian. She took the request to Mr. Bender and they refused to grant the leave on the basis of the Staff Manual, which states that no employee can have any vacation or time off until he has worked six months. I did not ask for a vacation, I merely want a leave of absence without pay.

I appealed to my supervisor to intercede on my behalf as it is mandatory for me to attend this convocation and she said that I would have to see Mr. Bender. I had a conference with him, told him that I was happy in my job and wanted to stay on but that if this leave isn't granted, I will resign. He told me quite bluntly that, while he respected my religious convictions, I would have to choose between my religion and my job. His decision not to grant the leave was technically correct as it adhered strictly to the written policy of the Staff Manual. However, I feel that policies should be more flexible so as to meet individual needs.

Will you please grant me this leave of absence? If you can't grant it, I will regretfully submit my resignation as of June 15. I would be happy to come to your office to discuss this with you.

ITEM - 7

PINK LADIES
May County Hospital

Mr. George Hoskins, Director June 7
May County Library System

Dear Mr. Hoskins:
    Our annual fund drive begins next week and we are hoping that we can count on the library employees to contribute generously to our program. I am enclosing a packet of forms to be filled out and sent in with contributions. Will you please assign one of your employees to distribute the pledge cards, collect the contributions and pledges, and bring them to us at the hospital?
    Thanking you in advance for your cooperation, I am

                  Sincerely yours,
                    Mrs. Zelda Abbott, Chairman
                    Fund Raising Committee

ITEM - 8

BANKS, FRITH, SOLTNER, FRITH, AND FRITH
Attorneys-at-law

Mr. George Hoskins, Director   June 7
May County Library

Dear George,
    Your presentation of the proposed library budget was excellent. However, I, as chairman of the Library Board budget committee, have been hearing some distressing news from other board members.
    It seems that the mayor has been quoted as saying, in reference to budgets, that this is the year for all governmental units to "pull in their horns." How much of this is just campaign talk, or how much of it is fact, I can't tell. Norma Segal tells me that some of her neighbors have complained that they aren't getting their tax money's worth of service out in that new little branch in Sandy Waters.
    At any rate, I think that you and I and the rest of the budget committee had better get together soon for a strategy planning session. The board meeting is scheduled for the 24th and if we expect them to approve the twenty-two per cent increase in budget we had better have some convincing justification for it.
    I would like a little more of your thoughts on the necessity of raising salaries just because a few troublemakers are threatening us with a union. On the whole I think your budget is a good one, but I am not sure that I have quite enough background to "sell" the board.

My suggestion is for a meeting Tuesday evening, June 16, at 8:00 p.m. I have to go to Washington on the 19th and I am not sure that I can work in another meeting before June 24.

Sincerely,
Joseph L. R. Frith
Attorney-at-law

ITEM - 9

May County Library   June 5

Dear Sir:
I would like to obtain some information on careers concerned with the library. Please send me also the educational qualifications needed for these jobs. Please send me this information at your earliest convenience.

Sincerely,
Anne Phillip

ITEM - 10

DAUGHTERS OF THE SONS OF THE FOUNDING FATHERS
Monroe Chapter

Mr. George Hoskins   June 6
May County Library System

Dear Sir:
It has been brought to my attention that all those old books, pictures, and artifacts which our group has given to the library over the years are never displayed and are not indexed or even appear in your catalog.
In view of what we read about the deplorable rate of loss and other misuse of books in your library, my board members wonder if the May County Library is the proper place for our treasures.
Mrs. Segal, who is one of our members and a member of your board, has suggested that I write to you expressing our concern. We have always supported the library through our taxes and by special gifts. If you do not wish our materials we shall remove them immediately, subject to a complete inventory by one of our staff members.

244 / Library Management

Perhaps instead of our annual contribution to the Friends of the Library Society, we would be better advised to start a museum and library of our own.
My board and I look forward to hearing from you at the earliest possible date.

                Respectfully,
                Mrs. Hiram Lawson, Grand Directress

ITEM - 11

To: Mr. Hoskins   <u>URGENT</u>   June 9, 9:00 a.m.
From: Eileen Egbert, Technical Services
In re: Arleen Henry
cc: Mr. Bender

    Here is a report on an unfortunate incident which occurred yesterday in the cataloging department. I want you to be fully informed because you may be involved in conferences on the problem.
    Arleen Henry was employed three months ago. She is in her mid-thirties, has a master's degree from a good library school, has had excellent experience as a cataloger, and came to us with good recommendations. We were very happy to get her because of her knowledge of languages, which we needed in our cataloging department. She is a superior cataloger and has a good grasp of the problems involved. We are happy with her work; she has a great capacity for work and accomplishes much more in a day than the average cataloger.
    We knew when she came to us that she had some problems with mental illness and was eager to come to this city in order to be under the care of the distinguished psychiatrist in our local medical school.
    Yesterday morning, while sitting at her desk, she suddenly became rigid and stared out into space. Several women working near her noticed her condition and talked to her to bring her out of this apparent trance. Their conversations evidently did not reach her and she remained unchanged. Her supervisor, Nelle, who knew her better, decided to see what she could do. Nelle tried to get Arleen to think about cataloging by asking her questions: "What is the title page of this book?" "Who is the author?" "What are we trying to do here?" This went on for about two hours and gradually brought Arleen back to normal. Nelle then went back to her desk. Half an hour or so later

Arleen went to lunch with some of her co-workers and Nelle thought Arleen was completely over her trouble. At lunch Arleen again became rigid and stared into space and her friends could not get her to budge out of her chair or to eat her lunch. One stayed with her and the others went back to work and reported to Nelle what had happened. Nelle's attempts to reach her failed, so she called Arleen's brother who came at once. After about three-quarters of an hour of forceful persuasion, he finally got her out of the restaurant and into his car.

Later, the brother called to report that he had taken her to the office of her physician who said that he had had her on intensive drug treatment but had concluded about a week ago that she was "over the hump" and had taken her off the drugs. This is what brought on the crisis. Her brother had no idea when she would be ready to return to work, as he had not discussed this with the physician.

If she does want to return to work, shall we keep her on? You know what a cataloging backlog we have!

ITEM - 12

MAY COUNTY LIBRARY SYSTEM
Interoffice Memo

To: Mr. George Hoskins
From: Fern North, Adult Services, Reader's Advisor
Subject: Maternity leave

I wish to apply for maternity leave starting on August 1. I hope to be able to return to work by November 15th. It was my understanding when I accepted the position with the library that this was regular policy. However, when I announced to Mrs. Shelley that I was going to have a baby she seemed very upset and said that she would have to find an immediate replacement for me.

As you know, my husband is still in school and it is necessary for me to continue working at least part-time. I have been with the library almost a year now and I have done, I feel, a good job in the adult services department.

I have taken this matter up with Mr. Bender, and he says that maternity leave must be approved by the department head. Mrs. Shelley refuses to do so, but she also refused to give any reason other than that she cannot constantly be training new employees.

I wish to return on a part-time basis in the

246 / Library Management

department. I am fully trained, and by Mrs. Shelley herself. I fail to understand what the real reason is. Could I please have a conference with you and Mrs. Shelley?

ITEM - 13

PROPERTY OWNERS IMPROVEMENT ASSOCIATION
Plainville

Mr. George Hoskins, Director
May County Library

Dear George:
  You probably don't even remember me, but we had several classes together in college and I remember you as a most persuasive and articulate speaker.
  Our group, which is concerned largely with holding down property taxes, but also with improving community services, sponsors a series of programs for our members and for our community. We have found in our town that the library is heavily tax-supported. Some of us would like to know what we get for this outlay.
  We wonder if you would address a meeting on the subject, "The Library and the Good Life." We, of course, would pay your traveling expenses here and would like you to be our guest at a dinner for our members before the talk.
  I hope you can make it. From all I hear, you and your library have a good life in May County, and you are considered the expert on public libraries in this state.

Sincerely yours,
George Fay
Program Chairman

ITEM - 14

METROPOLITAN TRANSIT COMPANY

Mr. George Hoskins
May County Library

Dear Mr. Hoskins:
  You will remember that several weeks ago we talked

at length about the possibilities of erecting bus shelters on the lawns of the branch libraries.
 I approached our general manager, Mr. Cahill, and he is greatly in favor of the idea. In return for permission to use part of the lawns of the three branches we will put up the shelter, pay for the cost of materials and labor, and maintain it. In return you may use the inside surface directly above the bench to post any announcements of library programs or news that you might think would be of public interest. We reserve the use of the outside of the shelter for our advertisements and our messages.
 You know we put up a high quality shelter and we maintain them well. Our suburban patrons are grateful for these little shelters in bad weather. No doubt many of your patrons are our patrons.
 I hope that you will let me have a favorable decision on this matter as soon as possible.

Sincerely yours,
Herman Dirk
Director of Public Relations

ITEM - 15

MAY COUNTY LIBRARY SYSTEM
Interoffice Memo

To: Mr. George Hoskins   June 8
From: Carl Kuhn, Maintenance
Subject: Cracked steps

The steps in front of the main library are badly cracked in two places. The boys cannot fix them with patching cement like those on the north and south sides because they are that funny colored brown marble.
 We could remove the steps completely and put temporary wooden treads in until we get new ones if you can tell us where to get the marble. I asked Mr. Bender and he said the steps have to stay because they are part of a bequest.
 I think it is dangerous, Mr. Hoskins. I see the kids teetering on the loose edge.

ITEM - 16

MAY COUNTY LIBRARY SYSTEM
Interoffice Memo

To: Mr. George Hoskins, Director
From: Wanda Clemens, West Side Branch
Subject: questions

       In your letter requesting the annual report for this year, you asked that problems be discussed, and I am taking the liberty of bringing a few of mine to your attention. I realize that in a large organization you cannot keep in touch with the many questions concerning the service that must arise throughout the system, but these problems are nonetheless real to me.

       I know from your remarks at branch meetings that many questions come to you, and while I do not wish to intentionally add to your burdens, I feel I should let you know of the questions and difficulties that confront me here.

       Our borrowers are asking for more of the new books; they expect me not only to be familiar with the books, but to tell them which titles will be added to our collection and when they will be here. It is frustrating to find myself unable to reply to these questions in a manner satisfactory to the readers or to myself.

       There was an article in the local paper recently about the new books at the branch, and the reporter was impressed when I told him of the million-volume collection that backs up the service outlets in this system. The special request service and the reference resources at Central, he said, should receive more publicity in the community.

       Borrowers ask me about books that are not in the library collection and they wonder why. On the other hand, questions are raised about some of the books that are on our shelves. All I hear from Central is that a given title is either not in the library or that it is being ordered; this is the answer I have to give the patron and it is not satisfactory.

       I have not seen my supervisor for several weeks and I am uncertain about the statement in the Branch Manual concerning the preparing of a time report. There has been a change in the form and it is not clear to me how the new forms are to be used or even why the change was made. At the last meeting of branch librarians, I recall that the new form was mentioned, but that is all I can remember about it.

ITEM - 17

MAY COUNTY LIBRARY SYSTEM
Interoffice Memo

To: Mr. George Hoskins   June 8
From: David Beason, Head, Bookmobile Services
Subject: Don Lane

 Mr. Lane has returned from his absence without leave and has asked to be allowed to continue his work on the bookmobile. He says he was absent because he caught the measles from his sister's children while he was visiting them on his vacation. Neither he nor his relatives had any means of notifying the library of his whereabouts.
 Mr. Lane is an experienced driver and a conscientious clerk. In view of his otherwise good work record, I recommend that he be allowed to continue his employment with us. Mr. Lane understands that another unexcused absence would be cause for dismissal. He assures me that this will not occur.

ITEM - 18

Box 85, Hart Hall
Sebastian University

Librarian
May County Library System

Dear Sir:
 I am writing in regard to summer employment in your library. Last June I completed an application form which is on file with you.
 I was called for a job last fall but by then I was away at school. I am a freshman at Sebastian University and for the first semester received a grade point average of 3 on a 4 point scale.
 I am again interested in employment for the summer, starting June 1, and would appreciate your reconsidering me for a position.
 Thank you for your consideration.

Sincerely yours,
Jeffry Shale

TITLE INDEX TO CASES

Case	Case No.	Type of Library
Arbitrary Architect	47	A
Baby-Sitting Service	6	P
"Bandaid" Work	39	S
A "Bargain"	35	A
A Branch in a Low-Income Neighborhood	31	P
Busy, Busy, Busy	19	A
Censorship	63	P/S
Central Information Desk	11	P
Church and State (Role Playing)	36	P
City Hall	61	P
Clearance Policy (Role Playing)	48	P
Confrontation (Role Playing)	53	P
Control of Special Appropriation	64	A
Data Packets	12	A
A Despotic Supervisor	3	A
Education Division vs. Library	29	
A Faculty Library Committee Member	58	A
Faculty Reading Lists (Skit)	40	A
A Fire	37	P
Flexible Scheduling	2	Sp
Fractionated Time	15	A
Fund Accounting	56	A
Gift Appraisals	34	A
A Gift with Stipulations	57	A
Harassment at Stonechat Branch	60	P
Hemlock High Resource Center	16	S
How Much Autonomy Should a Branch Librarian Have?	66	A
Identify Yourself	7	A
Individual Recognition (Role Playing)	45	A
Inflexible Rules	8	A

252 / Library Management

Case	Case No.	Type of Library
"Innovative" Cataloging	25	A
Interference with Student Discipline	9	A
International League Library	72	Sp
May County Library System	76	P
The Memo Writer	4	Sp
Mission of Research Libraries (Role Playing)	32	Sp
Misuse of Seabrook College Library	67	A
Momentum (Role Playing)	27	P
Need for Organizational Change	1	Sp
A New Community College	38	A
No Textbooks!	51	S
An Organization Chart	21	A
Overdues	62	P
Participative Management (Role Playing)	18	A
A Penitentiary Library	52	Sp
A Pilferage Racket	59	P
Planned Expansion	49	P
Popular Materials in a Research Library	28	Sp
Problems Inherited by a Young Administrator	22	A
Questionable Practices	71	A
Reorganization of Children's Services	24	P
Research Library Public Service	46	A
Resignation	14	P
A Schedule Change	13	P
School Reorganization	43	S
The Scribbler	54	S
The Sealed Envelope	65	A
Selection Committee	5	S
A Senile Public Library Board	55	P
Service to High School Students	70	S
Shawn Public Library	74	P
"The Shelf"	42	S
Short- and Long-Range Planning	33	A
Special Funding	30	S
Staff Concern	41	A
Study Center Requested	44	A
Technical Information Center	73	Sp
A Technical Services Department	26	A

Title Index / 253

Case	Case No.	Type of Library
Too Many Supervisors	17	A
Too Much Advice	68	Sp
The Tupelo Family	69	P
Tyson Hospital Medical Library	75	Sp
Volunteers (Role Playing)	20	P
Wanted: A Mover's Manual	23	P
Who Controls Library Space?	50	P
Work Assignments	10	A

Key to type of library designation: (A) Academic; (P) Public; (S) School; (Sp) Special.

SUBJECT INDEX TO CASES

	Case No.
Academic Status	
A Despotic Supervisor	3
Accreditation	
Control of Special Appropriation	64
Acquisition Policy	
A Penitentiary Library	52
Attitudes	
Confrontation (Role Playing)	53
Authority	
A Penitentiary Library	52
Volunteers (Role Playing)	20
Board of Trustees	
Overdues	62
Planned Expansion	49
City Hall	61
The Tupelo Family	69
Resignation	14
A Senile Public Library Board	55
Budget	
Control of Special Appropriation	64
Building Planning	
Arbitrary Architect	47
Business Office	
Fund Accounting	56
Cataloging	
"Innovative" Cataloging	25
Short- and Long-Range Planning	33
Censorship	
Censorship	63
Church and State (Role Playing)	36
Clearance Policy (Role Playing)	48
"The Shelf"	42
Chain of Command	
Control of Special Appropriation	64

Subject Index / 255

	Case No.
Data Packets	12
A Despotic Supervisor	3
The Memo Writer	4
An Organization Chart	21
Participative Management (Role Playing)	18
Volunteers (Role Playing)	20
Change	
Need for Organizational Change	1
Children's Services	
Reorganization of Children's Services	24
Confrontation (Role Playing)	53
Circulation	
A Despotic Supervisor	3
Overdues	62
A Schedule Change	13
City Council	
City Hall	61
Civil Service	
City Hall	61
Clearance Policy (Role Playing)	48
Reorganization of Children's Services	24
Collective Bargaining	
Flexible Scheduling	2
Committees	
A Faculty Library Committee Member	58
Selection Committee	5
Staff Concern	41
Communication	
Need for Organizational Change	1
The Memo Writer	4
Staff Concern	41
Dealers	
A "Bargain"	35
Delegation of Authority	
Busy, Busy, Busy	19
Too Much Advice	68
Participative Management	18
Discipline Problems	
Baby-Sitting Service	6
Confrontation (Role Playing)	53
Harassment at Stonechat Branch	60
The Scribbler	54
Service to High School Students	70
External Control	
City Hall	61

256 / Library Management

	Case No.
A Penitentiary Library	52
Financial Control	
Control of Special Appropriation	64
Fund Accounting	56
Questionable Practices	71
Fires	
A Fire	37
Floor Plans	
Hemlock High Resource Center	16
A Technical Services Department	26
Gifts	
Gift Appraisals	34
A Gift with Stipulations	57
Planned Expansion	49
The Sealed Envelope	65
Goals and Objectives	
A Branch in a Low-Income Neighborhood	31
Data Packets	12
Fractionated Time	15
School Reorganization	43
In-Basket Cases	
International League Library	72
May County Library System	76
Shawn Public Library	74
Technical Information Center	73
Tyson Hospital Medical Library	75
Insubordination	
The Memo Writer	4
Intellectual Freedom	
Clearance Policy (Role Playing)	48
Library-Community Relations	
A Branch in a Low-Income Neighborhood	31
Faculty Reading Lists (Skit)	40
Harassment at Stonechat Branch	60
Mission of Research Libraries (Role Playing)	32
Planned Expansion	49
Who Controls Library Space?	50
Library Tours	
Fractionated Time	15
Microforms	
A "Bargain"	35
Motivation	
Momentum (Role Playing)	27
Need for Organizational Change	1
Moving	
Wanted: A Mover's Manual	23

Subject Index / 257

Case No.

Mutilation of Materials	
The Scribbler	54
Service to High School Students	70
Organizational Structure	
An Organization Chart	21
Participative Management (Role Playing)	18
Participative Management	
Participative Management (Role Playing)	18
Staff Concern	41
Personnel Code	
Clearance Policy (Role Playing)	48
Planning	
"Bandaid" Work	39
A Fire	37
"Innovative" Cataloging	25
Momentum (Role Playing)	27
A New Community College	38
No Textbooks!	51
Penitentiary Library	52
Problems Inherited by a Young Administrator	22
School Reorganization	43
Short- and Long-Range Planning	33
Study Center Requested	44
Too Much Advice	68
Wanted: A Mover's Manual	23
Policy Statements	
Education Division vs. Library	29
Faculty Reading Lists (Skit)	40
Mission of Research Libraries (Role Playing)	32
Research Library Public Service	46
Political Interference	
City Hall	61
The Tupelo Family	69
Public Relations	
Baby-Sitting Service	6
Censorship	63
Confrontation (Role Playing)	53
Faculty Reading Lists (Skit)	40
"Identify Yourself"	7
Inflexible Rules	8
Planned Expansion	49
Service to High School Students	70
Reclassification	
Too Much Advice	68
Reference	
Central Information Desk	11

258 / Library Management

Case No.

Fractionated Time	15
Religious Literature	
Church and State (Role Playing)	36
Remodeling	
Hemlock High Resource Center	16
Reorganization	
"Bandaid" Work	39
City Hall	61
Data Packets	12
"Innovative" Cataloging	25
Need for Organizational Change	1
Problems Inherited by a Young Administrator	22
Reorganization of Children's Services	24
Short- and Long-Range Planning	33
A Technical Services Department	26
Reprint Publishers	
Questionable Practices	71
Research Libraries	
Faculty Reading Lists (Skit)	40
Mission of Research Libraries (Role Playing)	32
Popular Materials in a Research Library	28
Research Library Public Service	46
Rules and Regulations	
Baby-Sitting Service	6
How Much Autonomy Should a Branch Librarian Have?	66
"Identify Yourself"	7
Inflexible Rules	8
Interference with Student Discipline	9
Overdues	62
Service to High School Students	70
Scheduling	
Central Information Desk	11
Flexible Scheduling	2
A Schedule Change	13
Too Many Supervisors	17
Work Assignments	10
School and Public Library Relationship	
Who Controls Library Space?	50
Security	
Harassment at Stonechat Branch	60
Misuse of Seabrook College Library	67
No Textbooks!	51
A Pilferage Racket	59
The Scribbler	54
Service to High School Students	70

Subject Index / 259

Case No.

Selection of Employees	
Church and State (Role Playing)	36
The Tupelo Family	69
Selection of Materials	
"Bandaid" Work	39
Control of Special Appropriation	64
Popular Materials in Research Library	28
Selection Committee	5
"The Shelf"	42
Special Funding	30
Service to Industry	
Research Library Public Service	46
Service to Students	
Service to High School Students	70
Space Utilization	
Data Packets	12
Hemlock High Resource Center	16
Planned Expansion	49
Who Controls Library Space?	50
Special Collections	
A Branch in a Low-Income Neighborhood	31
Staff Associations	
City Hall	61
A Schedule Change	13
Staff Harassment	
Harassment at Stonechat Branch	60
Staff Manual	
Work Assignments	10
Staff Relations	
Individual Recognition (Role Playing)	45
Interference with Student Discipline	9
Momentum (Role Playing)	27
Staff Concern	41
Staff Utilization	
City Hall	61
Data Packets	12
Hemlock High Resource Center	16
Problems Inherited by a Young Administrator	22
Too Many Supervisors	17
Student Assistants	
Work Assignments	10
Supervision	
Busy, Busy, Busy	19
Central Information Desk	11
A Despotic Supervisor	3

260 / Library Management

Case No.

How Much Autonomy Should Branch Librarians Have?	66
Interference With Student Discipline	9
The Memo Writer	4
An Organization Chart	21
Too Many Supervisors	17
Wanted: A Mover's Manual	23
Work Assignments	10
Telephone Service	
Research Library Public Service	46
Termination of Employment	
Resignation	14
Unions	
Flexible Scheduling	8
Volunteers	
Volunteers (Role Playing)	20
Work Flow	
Work Assignments	10